BIOS
THEORETIKOS

TROND BERG ERIKSEN

BIOS
THEORETIKOS

Notes on Aristotle's
Ethica Nicomachea X, 6–8

Universitetsforlaget

Oslo — Bergen — Tromsø

ISBN 82-00-01585-8

Cover design: Bjørn Roggenbihl

UNIVERSITETSFORLAGET

Distribution offices:
NORWAY
Blindern, Oslo 3

UNITED KINGDOM
Global Book Resources Ltd.
37, Queen Street
Henley on Thames
Oxon RG9 1AJ

Printed in Norway by
Lie & Co.s Boktrykkeri, Oslo

To
ANFINN STIGEN

CONTENTS

INTRODUCTION

§ 1. PRELIMINARY REMARKS

During the last fifty years, the study of Aristotle has been strongly influenced by the theory of W. Jaeger on the development of Aristotle's thought.[1] Fruitful as his thesis may be to the philologist, its influence has not unambiguously promoted the philosophical understanding of Aristotle's thought. On the one hand, it directed the interest of the historian to the transition from Plato to Aristotle, and the research there has presented a new picture of the work of the later Plato and the early Academy. On the other hand, the impression of this thesis on the textual interpretation of the Aristotelian Corpus has been disappointing. Jaeger presented and promoted a kind of analysis that was primarily directed towards discovering phases, periods, steps, and stages in Aristotle's development. He and his followers assumed that the clue to Aristotle's thought was the reconstruction of his path from the Academy to the Lyceum. The fixed points here, however, are really scanty. The conclusions and presuppositions seem to depend on one another to the extent that most arguments must be circular. Jaeger contrived this on well-grounded authority, and his book is, in addition to this kind of investigation, full of important remarks on the most different aspects of Aristotle's work. But among his followers, using his method without having his knowledge, this way of analysis often degenerated into mere play. It seems necessary to leave this style of interpretation or, at least, to study the texts with other primary aims than constructing a chronology. J. H. Randall puts it pithily thus:

> For a generation it has indeed led to the expenditure of much time and effort in trying to determine just when Aristotle wrote a particular passage or book, effort that many scholars are beginning to suspect might well have been spent in analyzing what he said in it.[2]

Jaeger's approach was determined by the purpose of destroying the old picture of Aristotle's philosophy as a fixed system of thought. From the Middle Ages onwards, Aristotle had been read as the great systematic who covered the whole range of being with his conceptual matrices. His chains of thought offered clear structures which embraced everything that could be studied. Later, when the historians found contradictions and inconsistencies in his works, he lost the rest of his vanishing authority. They would rather call him a bad systematic than abandon the representation of him as a thinker with a system. This was the position of the great historian E. Zeller. He found two constantly opposite features in Aristotle's thought: form and matter, God and the world, the universal and the particular.[3] This observation he could not explain, but Jaeger, following his own preferences, interpreted this as one single opposition between two modes of thinking: the first one was metaphysical and religious, the second one rational and scientific. Jaeger wanted to show that the supposed inconsistency resulted from Aristotle's personal development. In a certain way, then, contrary to his intention, Jaeger kept and preserved the old picture of Aristotle as a systematic. He ascribed to him three periods of development, but within each of them, it was Jaeger's contention, Aristotle's thought had been consistent.

Since 1923 most interpretations have tried to improve on or turn down the thesis of Jaeger while sharing his general point of view. The commentators have presented many developmental constructions. Passages which were hard to interpret in their contexts, have been regarded as pieces written earlier or later than the rest, a contribution from a pupil or an editor. This implies that they often have attempted to solve philosophical problems by means of philological explanations. Against this practice, W.F.R. Hardie has reminded us of a simple principle of textual interpretation: "The developmental interpretation of doctrines can be helpful and illuminating. But, if it is offered as a way round philosophical difficulties, it needs defence in every case".[4] This is, in fact, a sentence passed on most of the research on Aristotle since Jaeger. For the present study, it is a basic principle that philosophical problems cannot be solved by means of philological dexterity. Moreover, our interpretation claims to offer a clue to some problems that previously have forced commentators into genetic, developmental hypotheses.

It is, of course,difficult to say if the problem at hand is a philosophical or a philological one. This, however, cannot be decided on beforehand. Both kinds of hypotheses have their own right, and both should be tried. But the historian of philosophy has to base his reconstructions on the texts and try to understand what is meant, what the author intends to say, whoever he is, whenever he has written the passage. This does not mean, of course, that he can despense with the work of the philologist. But often he not only lacks the competence to discuss matters of detail with him, but also has a need for a more direct access to the contents of the text. By discovering the author's chain of thought, the historian of philosophy can help the philologist in his work and, maybe, repay a part of his debts.

The difference between these two ways of analysis is most striking in the case of apparent inconsistencies. At this point the philosophical texts show their specific character. The philologist is often perplexed because he is not familiar with this phenomenon from the work on texts of other kinds. In a work of philosophy a contradiction does not need to be a flaw. On the contrary, it is often the mark of original thinking as distinguished from the writing of a mere pupil, of mere epigones. Philosophical thought is often nourished by tensions between positions that cannot be reconciled. For a thinker is a man who has a problem, not a man who has got rid of them all.[5]

This study intends to show that Aristotle is a man with at least one great problem, and, consequently, that a part of his apparent contradictions can only be understood from this point of view. Aristotle does not only struggle with philosophical questions. Philosophy itself has become a question for him. In the passage we are to comment, philosophy is the main theme. This section of EN has always been a puzzler, and the hypotheses are many - the last one assuming that parts of it originally belong to the Protrepticus.[6] We think that our difficulties in understanding it may reflect Aristotle's difficulties when he wrote it, that the problem arising depends on the theme which in itself was surely problematic for the author. It is our considered opinion that the difficulties of EN X, 6-8 cannot be solved by assumptions of form (e.g. that it is older or younger than the rest, spurious, or originally belongs to another work). The solution is to be found, if anywhere, in its contents, because the problem is rooted in its contents, not in its form.

The ethical thoughts of Aristotle are presented, one usually assumes, mainly in four treatises: the Protrepticus, Magna Moralia (MM), Ethica Eudemia (EE), and Ethica Nicomachea (EN). In this study, we are primarily occupied with a certain text and only secondarily with a theme in Aristotle's philosophy. A section of the last-named treatise is our subject, and the other three will be used to explain problematic passages in EN at the same level with the Topics, Rhetorics, Metaphysics, etc.

In spite of the work of, among others, Jaeger, Düring, and Schneeweiss, we have only an imperfect knowledge of the Protrepticus.[7] They have tried to reconstruct it from fragments, mainly in Iamblichus, but the results are, as far as we can judge, inconclusive. Without doubt we know single opinions that have been expressed in this relatively early work of Aristotle, but the sequence of its argument and its disposition is unknown.

As to Magna Moralia, F. Dirlmeier has argued for the genuineness of its contents.[8] To this it should be noted: if it is not genuine, also in its form, the treatise is of slight interest. Then, the genuineness of its contents must be decided from the other treatises, and that makes MM superfluous as a source. In its present form, however, it is undoubtedly the work of a pupil, and, we are tempted to add, not of an especially bright one. The style and arguments are clumsy and unphilosophic. The whole book gives a rather dull impression.[9]

The case of Ethica Eudemia is different. Its argument is clever, the disposition being mainly the same as in EN. J. Burnet says: "The undoubtedly Eudemian books only differ from their Nikomachean counterparts in matters of detail and emphasis".[10] The problem of its genuineness is too complicated to be discussed here. Be that as it may. This version is either written by Aristotle himself or by a person who knew him and his school better than anyone else did. The question, if it is genuine, is, then, an abstract question of mediocre interest. In every case we have, citing Burnet again, "in EE the most authoritative commentary on the Nikomachean".[11] In this way it will be used in the following paragraphs.

The present study has the form of a commentary, philosophical notes on the much discussed section EN X, 6-8. A complete philosophical and philological commentary would have turned out to be unreadable, apart from the fact that it must have been written by another person. We have got indispensable help, as the competent reader will note, from the commentaries of Grant (3rd. ed. 1874), Ramsauer (1878), Stewart (1892), Burnet (1900), Joachim (1951), Dirlmeier (5th ed. 1969), and Gauthier/Jolif (2nd. ed. 1970).[12] The present work, however, is not an attempt to pile up information on this section for its own sake. The notes are presented to support a hypothesis about the theme of this section: Aristotle's representation of the life of the philosopher. The form is chosen to argue as near the text as possible, and to make the interpretation of details more accessible to interpreters approaching the passages from other points of view.

It is an important virtue of interpretation to stop at the right moment. Often the commentators ask questions which are, and from their nature must be, strange or unknown to the author. Nevertheless, the texts are probed again and again to find a doctrine on the point in question. Where there is no direct support to be found, apologetics arise, with commentators who tell us what Aristotle has intended to say. Not always, but often, the obscurity and the inconsistencies that we discover result from our way of questioning. It is, of course, always possible to ask questions which cannot be answered by a text on the topic. And it is likewise impossible to write an account of a subject which can answer all possible questions. To understand the meaning of a text, we must, then, grasp the questions which the author intends to answer. From this point of view, most Aristotelian texts will appear to be good answers, not always to our questions, but to his.

The main theme of our passage, the life of the philosopher, is also treated directly and indirectly in other parts of the Aristotelian Corpus. EN X, 6-8 does not stand alone as an exception claiming some particular hypothesis. In fact, we are confronted with a similar puzzle in Aristotle's Politics, in his writings on psychology, and in the treatises known to us as his Metaphysics. Our text and those other texts will be discussed in the final chapters. We hold this theme to be irreducibly ambiguous in the contexts where it appears. In conclusion, then, we do not try to reconstruct Aristotle's doctrine on happiness and philosophy. On the condition that a doctrine is a harmonious system of well-grounded opinions, Aristotle has none of it on this subject. As was said above, it is often impossible to understand a philosophical text without discovering the tensions behind it. Owing to the character of the theme, the final task must be to give a representation of Aristotle's dilemma.

The introductory chapters will state the problem more clearly in its systematic and historical context. This is necessary because we think that it is possible to show that the dilemma did not arise from Aristotle's thought, but was an inheritance. In this, as in our main thesis, we will work out suggestions which have already been given by Jaeger, suggestions which till now have been paid little attention. Jaeger discusses Plato's ideal of the philosophic life and finds a contradiction between his ideal of the philosopher-king and "the actual dedication of his old age entirely to pure theoretical study". He continues:

> Thus gradually arose a set of problems which were inherited by
> Aristotle in their full gravity, and which threatened the essential unity
> of scientific knowledge and practical action that had been since Plato's
> Socratic period the presupposition of his research and therefore a
> foundation-pillar of his idea of the 'theoretic life'.13

To discover the dilemma of Aristotle, then, we have to take a short course to the previous Greek thought on the theme of the contemplative life, the life of the philosopher, and especially examine Plato's attempt to connect it with the political life. For, as Grant says, no books are more indispensable for the understanding of Aristotle than the dialogues of Plato.[14]

§ 2. PLATO AND THE PROBLEM OF CONTEMPLATIVE LIFE

The word theōrētikos as used to denote a certain form of life is firstly found in Aristotle. Plato does not make use of the word in this connection. But he knows, of course, the problems connected with the bios theōrētikos very well.[1] In any case, it is hardly right to say with Düring: "Erst bei Aristoteles finden wir aber das bekannte Schema der drei Lebensformen mit Genuss, bürgerlicher Tugend oder philosophischer Einsicht als höchstem Ziel".[2] The problem of the life of the philosopher, as distinguished from the life of the politically active citizen and the man of production, goes back to Plato, and, as we will see later on, only Plato has a plain scheme of three lives. The function and character of the similar doctrine in Aristotle are quite different.

The figure of the three competing lives must, however, be carefully distinguished from the discussions on the theme of the best life and from the ideal of __contemplative__ life. Each of the topics has its own history as well as some history in common.[3]

The early Greek poets reflect the ancient interest in the question: which life is the best one for man? In Heraclitus and Parmenides, Xenophanes and Anaxagoras, we find at least rudiments of the ideal of contemplative life. Thus the discussion in Plato and Aristotle is not only the beginning of a long tradition, but the conclusion of a permanent Greek discussion as well. The classical figure of the three lives presented to the philosopher a simple in- strument for the consideration of human possibilities.[4] But before this simplification was picked out by the reflecting philosopher, it was probably a well-known idea among common men.

The philosopher's way of life was at the same time admired and ridiculed by the common Greek. Many amusing stories show the absent-minded thinker in curious situations. Plato tells the story about Thales falling into the well while observing the sky (__Theaet__. 174a), and Diogenes Laertius records that Democritus once spent the day in the company of an ox without noticing it, because he was occupied with a problem.[5] There are many stories of the same kind concerning these figures and others, particularly Anaxagoras. Jaeger and Snell refer to most of them.[6] It may be true that these stories have a rather loose connection with the persons described, that they are, as we might say, mere inventions. But inventions also have a purpose. On this point Jaeger can be corrected when he says: "All stories that make the older philosophers conscious followers of the ideal of the 'theoretic life', either come directly from Plato's school or arose soon afterwards under the influence of the Platonic ideal".[7] It is hard to realise that an ideal among philosophers could have brought about stories of this sort. They were rather traditional, i.e. older than Plato, with the origin not in the Academy, but in the wonder of the common man, who did not understand this new form of life. Their character betrays that they must partly be jokes between the men in the street.[8] Jaeger has also noticed this, without remarking, however, that he undermines his own thesis. He says: it is clear "that stories of this sort were by no means merely the expression of a deep and sympathetic admira- tion of unusual intellectual concentration, but also give the folk's mocking view of absent-minded scholars".[9]

Plato may have used traditional stories to underline his points, but the representation of the life of research in Plato and the Academy is so problematic and ambiguous that it is, for that reason alone, unreasonable to suppose that he himself or his fellows could have impressed a simple ideal on the history of previous Greek thought to provide themselves with an illustrious ancestry. Jaeger seems to be wrong. But here, as often elsewhere, he knows so much that he himself presents the observations that destroy his oversimplified thesis.

Positively, it is not difficult to argue for the existence of an ideal of the life of research before Plato. The bios theōrētikos is a relatively late expression, as was said above, and so is theōria, denoting the study of nature and the stars. Before Plato, theōria is mainly used in religious contexts and for the traveller's study of strange countries and customs. But this does not, of course, imply that the subject-matter was unknown. Festugière, Joly, Wehrli, and Picht, among others, have examined the tradition behind Plato.[10] From different points of view their accounts indicate that philosophy as a new sort of activity and as a new form of life needed some kind of justification from the very beginning. The confession of, e.g., Xenophanes is too conspicuous to be ignored: sophia, he says, is better than strength and honour. A victory in the Olympics cannot give the city eunomia, but the wise man can.[11] The hostility against the old ideals of honour seems essential to the new consciousness. It is difficult to avoid the conclusion of Picht: "Wir erkennen also, dass die Antithese zwischen dem bios praktikos und dem bios theōrētikos der Antithese zwischen den adeligen Traditionen der archaischen Zeit und jener neuen Lebensform entspricht, die mit der Philosophie in Erscheinung trat".[12] That is: the philosophers have always tried to justify their business, and their immodesty with regard to their form of life is striking from the first moment on. The need for justification originated with the consciousness of doing something apart.

The ideals of life in Plato and Aristotle thus undoubtedly have a history. The theme of the bios theōrētikos in a wide sense occupied the thinkers before them. But this does not mean that Jaeger is all wrong in his contention. The deep originality of Plato cannot be effaced by pointing to the thoughts he had in common with his predecessors. In the Platonic dialogues the concept of theōria is developed in a new way, which came to represent a measure of what philosophy can and ought to be. In the criticism of previous Greek thought he and his students of course employed this metron. It was not more easy for them to avoid it than it is for us. We use, after all, the Platonic word 'philosophy' to denote the thoughts of men who probably did not know the term.[13]

In Plato the three lives are performed by the three parts of the body of the Republic where the three kinds of human beings are sharing the functions between them, some living the life of the philosopher, some the life of the warrior, and some the life of production. As is well known, this trinity is prefigured in the psychology of Plato (Rep. 580c-583a), the three classes of the Republic representing the three main faculties of the soul. This tripartition is not only found in the Republic, but also in the Symposium, in the famous speech of Socrates/Diotima. The kinds of "generation and birth in beauty", correspond to the three parts of the soul. Love can produce (a) children, (b) fame, or (c) wisdom, depending on the level of sublimation (Symp. 208e ff.). Both in the Republic and in the Symposium the life of reason is glorified and justified as the most valuable one. The correspondence between Plato and Aristotle on this point is, then, too striking to be a mere accident. There can be no doubt about Jaeger's contention:

> The trinity of pleasure, virtue and phronēsis, is in him (i.e. in Aristotle) connected with Plato's doctrine that the soul has three parts, from which he derives the three 'lives' and the three sorts of pleasure.[14]

The correspondence between Plato and Aristotle is not, however, a relation of mere inheritance. Their presentations of the three lives are also fundamentally different. In Plato the doctrine depends on his psychology, but in Aristotle the three kinds of human life are introduced as endoxoi protaseis: these are the three possibilities that men mention if you ask them what sort of life will make a human being happy.[15] In Plato each part of the soul has its own virtue, and therefore each of the three lives has a kind of isolated optimum. Contrary to this, Aristotle attempts, according to his method, to find a formula that could reconcile these three opinions, showing that all of them are both wrong and right (cf. EN 1095b13; EE 1216a27).

In the dialogues of Plato the theoretical man is not originally the fellow of Thales dropping into the well. Here, as elsewhere in his work, the point of departure is the phenomenon of Socrates. Plato's first description of the theoretical man and his life is given in the Apology of Socrates. "While I have life and strength", Socrates says, "I shall never cease from the practice and teaching of philosophy" (Apol. 29d). The reason that he gives is the conviction of both Plato and Aristotle: "The life which is unexamined is not worth living" (Apol. 38a). The philosophical practice of Socrates, however, was not the same as the practice of Plato or Aristotle. Consequently, this conviction needs a new legitimation from both of them.

The change in Plato's thought on the subject is most reluctant. In the Apology Socrates says that he is no student of natural philosophy. In fact, he does not know anything about such matters (Apol. 19d). In the Theaetetus, however, the figure of Socrates defends the ideal of the natural philosopher who has nothing to do with political affairs at all (Theaet. 173c ff.). Plato's picture of the philosopher in the Apology or the Phaedo is obviously not the same as in the Republic or in the Theaetetus.[16] Between the two last mentioned the tension is also remarkable. The statements here, together with the hints in the Gorgias, Politicus, and the Seventh Letter, give the impression of a gradual change in Plato's thought, which can undoubtedly be described and interpreted in different ways. We will restrict ourselves to some general statements.

In the Socratic inheritance of Plato, there is a notion of the philosopher's task as a political one, as a service towards the community. The Socrates of the Apology says that he always had done two things above all: a) 'inspected' Athens, as a general musters his troops (exetasis), stirred it awake as a "gadfly which God has given the state" (Apol. 30d), and b) made his fellow citizens "care for their souls" (Apol. 29d). In the Phaedo the second aspect of this practice is underlined, as the situation demands. But elsewhere the first aspect is the more important. In the dialogue Gorgias, Callicles attacks the life of the philosopher because it has nothing to do with politics directly, recalling the discussion in the Antiope of Euripides, where the two main characters, Amphion and Zethos, represent the practical and the theoretical life (Gorg. 484e, 485e ff.). The point of the dialogue is, however, to show that Callicles is wrong. The conclusion is reached that Socrates, the philosopher, is the one who is really engaged in politics, the one who is most familiar with the subject (Gorg. 521d). In this dialogue the care for the human soul (psychēs therapeia) is absorbed by the political art as its end and main goal (Gorg. 464a, 500e, 517a ff.). Callicles is a representative of the popular conviction that philosophy is something useless, and the dialogue must be understood as an attempt to justify the business of the philosopher vis-à-vis the misery of the surrounding world: political dissolution and disorder. Philosophy is not superfluous play at the border of the society. The city is in need of philosophy most of all, and the philosopher, in his turn, is convinced that the city is the primary field of his work.

This is, of course, the presupposition and the basic idea of the Republic: the way to philosophical insight is not completed before it works out emancipation among the citizens in the community. The path up from the cave makes sense only if completed in the work of drawing one's fellows the same way. This renowned parable is not only a picture of the way to wisdom, and of the way that the rulers of the ideal Republic have to go, but, and this is important, although it is well known: the parable is an interpretation of the life of Socrates (Rep. 514a-517d). Until the writing of the Republic, the two aspects of Socrates' practice are kept together in Plato's thought. In his paradox on the philosopher-kings,[17] the phenomenon of Socrates is universalised (Epist. VII. 326a ff.; Rep. 473c ff.; 499b ff.).

However, whereas Aristotle always maintains the practical character of politics, for Plato to rule right is a matter of theory: "Then, shall we say that the king has a greater affinity to knowledge than to manual arts or to practical life in general? - Certainly, he has" (Pol. 259c). The knowledge that Plato demanded from his philosopher-kings was often far from directly concerned with political affairs. When he himself, then, finally became disappointed as to the realisation of his political ideas, this knowledge became self-sufficient, valuable without any regard to its practical use. Jaeger describes the change in the ideal of the philosopher from the early to the late writings of Plato in this way:

> The detour through the fundamental questions, which Plato believed he
> must take in order to answer the Socratic question, led him more and
> more into a general doctrine of knowledge and being, and compelled him
> to add to his structure of theoretical science even the branches of
> mathematics and astronomy that he found existing. So phronēsis was

filled with the contents of this sophia, and out of the Socratic aporia and elenchos there grew a "theoretic life" devoted to the purest research. In Theaetetus, where the alliance between philosophy and mathematics is specially prominent, Socrates sings a veritable hymn to the life of the student, and paints an ideal picture of this life in colours borrowed from the type of the astronomer and mathematician.[18]

Festugière has made an attempt to show that theōria in Herodotus represents "un modèle de sociabilité", whereas in Plato it becomes "un type d'insociable". He says: "La vie théorétique du Phédon et du Théétète fait du sage un reclus".[19] This, as we have seen, is not true concerning all the dialogues of Plato. It is more appropriate to say, with Jaeger, that his ideal of philosophy embraces both political and contemplative aspects, and to add that a change of stress may be seen in his development.

The difference between the earlier and later Plato should not, however, be overstated. He is not replacing the state as the frame of reference with the adoration of the circular movements of the stars, in one blow. His cosmic religiousness is not the outcome of a conversion. On the one hand, the cosmic paradeigma of justice is already present in the concluding myth of the Republic. On the other hand, the passages on contemplation in the later dialogues are not that conspicuous. It may even be objected that the account in the Timaeus must be taken with a grain of salt, owing to the mythical and imaginative character of the dialogue. One may also refer to the Laws and contend that Plato's thought was determined by the political scope from his first to his last work.[20] However, even when we allow these objections their relative right, we cannot deny that the theme of theōria is stressed in a new way, e.g. in the Timaeus 47a. As to the Laws, contemplation there is completely detached from the arrangement and order of the state. The decisive point, however, is that the Timaeus, the Theaetetus and the Laws seem to give a coherent picture of the activity of the philosopher, a picture which is too different from the early Socratic dialogues to be ignored, and too similar to be turned away as a casual experiment of Plato's imagination.

The main idea is that the man who contemplates, imitates the object of contemplation. Because the totality of the course of the stars is a kosmos, a good order, the person contemplating it becomes kosmios, well-ordered. The aim of the spectator is to imitate the regularity of the life of the stars (Tim. 47c; 90c; Leg. 967e). The heaven and its bodies have a soul (Leg. 898a ff.), and the human soul can win the fight with the passions and the bodily disturbances by making itself uniform with the divine, cosmic soul. To become _kosmios_ is thus to become sort of _athanatos_ and _theios_.[21] The concept of philosophy in the later Plato is, then, centred around the notion of _homoiōsis tō theō,_ to make oneself uniform with God (Theaet.176b). This is also an essential part of Aristotle's concept of philosophy as presented in EN X, 6-8. As an introduction to its historical background, this may suffice. Later the thoughts of Plato will be considered in connection with the similar themes in Aristotle. Here is the place for a summary.

Socratic thought had been ethical and political through and through.[22] Plato had also ascribed to philosophy a political task, but when the opportunity for the realisation of his ideas failed to appear, this aspect shrank into a parenthesis. Jaeger puts it thus:

> Plato's personal development and the inner tendency of Platonic science worked in the same direction ... Plato's early philosophy had pressed still more determinedly towards participation in actual life and in the state. But in the course of Plato's development the drive towards knowledge had immeasurably extended its range. Late Platonic science did indeed appear to have developed quite organically out of the Socratic seed by a process of constantly incorporating richer theoretical contents; but its field was no longer exclusively political ethics as it has been in the writings down to the Republic. Ethics had become a mere "part" of philosophy, co-ordinate with logic and physics.[23]

In this way the Socratic synthesis broke up, dissolved, and Aristotle is faced with a new problem. The justification of the life of the philosopher in the earlier Plato was based on the supposed unity of practical and theoretical thought. How can this life be justified now when the Socratic unity is decomposed into a plurality of different sciences?

We have used different names for the life of the philosopher, the _bios theōrētikos_: 'the contemplative life', 'the life of reason', 'the life of research', 'the theoretic life'. The plurality of terms corresponds to the obscurity of the subject. Sometimes this life seems to consist of the study of astronomy or the study of metaphysical principles. At other times we must think of the life of reason in all its forms or a blessed recognition of God. As to Aristotle, §14 will be an attempt to clear up the confusion.

§3. THE METHOD OF ARISTOTLE'S ETHICS

Some insight into the method of Aristotle, his methodological intentions as
well as his actual procedure is indispensable for an adequate understanding
of EN both in detail and as a whole. This is the more important because the
method of Aristotle does not only mean a technique of investigation or exposition, but mirrors his notion of truth in the field concerned, its source and
nature. Without a general knowledge of his method we should have difficulty
in deciding where his share is to be found in the complex arguments.

In Plato, dialectics was the most noble science. Aristotle, however,
judges differently.[1] He hardly regards it as a science at all. What he meant
by 'dialectics', we read in the Topics. The considerations there may be
understood as a preparation for his ethical treatises, but the actual procedure
in EN is at the same time both more minutely thought out and marked by other
principles as well. Burnet, in his useful commentary on EN, underlined the
importance of methodological studies for the understanding of the style and
structure of this treatise. He says in his preface:

> I had come to the conclusion that most of the difficulties that have been
> raised about the Ethics were due to the fact that, though the dialectical
> character of many passages had long been admitted, commentators had
> never thoroughly recognised that the treatise was dialectical throughout.[2]

On some points, however, Burnet's work was consciously provoking.
because he wanted to attract attention to this new clue. In details, then, he
needs some correction, and he has it, first and foremost from the commentary of Greenwood on EN Book VI.[3] Here we can only refer to the main points
of the discussion and add some observations of our own. The treatment must
be imperfect, but we would have been led astray in the commentaries on
particular passages if this aspect had been ignored.

In EN the statements of Aristotle ex professo on the subject of method
are scanty. But a collection of the scattered remarks will show that he has
given the question more serious consideration than it seems at first. Grant
remarks that EN does not begin with a review of the contribution of previous
thinkers as does the Metaphysics in our arrangement. De Anima also starts
with a short discourse on previous theories, and the programme for the
Politics, at the end of EN, suggests a similar order there. The reason for

this, Grant says, is that "morals had never yet been clearly separated from politics".[4] In the introductory book of EN, however, Aristotle discusses Plato's theory of the Good in itself. Still, it is true that Aristotle is the first to have studied ethics as a separate branch of knowledge. But in his practical philosophy ethics is subordinated to politics. This relation we will examine later (cf. §35). Here it is sufficient to note that in EN there are many references to the treatise on politics, and that the disciplines have a common end in the happiness for man. In general the inquiries follow the same methodological directions.

As is well known, Aristotle distinguishes between practical, productive, and theoretical thought (Meta.1025b25; Top.145a15). Ethics and politics are practical sciences, i.e. their end lies in things to be done. This does not mean that ethics and politics are mainly or exclusively concerned with action, but it surely implies that their insights are apt to affect our way of life. Aristotle says: "Will not the knowledge of it (i.e. the chief good), then, have a great influence on life? Shall we not, like archers who have a mark to aim at, be more likely to hit upon what is right?" (EN 1094a22). This improving influence on our living is the end of the practical sciences. For they are studied, as Aristotle says, not in order to make us know what virtue is, but that we may become good (EN 1103b26; 1095a5; 1179a35ff.; cf. Meta.993b20).

In so far as they have to do with becoming rather than with being, practical sciences are relatives to art (An.Post.100a9), for both concern things which have to be moved from outside as distinguished from natural science which deals with things that have their cause of motion in themselves. In Aristotle, the practical sciences are not regarded as sciences in the precise meaning of the word, because their procedure is non-syllogistic. The subject-matter cannot be conceptualised to the same extent as the subject of metaphysics or natural sciences. For the subject of practical knowledge is 'things that may be otherwise' (EN 1139a6-8; cf. 1094b14ff.).

The end of the Aristotelian science is to understand things in their necessity, to find out why things are as they are. It is not a science of discovery, but a science of understanding. Its aim is not to control the real world, but to see the properties of everything in their dependence on the topos of the subject in the structure of being. Randall puts it in this way: "The scientific explanation, the 'reason why', the dioti or ,cause', will when found form the premise from which that observed fact can be demonstratèd as conclusion. Thus scientific syllogism derives facts already known through observation".[5] Ethics also tries to understand the various moral judgements, the good and the bad man. But matters of conduct are relative, and Aristotle is forced to build a probable structure to understand human action. This structure is based on the actual acts of men and their relation to accepted values. So EN and De Anima offer a framework for the understanding of human decision and its mechanics. As to their contents, however, the decisions are unpredictable.

It is obvious, then, that the ethical arguments lack the precision and exactness of the scientific proofs. Aristotle explains this in the famous passage of his introduction to EN:

> We must be content, then, in speaking of such subjects and with such premises to indicate the truth roughly and in outline, and in speaking about things which are only for the most part true and with premises of the same kind to reach conclusions that are no better. In the same spirit therefore, should each type of statement be received; for it is the mark of an educated man to look for precision in each class of things just so far as the nature of the subjects admits; it is evidently equally foolish to accept probable reasoning from a mathematician and to demand from a rhetorician scientific proofs (EN 1094b19ff.; cf. 1098a25ff.; Rhet. 1357a25ff.).

This not only implies a resignation as to the claim for exactness,[6] but also a restriction concerning the listeners to the lecture. They have to be educated men, because Aristotle is convinced that folly in methodological questions and in the listener's expectations is due to apaideusia, lack of education (Meta. 1006a6). His demand on his listeners, that they should be experienced, educated men (EN 1095a2), corresponds to his methodological point of departure: to find the right principle of moral action we must "pay attention to the unproved statements and beliefs of experienced and elderly people" (EN 1143b11).

Aristotle did not try to say something completely new or to change men's notions of what is good and bad. Caird formulates his intentions thus: "The value of scientific ethics is ... that it brings into clear consciousness the ideas which underlie the unreasoned ethics of the ordinary good man and good citizen".[7] This is the reason why Aristotle has to discuss the beliefs of the many. He does not wish to make any revolution, but to reformulate traditional opinions to bring forth a hidden consensus.[8] In the natural sciences, ta phainomena or ta hyparchonta represent the starting-point and the touchstone of the theories. In ethics, ta dokounta play a similar role, because "every man has some contribution to make to the truth" (EE 1216b31; EN 1145b3-6; Meta. 993b1-4; Soph. Elen. 183b17-32). And the more experienced he is, the more educated he is, the better the reason to listen to him. EN I, 8 may serve as an instance of this sort of investigation. There, as elsewhere, Aristotle attempts to show that his contentions are far from paradoxical. On the contrary, he takes pains to show that the opinions on the best life for man, different as they may be, are all right or at least understandable from a certain point of view. The happy activity correctly understood, includes both virtue and pleasure.

The reason for this procedure is certainly not to be found in a democratic temperament that gives everybody his right of voting. It may depend on a curious conception of history. In the Metaphysics, he says:

> In all probability, every art and science and philosophy has been over and over again discovered to the farthest extent possible, and then again lost, and one may conceive these opinions to have been preserved to us as a sort of fragment of those lost philosophies. We see, then, to some extent the relation of the popular belief to those ancient opinions (Meta. 1074b10ff.).

It must be admitted, however, that this confession to anamnēsis is a somewhat singular passage in the Aristotelian Corpus. The reason for the procedure is rather to be found in the characteristic feature of Aristotelian science mentioned above: he just wants to find out why things are as they are. He does not want to improve on mankind by introducing new principles. The right actions, he thinks, are promoted by showing why and how certain actions actually are right.[9]

In Plato, the cognition of the Good in itself was the source of right action. Ethics is thus identified with metaphysics. In his search for a hidden consensus as a starting-point, Aristotle separates his ethics from his theoretical philosophy. He denies the necessity of using metaphysical principles to explain or regulate human action. This is the reason for his rather harsh polemics against Plato (EN I, 6). The rejection there presupposes the doctrine of the categories in some form, but Plato's conclusions are already tacitly rejected in the previous chapter, where Aristotle discusses the beliefs of the many more seriously than Plato ever did. Like Isocrates, the rhetorician, Aristotle apparently gives up any theoretical or metaphysical foundation for his ethics.[10] Isocrates asserts that there is no strange or exclusive knowledge that can guide human action, like, e.g., Plato's knowledge of the Good in itself. Everybody agrees on what is good and bad, Isocrates says (Antid. 84-85). Aristotle too appeals to a consensus, but it is not there yet. It must be detected in the beliefs of the many and the opinions of the wise.

This does not imply, of course, that Aristotle forgets his familiar conceptual matrices in dealing with ethics. But they are primarily used as instruments in the clearance work on ta dokounta, i.e. to solve the contradictions and difficulties, aporiai, which arise from them. This is what needs to be done, "for if we both refute the objections and leave the common opinions undisturbed, we shall have proved the case sufficiently" (EN 1145b1ff.).

That the inquiry is dialectical not only means that it lacks exactness and that its conclusions are only valid for the most part. It also and particularly means that it is wedged in between previous opinions, that it answers questions asked by previous thought. In EE this principle is stated in plain words. Aristotle (or his best commentator) says:

> We must, then, find a method that will best explain the views held on these topics, and also put an end to difficulties and contradictions. And this will happen if the contrary views are seen to be held with some show of reason; such a view will be most in harmony with the facts of observation and both the contradictory statements will in the end stand, if what is said is true in one sense, but untrue in another (EE 1235b12ff.).

The first task of the dialectician is to show the fundamental agreement between the opposing contentions. He starts from the opinions that are "true, but not clear" (EN 1138b26). These opinions are then attacked by different patterns of distinction: the more and the less, the essential and the accidental, the potential and the actual. In this way the dialectician attempts to dissolve the contradictions by means of qualifications. It is important to note that Aristotle is a man of compromise.

Aristotle often gives more than one solution of the difficulties which arise from the contradictory opinions. He follows a certain line to a rough conclusion, and then he says: let us start anew. This point may also be presented in another way. Then he continues till the conclusion is made acceptable. Burnet comments on this procedure with an overstatement:

> If it can be shown that these apparent duplicates are really successive applications of the different dialectical topoi appropriate to the subject, the critical problem does not arise. Aristotle is not committed to all or any of the solutions he gives any more than Plato is committed to the successive definitions of knowledge given in Theaetetus. Nor can we even assume that the true solution is necessarily given at all. It is often given, but it was contrary to Aristotle's own principles to base the exposition of Politics on his metaphysical system.[11]

Burnet is right in emphasising the positive meaning of the plurality of solutions in EN, but it is inaccurate to say that Aristotle is not committed to all or any of the solutions given. He is, surely, not committed to anything else either. It is not that difficult to find out what he means.[12] The plurality of solutions is not an argument for their invalidity. On the contrary, they are all valid in their point: to show that there are no absolute contradictions in the traditional views on ethical problems.

The picture of Aristotle as a system-thinker was fundamental for the Thomistic use of him and for the developmental constructions. Against this, Burnet says rightly about the procedure in EN:

> There is a higher art in Aristotle's apparent confusion, and the spirit of the Platonic dialogue with its tentative arguments and provisional conclusions still lives in his dialectical procedure. He is seeking the truth along with his hearers and not expounding a ready-made system.[13]

This is not only true about the ethics, but also, if not to the same extent, about his Metaphysics. In the dialectical character we do not wish to underline the looseness and lack of precision Burnet found everywhere, but rather the open dialogue with tradition and the common opinions. In this sense, his Metaphysics is also worked out through a partly dialectical process, as is seen in Alpha.[14] The difference is that in the Metaphysics he is committed to previous thought in the statement of the problems, whereas in his ethics he is also committed to the beliefs of the many and the opinions of the wise for his solutions, because these opinions already represent the truth which, however, is not yet clear.[15]

The method of Aristotle's ethics is not a strictly followed course which can be recognised anywhere in EN. His references to the traditional opinions are often hidden in the treatment of the language in its traditional use.[16] And often the investigation is promoted by arguments of another kind, e.g. by considerations from analogy. This sort of thought is especially interesting in Aristotle and hitherto far from fully investigated.[17] The compulsion of analogy must have been as strong for him as for the Greek thinkers before him. It even forces him to apparently absurd conclusions, e.g.: "To see a friend is as pleasant as anything can be (i.e. because in the friend you perceive and know yourself), and, indeed, to see him ill is pleasant if you are ill yourself" (EE 1246a17ff.). In the section of EN that we are to comment, this sort of inference from analogy is very important. But the passages will be commented on in their turn.

An idea of Jaeger deserves some attention because it makes a convenient angle for a new discussion on the method of EN. Jaeger attempts to determine the character of Aristotle's practical science as a whole by referring to the apparent analogies with medical science. Medicine, he contends, is the kind of scientific knowledge that comes closest to Aristotle's concept of an ethical science.[18] For readers of Plato, this is no surprise. We remember from the Phaedrus the praise of Hippocrates' method as the classical model for the dialectical method of the philosopher (cf. Phaedr. 270c-d), and the expression psychēs therapeia from Gorgias. Jaeger says:

> Strength and health are the 'virtues of the body'; they had already been paralleled with the 'virtues of the soul' by Plato in the Gorgias (496b, 499d, 504c), where he carries out his comparison of the 'political art' with the art of the physician.[19]

This analogy does not mean exactly the same to Aristotle as to Plato. The considerations of EN are the work of phronēsis, not a science in the strict sense as Plato claims his dialectics to be. On the other hand, the analogy does not apply to the physician, because the physician's work for Aristotle is a simple technē, an art. As phronēsis has its place between epistēmē and technē (EN 1140a25-b8), Aristotle tries to make room for his ethical science

between the metaphysical ethics of Plato and the dexterity of the artisan.
The analogy applies to medical science, because this science shares with
EN the intermediate position between pure science and art. As the art of
medicine depends on medical science and serves health, so the practical
wisdom applied depends on practical science and serves philosophical
wisdom, sophia (EN 1145a6ff.; cf. Pol. 1282a1-7).

The origin of this analogy does not need to concern us here.[20] The
point is that this interpretation is expressly supported by Aristotle, and the
analogy has probably meant more to him than it appears at first sight. He
says:

> The things concerned with action and that which is useful have nothing
> stable in themselves, just as it is in the matters of health. If, however,
> the general statements are of this nature, there is even less accuracy
> in the statements about particular cases, since they fall under no art
> or precept, but the person who is acting must himself always keep in
> mind the special circumstances of the moment (ta pros ton kairon) and
> what they require. This is also true of medicine and the art of naviga-
> tion (EN 1104a3-10; cf. EE 1247a5).

This might be an echo of Hippocrates, as Stewart and Burnet presume.[21]
But it might also mean more than that. The art of medicine and the art of
navigation: thus Aristotle is perhaps including the politics in the analogy.
As is well known, the representation of the state as a ship was familiar among
the Greeks.[22]

Be it as it may. There can be no doubt about Jaeger's judgement as far
as EN concerns: "The example of medicine is used not only as a model of
method for the theoretical analysis of ethics, but equally for its practical
application in human life and education".[23] The use of medical science was
tempting because it was a new science with distinctive features differing from
the strict sciences. It was far from a casual analogy. We have seen it prefigured in Plato and can reconstruct its tradition. But to Aristotle the philosophical motives of his own position were decisive. Lloyd, who has recently
extended and improved on Jaeger's thesis, concludes:

> The analogy of health or physical well-being helps Aristotle, then, to
> make the important point that moral excellences may be determinate with-
> out being invariable constants, and to adopt a judicious position inter-
> mediate between those on the one hand who advocated fixed and univer-

sally valid moral rules, and those on the other who argued that the difference between right and wrong is purely subjective.[24]

Thus Aristotle succeeds in making room for his new science between metaphysics and art, between the dogmatism of Plato and the moral relativism of his age.

For our purpose this analogy to medical science is helpful in deciding the relation between practical wisdom and philosophy. This relation will be discussed in the next chapter.

§4. ETHICS AND THE DOCTRINE OF MAN

In the commentary, we will primarily examine the writings concerning ta anthrōpina, the 'things human' : ethics, politics, and psychology. Their common subject is man, and we may stop for a while to consider the fundamentals of Aristotle's anthropology, before we investigate the dilemma of his ethics. The characteristics of Aristotle's doctrine of man are perhaps best seen as distinguished from the early teaching of Plato.[1]

In the Phaedo, the ethics of Plato and the doctrine of the best life rests on what we might call a dualistic anthropology, or better: in the Phaedo the anthropology is still mere psychology. For the body is not really man. It merely plays the role as the dramatic counterpart of the soul. Human life is the struggle of the soul for clarity and redemption. The body, like matter, is something incomprehensible and strange. The real human being is that which thinks and has consciousness. The soul, then, is not only different from the body, but tries with all its manifestations to come out of it, to be released from it.

In this way, man as he is becomes something unfinished, incomplete, which finds its aim and end outside itself. Even in the Phaedo, man is body and soul, but he fulfils his destination by refuting the body and cleansing the soul. This happens when he recognises being with pure thought, without any help from the senses. Actual man in the Phaedo is merely a transition, a wish for something else.[2] The desire is particularly strong in the philosopher, the lover of wisdom. Consequently, the philosopher is regarded as the human being par excellence, and Plato's doctrine of man becomes mainly a doctrine of the philosopher.

At first glance, Aristotle presents a totally different picture of man. He regards him, one usually says, as a natural phenomenon, a living being, and analyses him as he analyses other species of nature. In Plato the point of view of value dominates the representation of man completely. Aristotle, however, notes the specific characteristics of man and tries to determine his topos in the relations of nature. This does not mean, of course, that Aristotle's description lacks the point of view of value, but he finds the destination and task of man by examining his faculties. Man, for Aristotle, is primarily what he seems to be, the unity that can be seen by all. Soul and body are always given together, and the specific function of man is given with his qualities. In the early Plato, man was a stranger in the world and a guest in his own body. From its prison, the soul could get glances of real being and thus forget its condition in the world. In Aristotle, however, man has a certain topos in the world; he belongs to a meaningful whole, where nothing happens in vain. Human beings are restricted by their conditions, but they take these restrictions into account when they try to find out which life is the best, and they can be compared with higher and lower beings to discover what is in their power and what is not (cf. EN I, 6; §28).

Aristotle's doctrine of man thus becomes more than reflections on the phenomenon of the philosopher. He describes all human faculties thoroughly and sketches many possible forms of life. Even Aristotle estimates philosophy as the highest possibility, but he does not, for that reason, regard other forms of life as failures. The task of man is to bring his species into operation, but the particular man must to the same extent consider his personal abilities in the framing of his life. This is a definite condition for the establishment of the state. Aristotle says:

> Again, the state, as composed of unlikes, may be compared to the living being: as the first elements into which a living being is resolved are soul and body, as soul is made up of rational principle and appetite, the family of husband and wife, property of master and slave, so all these, as well as other dissimilar elements, constitute the state; and, therefore, the virtue of all the citizens cannot possibly be the same, any more than the excellence of the leader of a chorus is the same as that of the performer who stands by his side (Pol. 1277a5ff.).

This is mainly the same thought as in the Republic of Plato. The difference is that Aristotle also seems to be seriously interested in other sorts of human beings than only philosophers.

In Aristotle, then, we do not expect to find a sharp distinction between the philosopher and the common man. In Plato, the common man was, compared to the philosopher, like an unhealthy person, a phenomenon of decay. Even Aristotle employs the analogy to health, as we have seen, and also in him the philosopher is the person who realises the highest human faculties; but he emphasises that it is a life on the border of what is human (cf. §22). It can only come about in spite of human limitations, and, therefore, it should not be more typically human than the other forms of life in which man uses his faculties, e.g. the life of the politician. But, on this point, Aristotle presents the puzzle.

In the first book of EN, he asks: what is the telos, the end, for the life of man? and he finds that everybody agrees on the answer: it is happiness, eudaimonia (I, 4). This answer, however, is not a final solution. For wherein consists happiness, then? To answer this question Aristotle gives his preliminary definition: "Human good turns out to be activity of soul (psyches energeia in accordance with virtue, and if there is more than one virtue, in accordance with the best and most complete" (EN 1098a17). But even this answer needs some addition. For what is virtue, then? The answer is given in Books II-X, which formulate the Aristotelian concept of virtue and present his classification of the different sorts. All this is done to establish the conditions of human happiness. Adkins formulates the old problem thus:

> Accordingly, we might expect Aristotle to include in his definition of eudaimonia the possibility that its nature might be complex, and include several aretai. In EN from Book II to IX, such a view seems possible, despite the definition of Book I. The practice of the aretai so carefully analysed must surely be eudaimonia, or essential to it; and yet Book X, reverting strictly to the dangerous definition quoted above, gives a very different answer.[3]

Adkins has stated the question as it meets the reader at first sight. He is, of course, not the first one to note the difficulty. It is well known that section EN X, 6-8 seems to give statements and ideals contradictory to the rest of EN. We consider it a main task to determine the nature of this supposed inconsistency.

The first thing to remember is that it is definitely un-Aristotelian to construct a doctrine of the first nine books of EN and then compare it with the problematic passage EN X, 6-8. The structure of action and the varieties of goodness cannot be a measure for the criticism of the account of happiness. Happiness is the telos of human action, and the structure of action must, then, be understood from the point of view of its end, not the other way round. Like the Republic of Plato, EN can only be understood from its summit. We should not ask if EN X, 6-8 is intelligible in the light of what is said before, but rather if EN X, 6-8 renders the former books intelligible.

Secondly, our section does not come as a sudden intrusion. It is referred to and obviously presupposed at any rate in Books I and VI. Moreover, the account of happiness is neatly prepared for in the first chapters of Book X. Further, the Politics assumes both the formal treatment of happiness and the doctrine of theoria in EN X, 6-8 as regards contents (cf. §§21 and 35).

Thirdly, there is no lack of explicit doctrinal conjunction between the two parts. EN VI, 13 makes it clear that moral virtue and the intellectual virtue of phronesis are means to the supreme virtue of theoria. On this point we may with profit adopt the distinction of Greenwood between 'component' and 'external' means: "To take a trivial example, fire and basin and cloth are means to pudding in the latter sense, suet and flour and currants in the former".[4] The question is: in what way is phronesis a means to theoria? Stewart thinks that phronesis is a 'component' means. Greenwood contends that it is regarded both as 'component' and 'external' means, because Aristotle never made the distinction.[5] If we could state the reason for a decision on this score, our main problem would be at least partly solved. In general form, we will anticipate some of our conclusions.

On the one hand, we can easily infer that a man cannot reach the happiness of theoria without being phronimos to a certain extent. On the other hand, it is certainly one of the main tasks of the phronimos politician to secure the possibility of the life of the philosopher. Thus it is difficult to disagree with Greenwood's opinion that Aristotle regards phronesis as a means to theoria both in the 'component' and the 'external' sense. This does not mean that a man must be a politician before he can be a philosopher. He must, however, have the minimum of phronesis demanded from a man who will be his own master. Therefore, it is not right to say: the more phronesis you have, the nearer you are to the happiness of theōria. The phronēsis of the politician is rather to be regarded as a specialisation which bars the path to supreme happiness for the man in question, but, nevertheless, is a condition for other men's happiness in the state. We will, therefore, rather stress the 'external' relation between phronēsis and theōria.

Contemplation cannot supply us with rules for moral action. The freedom and pleasure of theōria are rather the skopos of the acting person. If theōria could tell us what to do and what should be avoided, it would be useful for something. But Aristotle insists: "All the sciences, indeed, are more necessary than this, but none is better" (Meta. 983a10). It is chosen plainly for its own sake. It is a thing apart, an appendix to the structure of human life as determined by necessities, an addition that is supremely valuable in itself in spite of or, rather, because of its uselessness. Philosophy or theōria is primarily justified from above with the analogy to the life of the gods and not from below by pointing to political or ethical necessity. But both kinds of arguments are represented.

Theōria is different from phronēsis in the same way as the mark is something other than the archer, as health is another thing than medical art or science.[6] On this point there is no plain inconsistency between EN X, 6-8 and the rest of EN. Greenwood states the relation between the end and the means thus:

> To keep one's eye on the skopos, to measure by means of the horos, signifies to consider precisely what the final end is, and to fix the meson accordingly between excess and defect signifies to decide what moral states or moral actions are the best means towards the attainment of the final end. VI gives an explanation fully but implicitly that X makes explicit and perfectly clear.[7]

It is undoubtedly an exaggeration to say that EN X, 6-8 makes anything "perfectly clear". No doubt, it represents a problem, and till now we have made clear what this problem does not consist in. Now we will try to state it positively by turning back to our remarks on the anthropology of Aristotle.

In the first part of Book VI, phronēsis is depicted as the main virtue because it lets the human faculties work together in a well-ordered whole. So the political or practical wisdom is the most honourable virtue, and we should expect that this virtue could make men happy. For in the person with

practical wisdom, the faculties of human soul work together at their best.
This, then, should be the species of man in operation, the ergon of man,
because Aristotle insists that man is all his faculties, the reason as well as
the desire which is guided by reason. The desire gives its contribution to the
well-ordered whole of man just by being guided. This is said ex professo:
"It seems that the irrational passions are not less human than reason is"
(EN 1111b1). So far, Aristotle says what we rightly or falsely expect from
him. So far, his account is 'Aristotelian', bound to the observations on man
as a natural species, common-sensical and 'modern'. But, and this is the
crucial point, so far, there is no urgent need for philosophy in the grand
manner, and no place for it in the human life.

As far as we were concerned with phronēsis, Aristotle's ethics seemed
to rest on an anthropology which could easily be contrasted with the anthropology of Plato's Phaedo. The section EN X, 6-8 makes this contrast more
obscure. It is, in fact, not easy to detect any difference at all. In his treatment of happiness and the contemplative life, Aristotle identifies man with
his reason in its theoretical use. On this supreme virtue, he advances two
apparently contradictory statements: a) this virtue is the specifically human
one (cf. §24), but b) it is due to man only as far as there is something
divine in him coming in from outside (cf. §§22 and 26).

Surely, man is a species of nature in Aristotle's thought. And as a
species he can be described as to his distinctive features and compared with
other living beings. But man is more than that. There is a break in Aristotle's
anthropology. Man is not as completely comprehensible as other living beings.
To put it another way: except for his faculty of comprehension, man is wholly
comprehensible. But this faculty places man between the natural species and
the gods. And so does his habit of living in a city (Pol. 1253b4, 53b25-30). It
is, indeed, one of the chief tasks of the city to secure this more than merely
human life of man.   The philosopher crosses the border of his natural topos
as a man, because nature is the things that can be understood, whereas man,
at his best, is the curious being which can understand it all.

The justification of philosophy in Aristotle's ethics is a justification of
man and human life. The difference between his thought and Plato's Phaedo
is hardly a difference in enthusiasm, but a difference in arguments. Whereas

in the Platonic dialogue Socrates stresses the purification from the body,
Aristotle underlines the happiness of <u>nous</u> grasping the truth in <u>theōria</u>.
Aristotle has no embarrassment on the score of the body. He understands
how it works. His wondering, however, concerns the life of reason, which
is a thing apart (cf. §26).

The treatment of section EN X, 6-8 has often missed the point because
the peculiarity of the section was not made clear first. From the foregoing
statement of the problem, it should be obvious that there is no reason whatsoever to refer to the early Aristotelian writings and suppose that the section
is an excerpt from the <u>Protrepticus</u> or <u>On Philosophy</u>.[8] Suppositions like
this are, of course, merely answers born of perplexity. Yet they may depend
on a right observation: the passage in question has a protreptic, adhortative
character. The contemplative life is not described primarily as something
given, but it is defended against suspicion and attacks. More than that:
Aristotle tries with all his might to establish the 'life of the philosopher' as
the most important form of human <u>energeia</u>.[9]

There have been various attempts to state the relation of the problematic section to the rest of EN, starting from its contents. Gauthier's concept
of 'la vie mixte', which is more superfluous than false, will be discussed
later (cf. §25). The most courageous attempt is that of Burnet, who en passant
presents a new hypothesis in his notes of friendship:

> We can see, then, how the treatment of <u>philia</u> is quite in its right place
> here, and we shall see later how it leads us naturally through the stages
> of love for the good as such, and love for our own 'best self', to its
> highest manifestation, the <u>amor dei intellectualis</u>. It is, in fact, <u>philia</u>
> and <u>philia</u> alone that can bridge the gulf between <u>phronesis</u> and <u>sophia</u>,
> the practical and the theoretic life.[10]

Burnet wisely leaves it with the mere contention. There is, it is true,
a hidden connection between the account in question and the books on friendship (cf. §34). But it is more smart than appropriate to base a comprehensive
reconstruction on this scanty relation. And it should be added: <u>philia</u> is not
the main word in EN. We may also distrust the candidacy of <u>praxis</u>. Stigen's
supposition that an analysis of <u>praxis</u> would give us the clue to EN, however,
is not far from the mark. The supposition is based on the common Aristotelian
anthropology: to act is something peculiar to man.[11] Aristotle says: "Man

alone of animals is also the source of certain actions; for no other animal would be said to act" (EE 1222b18). But it must be remarked that the notion of praxis is not being used in the definition of happiness; and besides, the books on friendship and the section on contemplation seem to disappear or to be ignored when the investigation takes its starting-point in the concept of praxis.

Of course, 'duty' and 'conscience' are not the main words either. Gauthier's mixing of the concepts of 'duty' and 'conscience' into the ethics of Aristotle is not only confusing, but ignores the character of Aristotle's ethics as a whole. These curious christianisms blur the Greek temper of Aristotle.[12]

The main word in EN, giving a clue to its structure, is the same as the main word in the definition of happiness in Book I: energeia, the activity which realises the faculties of man and shows him at his best, i.e. exercising his ergon, performing his arete. From this point of view the plurality of virtuous actions is no mystery. This idea claims, too, a treatment of friendship as a condition for the realisation of man, and the account of contemplation as well as other sorts of human activity. The break and the dilemma are not cleared out, but thus the section EN X, 6-8 is not a priori a strange part in the Corpus. Its curious anthropology must be explained, but the problem consists in other things than the lack of contribution to an analysis of praxis or in its indifference concerning the question of 'duty' and 'conscience'. Not surprisingly, the stressing of the importance of energeia is the first point made by Aristotle in the section in question.

Aristotle is well aware that EN X, 6-8 treats another kind of activity, another level of action than the sort previously examined. Already in the introduction in Book I, he distinguishes between the two levels: "For always, or by preference to everything else. he (i.e. the virtuous man) will be engaged in virtuous action and contemplation" (EN 1100b19). In the passage immediately previous to EN X, 6 he repeats this:

What kind of pleasure or what pleasure should be said to be that proper to man? Is it not plain from the corresponding activities? The pleasures follow these. Whether, then, the perfect and supremely happy man has one or more activities, the pleasures that perfect these will be said in the strict sense to be pleasure proper to man, and the rest will be so in a secondary and fractional way, as are the activities (EN 1176a22-29).

This statement anticipates the opening contention of EN X, 8 that the virtues of action are secondary (cf. §25). Aristotle himself warns us, then, repeatedly, that there is a structural transition here. He is puzzled himself, and the dilemma is no mere inconsistency.

The perplexity of the commentators as to EN X, 6-8 should not be explained away or hidden in the last moment with a courageous hypothesis. We think that our perplexity is a most valuable one, reflecting the perplexity of Aristotle. As was said above, a kindred ambiguity and a similar problem can be noted in other writings of the Aristotelian Corpus as well. At the end of this book, we will examine the Politics, De Anima, and the Metaphysics. Concerning parts of these writings, there has been a discussion like the discussion of EN X, 6-8. In the conclusion we will make an attempt to explain all these obscurities. For if there is a similar dilemma in some of the other writings concerning ta anthrōpina, the dilemma of EN X, 6-8 cannot be understood isolated from the other ones. In fact, we must claim that the hypothesis should give a solution to the similar problems in the other writings as well.

These breaks make us the more watchful because the passages which thus make themselves conspicuous fit very well together. The sections which break with their respective pragmateiai much in the same way as do EN X, 6-8, have a common theme: they are all about philosophy, and the passages presuppose more or less the same anthropology as the passage of EN in question. The doctrines of scholē in the Politics, of nous in De Anima, and of noēsis noēseōs in the Metaphysics stand in some sort of connection. The nature of this connection has to be examined to understand the peculiarities of EN X, 6-8 (cf. §§35-38).

Our commentary has the headings: 'What is Happiness?', 'What Makes Man Happy?', and 'Who can be Happy, then?' They are meant to show the disposition of Aristotle's treatment of happiness from our point of view. As we shall see, the section repeats in the most conspicuous way the structure of EN on a smaller scale. Burnet says in his Introduction:

> The starting-point of Politics will be a definition, not of something that is, but of something that is to be ... we assume the construction is made, and ask what are the conditions of its being made until we come to something that is in our power.[13]

This is exactly what happens in EN X, 6-8. A definition of happiness is given, and it is asked for its conditions. The whole section ends up with an enkōmion or makarismos of the life of the philosopher, i.e. something that it is in our power to be. This last point gives the passage its protreptic, or quasi-protreptic character: the ideal is not easy to gain, but we are invited to it. If you can make yourself 'immortal' by means of theōria, you will be the favourite of the gods, and thus supremely happy.[14] The account, however, is not directed to philosophers in spe, but to lawgivers in spe. This justifies the expression 'quasi-protreptic' (cf. §35).

§5. HAPPINESS IS NOT A DISPOSITION

<u>1176a30-35</u>. Chapter X, 6 starts with a summing up and a programme. We have treated the virtues, friendship, and pleasure, Aristotle says; what is left is to examine the nature of happiness. This examination appears as an independent part of the structure of EN. It comprises EN X, 6-8 and ends with a new summing up in the introduction to X, 9. But the section is not independent in the sense that it can be regarded as an extraneous matter in the treatise. Firstly, it fulfils and completes the programme stated in Book I. Secondly, it is referred to on the way. And, thirdly, the transition from the examination of pleasure in X, 1-6, to the examination of happiness here, is prepared with neat rhetorics. The section on happiness had to come just here. It gives an account of the completion and perfection of human life, and with this, the task of EN is fulfilled. More striking is the vagueness of Aristotle's conclusion and more conspicuous the tension between the main lines of his ethics and the conclusive remarks.

It is, of course, wrong to stress the introductory account of X, 6 of what is treated previously. Gauthier finds only one of the discussions of pleasure mentioned and says ad loc.: "On remarquera que le traité du plaisir du livre VII est omis, preuve que ce n'était pas l'intention d'Aristote de le laisser là". A too hasty conclusion. Aristotle does not mean to give a list of the contents. He only reminds us that the opportunity has come to treat something hitherto neglected. He is to pick up a new theme and contends that it is a <u>main</u> theme by placing it on a level with the treatment of the virtues, friendship, and pleasure. But we may do well to note the scepticism of Stewart:

Connecting-passages like these must be interpreted with great caution. They are evidence only for the order which existed when they were written, and, in many cases, are demonstrably late interpolations. The two passages before us may well belong to the time when EN as we have it, with the two treatises on hēdonē, was made up; for the editor, having just left the subject of hēdonē (as treated in X, 1-5), would naturally put it last in his list of subjects hitherto discussed.[1]

Without doubt, happiness is a main theme, but it is not easy to explain why the treatment is so compressed. The virtues, friendship, and pleasure were considered in chapters and books, while happiness gets some scanty passages. Already in Book I, however, Aristotle is rather reserved concerning happiness: "Since happiness is an activity of soul in accordance with perfect virtue, we must consider the nature of virtue; for perhaps we shall thus see better the nature of happiness" (EN 1102a5ff.). Here, he gives us a warning with the expression typō dielthein (76a31), and this can, maybe, explain something. With this expression he reminds us of a passage from the introduction in Book I: "We must be content, then, in speaking of such subjects and with such premises to indicate the truth roughly and in outline (typō)" (EN 1094b19, 1094a25).

Here, as elsewhere, the methodological principle of Aristotle, that the treatment should correspond with the subject in question, is carried out. Typō does not need to imply that the section is provisional, that it prepares for or sums up another account. It rather means that the subject of the investigation, happiness, does not allow a more detailed and exact account. The reserve as regards the summit of his ethics may also result from another statement of the introductory book: "The end aimed at is not knowledge, but action (praxis)" (EN 1095a5). In this context, praxis probably includes theōria (cf. §35).

Aristotle is convinced that nobody will be happy by knowing more about happiness. He is also convinced that happiness is not due to the same condition in all kinds of men. Therefore, it is impossible to speak as generally about happiness as about the virtues, friendship, and pleasure. When in this section, however, Aristotle stresses one virtue, one sort of friendship, and one kind of pleasure at the cost of all others, it is not a sharply framed doctrine. He keeps, as will be seen, other possibilities for happiness open, even though he gives them an inferior rank. The eudaimonia of contemplation is the happiness par excellence. But Aristotle often mixes the question of what happiness consists in with the question of what the supreme happiness consists in. He defends the life of the philosopher eagerly. Therefore, in this section, he often makes happiness more exclusive than his theory for the rest admits.

The commentary will lead us to the core of Aristotle's anthropology for one important reason. The examination of happiness comes at the end of EN because happiness is the telos, the completion and aim of human life, the end towards which all men direct their actions. Even bad men seek for happiness with their bad actions. Their failure is due to the flaw that they do not know the proper conditions for eudaimonia. When Aristotle says that happiness is the end of human nature, he also means that it is in the account of happiness that we may discover what man really is, what he is to be: "For each thing is defined by its end" (EN 1115b22).

In EN X, 6-8 the different lines and topics of EN are united again. Here, for the first time, we meet the good that "every art and every inquiry, and similarly every action and pursuit, is thought to aim at" (EN 1094a1ff.). In these chapters, Aristotle fulfils the promise from the introduction, so far delayed. Accordingly, he reminds the listener and reader of the introduction by repeating the methodological principles. In the same way he recalls the preliminary definition of happiness in Book I. Ta proeirēmena (76a32) includes merely points that have been made in the introductory book. This does not, of course, mean that Book I and this section originally have formed one treatise without the rest of EN.[2] On the contrary, the repetitions and admonitions show that originally there has also been a certain distance between them, that EN X, 6 consciously picks up a theme which has been left in the introduction.

The section treats the end of human life, and we may stop for a while to consider Aristotle's concept of telos and teleios. An admirable little book by W. Theiler gives an account of the history of the concept with some remarks on its nature in Aristotle.[3] The agreement of this idea with Platonic and Socratic thought cannot be ignored. But, especially in the ethics, the Aristotelian concept has strikingly original features. Plato's doctrine of the Good in itself concerns something partly hidden or seldom found. In the Republic, Plato refers to this end:

It is what every man pursues and makes his aim, having a presentiment that there is such an end, and yet hesitating because neither knowing its nature nor having the same sure proof of it that we have of other things (Rep. 505e).

In Aristotle, however, the end is not a strange thing, but the completion and aim of the particular species, animal and man alike. It does not transcend ordinary experience, but determines it as its own distinctive rationality. Aristotle always turns down the concept of infinite regress and progress. There must be a stop somewhere. Otherwise nothing could be understood, owing to the lack of principles (Meta. 994a1, 994b9, 1000b28; EN 1094a20; Gen.Corr. 332b12).

The natural species are to be described from the point of view of their telos, their completion or end. For living beings have not only a source of motion in themselves, but also a source of rest (Phys. 192b13; Meta. 1013a29; Gen.An. 776a35). On this source of rest in human life, Grant says: "The end-in-itself renders life a rounded whole, like a work of art, or a product of nature. The knowledge of it is to give definiteness to the aims".[4] The telos of man may, then, be described in two ways: it is both the actual completion of man and the end of his ambitions. It is hardly possible to formulate this composite nature of the notion of the human telos better than Grant did:

> The ethical telos not only exists in man, but also for man; not only is the good realised in him, but it is recognised by him as such; it is the end not only of his nature, but also of his desires; it stands before his thoughts and wishes and highest consciousness as the absolutely sufficient, that in which he can rest, that which is in and for itself desirable.[5]

This makes human completion different from the completion of other species. The human telos is marked by and depends on the consciousness, the interest of the person. The matter, therefore is, more complex than the completion of plants and animals. Plants and animals do not reach their telos automatically. They may be disturbed by external conditions. But in man the perfection and completion depend on his decisions as well. Far from accepting Gauthier's interpretation on the point of duty (cf. §4), we have to quote him when he says: "Le bonheur est bien en effet la fin à laquelle doit tendre toute notre vie".[6] The idea of telos in Aristotle's ethics may thus be understood as an interpretation of the famous dictum of Pindar: become what you are! (Pyth. II, 72f.). A greater distance from the Kantian concept of duty can hardly be imagined.[7]

In Aristotle the terms telos and teleios do not, then, denote a state or disposition totally different from what is given. The telos is rather what makes man a complete thing. This meaning of teleios is explicitly confirmed by Aristotle (De Cael. 268a21). A thing is complete when all parts of it give their contribution to the whole, as an art or science is complete when it considers all parts of a subject (Pol. 1288b11). In the Metaphysics, Aristotle states the point thus: "Excellence (aretē) is a completion (teleiōsis); for each thing is complete and every substance is complete, when in respect of the form of its proper excellence it lacks no part of its natural magnitude" (Meta. 1021b21ff., 1055a10; Phys. 207a9). The concept of telos and teleios, then, renews the dilemma pointed out in §4: the telos for man should be something enbracing his whole nature. But the actual account of EN X, 6-8 seems to forget this point.

One could believe that aretē, virtue, perfection, or excellence, was the supreme good for man. But in Book I Aristotle twice rejects this supposition emphatically (EN 1095b31ff., 1098b31ff.), and in addition he finds that the distinction between virtue and happiness is already made in our use of language: "No one praises happiness as he does justice, but rather calls it blessed, as being something more divine and better" (EN 1101b26). Aristotle apparently knows the thought that virtue is happiness, as common or at least present in his environments, and he wishes to make it clear that it is not his opinion. The difference, he says, between this idea and his own is not an absolute one, but it is decisive. If virtue were happiness, then happiness could be had like a piece of property. But happiness means for Aristotle activity and realisation of human nature, in one word: energeia. He says:

> But it makes, perhaps, no small difference whether we place the chief good in possession or in use (en ktēsei ē chrēsei), in state of mind or in activity (en hexei ē energeia). For the state of mind may exist without producing any good result, as in a man who is asleep or in some other way quite inactive, but the activity cannot (EN 1098b31; EE 1219b9).[8]

This is polemics without mentioning the name of the counterpart.[9] In this practice we discover the central idea of his dialectics: to develop his own thought in constant discussion with his predeccessors. Burnet says ad 1098b31: "This is where Aristotle parts company with Speusippus, who defined it as ktēsis tēs oikeias aretēs ... His advance on the Academy consisted in the substitution of energeia for hexis, or what comes to the same thing, chrēsis for ktēsis". If Burnet is right, then the Academy was the target of Aristotle's polemics. It should be granted that the criticism hits Speusippus and Xenocrates as recorded in Clemens Alexandrinus (Strom. II, 21-22). We must add, however, that it also might be directed at expressions in Plato himself, e.g. in the Philebus, where Socrates says: "Shall we further agree that we will both try and discover some state (hexis) and disposition (diathesis) of the soul, which is able to make the life of all men happy; will not that be our aim? - Yes, that will be our aim" (Phil. 11d). In the Symposium Plato lets Diotima make a similar statement on the condition of happiness, using the word ktēsis (Symp. 205a). Against this opinion, Aristotle here repeats two arguments from Book I (EN 1095b32ff.). Both of them are meant to show the absurd consequences following from the idea that virtue is happiness.

(1) "If it were, happiness might belong to someone who was asleep throughout his life, living the life of a plant" (76a34). To this we may ask: why should not a man spending his whole life asleep be called happy? As is well known, sleep and consciousness are used in the early Greek philosophy as representations of the ignorant and the knower. This distinction is especially sharp in Heraclitus.[10] In Aristotle, sleep is also an instance of irrationality and passivity. The sleeping man is beyond good and bad. He lacks, among other things, the moral consciousness which makes man a man (EN 1102b2). Sleep does not bring about the specific human.[11] On the contrary, it activates the irrational functions of the human soul, the functions that it has in common with other living beings. Therefore, the sleeping man is compared with the lunatic, the drunkard, or with a man under the influence of passions (EN 1147a13). This identification of sleep with the reign of the vegetative part of the soul is clearly expressed in EE:

> Nor likewise would anyone desire life for the pleasure of sleep either; for what is the difference between slumbering without being awakened from the first day to the last of a thousand or any number of years, and living a vegetable existence (zēn onta phyton) (EE 1216a2ff.).

For Aristotle activity and human life belong together. It is, then, not the completion of human life to have this or that virtue. This is emphasised in the considerations on the liberal man (EN 1120a8) and the just man (EN 1129b31): the virtues have to be used, employed. It is never enough to have virtues, faculties, or knowledge. To live is to act in the way that the possibilities are turned to account. On this opinion Aristotle constructs the correspondence between the ergon of human life, its arete, and its eudaimonia (EN I, 7). Happiness is brought about when the task is executed in virtuous activity.

This opinion is mirrored in the statements about the gods. They must be active. They cannot sleep like Endymion (EN 1178b18). They must think of something: "for if the divine thought thinks of nothing, what is there here of dignity? It is just like one who sleeps" (Meta. 1074b17ff.). If you can think, but actually think of nothing, then you are like one who knows, but does not use his knowledge, i.e. you are asleep (EN 1152a15).

A sleeping man cannot be happy. This is not merely because he is beyond good and bad, but also because he does not activate his human faculties. The most famous passage on sleep in Aristotle is found in Gen.An. There he comments on the different degrees of potentiality. Everybody knows what a mathematician is, and that his proper task is to study mathematics. He can, however, also let it be. But a mathematician who is not studying, is not actual qua mathematician, Aristotle contends. The not-studying relates to the studying as a sleeping mathematician to one awake (Gen.An. 735a9-13). It follows, then, that man is man first and foremost in executing his ergon, his proper task.[12]

(2) The other argument against the opinion that virtue is happiness is also repreated many times. For Aristotle, virtue is a hexis, i.e. a disposition or state of mind. The opinion expressed must involve, then, that happiness is a hexis too. But if happiness were a hexis, even the most unlucky man could be happy. Then happiness could be brought unharmed through the greatest sufferings. Aristotle has, however, a more realistic view of the conditions of happiness. Eudaimonia is not due to luck, prosperity, or external conditions, but all the same it cannot be preserved completely without them. The instance of illustration is Priam, the king of Troy when it was sacked by Agamemnon (EN 1100a6ff., 1101a6ff.). No one could expect him to remain happy when everything he had was destroyed.

Happiness can, apparently, be affected by the possibilities of human realisation, because the realisation of our faculties is directed towards a world that can be different. According to common opinion, Aristotle nowhere contends that man can realise himself in the contemplative life in the way that he could be happy by means of inner acts precluded from the rest of the world. This isolated and protected way to happiness should, then, belong to the wisdom of the later centuries. It must be admitted that Aristotle's representation of the active human being mostly presupposes an open relation to the environment, the state, and its duties. In this context, lucky occurrences can make human life happier (EN 1100b25), because the conditions of most human realisation may be improved this way.[13] However, the bios theōrētikos is thought of as a sort of exception (cf. §§20 and 21).

§6. AN ACTIVITY DESIRABLE IN ITSELF

1179a35-36. Happiness is not a hexis, but an energeia, an activity that realises human nature. This is also clearly expressed in Book I. Aristotle found that happiness was the supreme good for man. But it had to be defined more exactly (EN 1097b23), because there are different opinions as to what happiness consists in. It is brought about when man is executing his proper task, Aristotle said, the task which results from his faculties as distinguished from the faculties of other living beings, the faculties man has in addition to those which he shares with plants and animals: "There remains, then, an active life of the element that has a rational principle (praktikē tis tou logon echontos)" (EN 1098a3). Shortly afterwards, he again emphasises the active aspect of this life: "We must state that life in the sense of activity (energeia) is what we mean" (EN 1098a5). Then follows his famous definition of the human good: an activity of soul in accordance with virtue (EN 1098a13).

Both in EN and in the Politics Aristotle often substitutes eudaimonia with the expression eu zēn to stress that it turns on a sort of life and not on an inner constitution of mind or a set of right opinions (cf. EN 1095a19, 1098b21, 1140a28). The discussion of happiness in the Politics is marked by the same basic determinations as in EN, even though the framework of the investigation is different (cf. Pol. 1328a38ff.).

The definition of _eudaimonia_ as an activity results from the Aristotelian ideal of life (EN 1100a12ff.). It is not true that the happy man does not need friends, he says, for happiness is not a thing that we can keep for ourselves. It is not "present at the start like a piece of property" (EN 1169b25ff.). _Eudaimonia_ comes to the one who activates his faculties. Otherwise it would belong to that which is merely possible. But all possible things are incomplete They may become something which is not there yet, or they may serve something else, find their completion in an end. But this is not the case with happiness. We praise the things which serve their end well, but we never praise happiness or the gods, Aristotle says (EN 1101b10ff.). The reason is that happiness does not consist in having a faculty, "it is not to be placed among potentialities (tōn ge dynameōn ouk estin)" (EN 1101b12).

The logical connection between the determinations of happiness as (a) an activity from which the sleeping man is excluded, and as (b) an end in itself, is given with Aristotle's doctrine of possibility and actuality. Happiness must be completely actual, therefore it is its own end. It is an activity desirable for its own sake, not for the sake of something else. It can neither be a _hexis_ which is to be activated nor an activity which is to be appreciated by its results. _Eudaimonia_ must be something final, complete. This point is underlined in the _Metaphysics,_ where Aristotle distinguishes between two kinds of actions. One is aiming at a result apart from the exercise,

> but where there is no product apart from the activity, the activity is present in the agents, e.g. the act of seeing is in the seeing subject and that of contemplation in the contemplating subject and the life is in the soul, and therefore happiness also; for it is a certain kind of life (Meta.1050a22-37).

This is the basic argument of EN X,6 in a nutshell.

The definition of happiness as something final (teleion ti), is not surprising. Book I begins with the question of what is desirable for its own sake, the good at which "all things aim" (EN 1094a3ff.). From this definition one could believe that happiness was the only thing desirable for its own sake. But this is not the opinion of Aristotle. There are many other things which are not wished for or aimed at for the sake of something else (cf. EN 1174a 4ff., 1096b16ff.). Happiness, however, is the final end because it is merely wished for for its own sake. This does not mean, of course, that other things

could not both be wished for for their own sake and serve a further end,
depending on the situation. The best actions are not the actions that are
good for nothing, but the actions that include their good aim in themselves.[1]
For these actions, the condition is <u>scholē</u>, leisure (cf. §20). Only in
<u>scholē</u> is man his own master, not serving anybody except at his own wish.
<u>Scholē</u> is desirable in itself, but also desirable because it makes happiness
possible. <u>Eudaimonia</u> is, however, the only thing desirable exclusively for
its own sake and, accordingly, the most final end. This is inferred from the
actual use of the word <u>teleios</u> (EN 1097a30ff.).

If Hardie is right, this point includes polemics against Plato: "Aristotle
might have recalled that, at the beginning of the <u>Republic</u>, Book II, the goods
said to be the fairest of all are those which are desired both for themselves
and for their consequences (357b-58a)".[2] In Book I, Aristotle attacks Plato's
doctrine on the Good in itself (EN I, 6), and we have seen that his rejection of
the opinion that happiness could be a <u>hexis</u> is directed against Plato as well
as against members of the Academy. If this last point is also to be understood as polemics against the teacher, this must restrict the judgement of
Düring: "Im Schlussteil der Nikomachischen Ethik ist der geistige Einfluss
Platons stärker als in irgendeiner seiner Schriften".[3] The objects of attack
mentioned above are what most decidedly determine the account of happiness
in Book X.

In the introductory book, happiness is defined as "that for whose sake
everything else is done" (EN 1097a19) and then follows the qualification from
"the point of view of selfsufficiency" (EN 1097b8). This is, as can be seen,
the same order of representation as in the summary of Book X. For happiness
is not only exclusively desirable for its own sake; it is what is most desirable
of all things. Nothing can be done to increase it if it is there (cf. EN 1097b
17ff.). This is, as it seems, contradictory to the grades of happiness which
are presented elsewhere, when Aristotle mentions 'supreme' happiness,
happiness 'in a secondary sense', or distinguishes happiness from blessed-
ness (<u>makaria</u>), as in the judgement about Priam (EN 1101a6ff., 1176a25).
For if happiness is complete, without any defects, can there be, then, many
forms of happiness or grades of happiness?[4]

That <u>eudaimonia</u> is the most final end is repeatedly stated in Book I
(EN 1097a30ff., 1097b7), and Aristotle defines it there in just the same way

as in Book X: "The self-sufficient (to autarkes) we now define as that which
when isolated makes life desirable and lacking in nothing (mēdenos endea).
And such we think happiness to be" (EN 1097b14ff.). Grant contends that
this is crumbs from the table of Plato. In the Philebus he makes Socrates
say:

> Is the good perfect (teleon) or imperfect? - The most perfect (teleota-
> ton), Socrates, of all things. - And is the good sufficient (hikanon)? -
> Yes, certainly ... - Let there be no wisdom in the life of pleasure, nor
> any pleasure in the life of wisdom, for if either of them is the chief
> good, it cannot be supposed to want anything (mēdenos eti prosdeisthai)
> ... (Phil. 20c-e).

In this passage, Plato gives the basic determinations of happiness, which
Aristotle repeats in our text. Even though they use almost the same words,
there seems to be a certain difference. Grant comments:

> It is to be observed, however, that Aristotle analyses the term teleion,
> and gives it a more philosophical import than Plato had done. Plato
> probably meant nothing more than 'the perfect'. Aristotle analyses this
> into 'that which is never a means', 'that which is in and for itself
> desirable'.[5]

We note that Aristotle shares the predicate teleion about the supreme
good with the Philebus, but he defines it in such a way that it contradicts the
definition of the chief good in the Republic, as was mentioned by Hardie above
This supposed dependence on the Philebus, then, does not put this section
nearer to the world of Plato, but, on the contrary, evinces Aristotle's
conscious elaboration of an alternative. That the contention of Düring is
wrong as a general statement of the character of EN X, 6-8, is evident from
the concept of autarkeia, on which the whole argument of this section
depends.[6]

The ideal of self-sufficiency is one of Aristotle's deepest convictions.
In EN is mirrored in the distinction between poiēsis/technē on one hand, and
praxis/energeia on the other.[7] Aristotle thinks that making or producing
something is the mark of an unfree man, if it is the contents of his life. The
free man does noble deeds which in themselves are desirable to execute. His
main consideration is not that of utility (cf. Protr. B42, B25). The ideal of
self-sufficiency determines the Aristotelian concept both of the best action,

the best man, the best city, and the best life. We will later consider the
self-sufficiency of contemplation (cf. §18) and its condition in the self-
sufficient life of schole̅ (cf. §20). Here we merely note that the ideal
corresponds to the basic ideal of the Greek polis. Self-sufficiency does not
mean, then, an ideal of isolation or exclusion from the rest of the world.
The ideal of autarkeia is the ideal of freedom: to be one's own master both
in the relation to other men and to the necessities of life.[8]

The distance from the ideal of life expounded in Plato's Phaedo is
evident. In the Phaedo man is a being who is out for something else, a
being who can only justify his life by attaining something beyond it.
Aristotle's acceptance of man as a species on his own awards him a certain
value as he is. Human life is no more an escape of the soul from the body,
taking refuge in the contemplation of the divine. However, when Aristotle
talks about philosophy and the philosopher, this autarkeia is no more
ascribed to man with all his faculties. It is reserved for the highest part of
his soul.

This may be understood as an inheritance from Plato, as Düring apparently does. But the differences should be underlined as well. In Aristotle, the
divine object of contemplation nearly disappears at the expense of the act of
contemplation, because man has his end in himself. Consequently, Aristotle
contends that it is possible for man qua man to settle down well in this world.
That which is beyond is as indifferent to him as it was to Epicurus.[9]
Aristotle's praise of the proper energeia of man is a confession of human
life at its best. Grant gives a beautiful comment on the import of this thought.
He says: energeia

> is the mind itself called out into actuality. It springs out of the mind and
> ends in the mind. It is not only life, but the sense of life; not only waking,
> but the feeling of powers; not only perception or thought, but a conscious-
> ness of one's own faculties as well as of the external object (EN 1170a28
> ff.).[10]

§7. VIRTUOUS ACTIONS AND AMUSEMENTS

<u>1176b6-11</u>. Happiness was something desirable in itself, something self-sufficient and final, Aristotle said. In addition, it was not a <u>hexis</u>, but an <u>energeia.</u> He goes on, then, to examine the different activities that may be regarded as candidates for the task: to make man happy. As we have seen, virtue alone does not make man happy, because virtue is a mere <u>hexis</u>. But, maybe, virtuous actions do? These are activities of the nature that Aristotle has claimed as desirable for their own sake. The discussion is not, however, finished with this, for there are other activities that are done for their own sake. The first to be mentioned are the pleasant amusements, and later contemplation is considered. Thus the three candidates for the proper <u>energeia</u> of human nature are (a) virtuous actions, (b) pleasant amusement, and (c) contemplation. These activities correspond, as can be seen, to the three forms of life presented in the introductory book (EN 1095b17ff.).

Section EN X, 6-8 does not, then, strictly speaking, turn on contemplation, but on happiness. <u>Theōria</u> is only one possible way to human happiness, but it is probably the most important. The disposition of the section may be reconstructed in different ways. The apparent structure, however, is given in Book I, in its programme to examine the three possible or typical forms of life as to their force to bring about happiness.[1] In this section Aristotle repeats on a reduced scale the structure of EN as a whole by reconsidering the conclusions about virtuous actions and pleasant amusements before the account of the third activity, contemplation, as promised in Book I (EN 1096a4).

Both virtuous action and contemplation are pleasant (cf. §17), but Aristotle distinguishes between the life of pleasure and the life of virtue by naming the good action and the good man <u>spoudaios</u>. This is apparently stressed on the points where the difference between those two forms of life could otherwise be confused. When Aristotle says that virtuous actions are pleasant, he always adds: pleasant to the man who is <u>spoudaios</u> (cf. EN 1099a21ff.). To act virtuously is not an amusing game, but a serious thing which deserves consideration, and, then, as a reward, gives the agent a certain satisfaction. Probably this pleasure results from the doing of a free act, and the virtuous act is free.

On the use of spoudaios here, Gauthier says ad 1176b8:

Aristote dans tout ce chapitre va jouer sur le double sens du mot spoudaios: est spoudaios ce qui réclame des soins empressés, ce qui demand effort, ce qui exige de l'application; d'où le double sens du mot: d'une part, "soigné", "bien fait"; "excellent", "vertueux", et d'autre part, "sérieux", "consciencieux". Ainsi l'activité vertueuse, spoudaia, parce qu'elle est excellente apparaîtra du même coup comme sérieuse, et s'opposera ainsi à l'activité de jeu.[2]

In the passage at hand, virtuous actions are confronted with pleasant amusements, because both of them are desirable for their own sake. The question is which of them makes man happy. Naturally, the virtuous action is set off at the expense of the amusements. When we wish amusements for their own sake, Aristotle says, the reason is that they are good for nothing else. They are desirable in themselves because that is what is left when they do not serve any end (EN 1176b10). Here Aristotle exaggerates the worthlessness of pleasant amusements in such a way that he contradicts the statements in EN 1176b33-77a1 (cf. §11). There the amusements are defended as relaxation between the periods of work.

The positive part of Aristotle's judgement about amusements is not an opinion of his own; Rodier says ad loc.: "C'est l'opinion commune (dokousin) qu'Aristote exprime ici, et non sa propre pensée". Rodier tries to argue for this contention by referring to EN 1176b17: "Now these things are thought to be of the nature of happiness because people in despotic positions spend their leisure in them". The opinion that amusements can give happiness is, of course, a serious mistake. But this assertion is quite different from the conclusion Rodier wished to prove. Aristotle starts with the contention that amusements are desirable in themselves, and that is just what he means. On this contention rests the analogy between the three forms of life, the three activities that are candidates for the contents of the best life. It is too easy to say that Aristotle does not actually mean what he contends. Here neither Rodier, Burnet, nor Stewart has discovered the point that Aristotle wants to make. Both amusements, virtuous actions, and contemplation are actually wished for for their own sake, otherwise they could not satisfy the minimum claim in the definition of happiness. Because they do, Aristotle regards it necessary to consider all of them.

In the Rhetorics, Aristotle gives a sort of reason for the opinion which
Rodier thought to be common and not his. He says:

> Again, that is pleasant which is not forced on us; for force is unnatural,
> and that is why what is compulsory is painful, and it has been rightly
> said: All that is done on compulsion is bitterness unto the soul. So all
> acts of concentration, strong effort, and strain are necessarily painful;
> they all involve compulsion and force, unless we are accustomed to
> them, it is custom that makes them pleasant. The opposites of these
> are pleasant; and hence ease, freedom from toil, relaxation, amuse-
> ment, rest, and sleep belong to the class of pleasant things; for these
> are all free from any element of compulsion (Rhet. 1370a9-16; cf. EE
> 1223a30ff.).

This is no irresponsible liberalism which feels contempt for necessary
actions and necessary work. The point of the argument is that force is
unnatural, and therefore (a) pleasure is, as a rule, excluded from compulsory
acts; (b) amusements and relaxation are not forced on us and, accordingly,
they can be pleasant. But (c) it is most pleasant to transcend the sweet life of
amusements and act according to the propulsions of human nature, that which
protrudes from its proper faculties.

It is not right to say that Aristotle rejects the pleasure in life or even
that he does not consider it as a serious candidate for the contents of the best
life.[3] It is right that a life spent in amusements is not good enough for
Aristotle, but that is partly because it is not pleasant enough. The best life
is the most pleasant life. He does not, then, reject pleasure as a compound
of the best life; on the contrary, he shows that hēdonē is included in the form
of virtuous life. The point of the passage at hand is to show that they who
seek for pleasure in amusements, look for it in the wrong place. It is not
false to pursue pleasure, but it is wrong to do it in the amusements, even if
they are analogous to the best aims of life in the way that they are wanted
for their own sake.

Stewart makes nearly the same mistake as Rodier. Of Aristotle's contention that amusements are desired for their own sake, he says ad loc.:

> This, of course, it not Aristotle's own opinion. His answer to the argu-
> ments for regarding amusement as an end in itself begins with ouden
> d'isōs etc. (b17); and in §6 he states his own view of the place of
> amusement in life - that it is relaxation, a means to the better perfor-
> mance of earnest work.

But it is said nowhere that amusements are ends in themselves. That would, of course, have been a popular opinion not shared by Aristotle. What is said is that amusements actually are wanted, desired for their own sake. And that is something quite different. What is later said about relaxation as a means is wholly compatible with the knowledge that people choose it for its own sake. The two passages do not differ in the way that Aristotle firstly presents the common opinion and then gives his own, but rather in the way that he first mentions what amusements are, and then what they should be. Dirlmeier seems to be the only one who judges rightly on this point:

> Das Spielerische gehört zwar qua energeia, die wegen keines weiteren Zieles gewählt wird, in die gleiche Kategorie wie das ethische Handeln; aber da ist ein grosser Unterschied: während beim ethischen Handeln der Verzicht auf weitere Zwecke etwas Positives ist, führt der "Verzicht", den der Spielerische leistet, wie die Erfahrung lehrt, zu Negativem. Eine Sache um ihrer selbst willen tun, ist also nicht a priori etwas Wertvolles.[4]

We should be careful, however, in distinguishing between the opinions of the many and Aristotle's own contentions. Unlike most of the Greek philosophers, he shows respect for opinions that have been expressed before. Aristotle never mentions the common opinion contemptuously. His own task is merely to think the common opinions through, to show the consequences that are included in them. Aristotle only finds what people were always out for. He articulates what they tried to say. So also on this point: they are wrong who hope to find happiness in pleasant amusements, but the contention is nevertheless in a way understandable, because pleasant amusements are, like happiness, wanted for their own sake. And that which brings about happiness is pleasant (EN 1099a25; cf. EE 1214a1ff.). Aristotle's point of departure is the common opinion, not because it is wrong, but because it includes a sort of presentiment of what is right and true.[5]

§8. THE TYRANTS SPEND THEIR LEISURE IN AMUSEMENTS

<u>1176b12-21</u>. We have seen that pleasure and amusements are often chosen for their own sake or, at least, not for the sake of anything else. But Aristotle admits openly that he has scruples concerning this candidate for attaining the best life of man. Certainly, he hesitates in some passages before the final judgement, but immediately he tries to explain how people can believe that happiness consists of amusements. The most obvious reason we have mentioned already, and he reformulates it thus in the <u>Politics</u>:

> It sometimes happens that men make amusement their end, for the end probably contains some element of pleasure; but they mistake the lower for the higher, and in seeking for the one, find the other, since every pleasure has a likeness to the end of action (<u>Pol</u>.1339b31ff.).

In this way Aristotle will explain how people are led astray in their search for happiness. Those who devote themselves to amusements are looking for the same thing as those who cultivate their virtues. The pursuit of happiness is common to all men; nobody wishes to be unhappy. Therefore it is urgent to explain why most men do not attain their end. This happens, Aristotle says, when they mistake this end for something else which is similar to it.

In the present passage still another reason is given. Most men identify happiness with amusements because tyrants spend their leisure in this way, Aristotle says. For people believe that the tyrants are supremely happy. Why people believe that, Aristotle does not say, but Burnet suggests: "because they are able to choose freely" (ad EN 1095b21-22). Maybe this is common sense. For Aristotle, however, this kind of freedom is no mark of perfection. Occasionally, Aristotle mentions "unimpeded activities" as bringing pleasure and as being similar to the chief good (EN 1153b9ff.). But this freedom does not exclude discipline, it only negates compulsion from outside. Freedom without any rules is as abhorrent to Aristotle as it was to Plato. In the ethics of Aristotle it is wrong to follow every chance thought because it is contrary to nature. Rodier comments on this idea: "Liberté et contingence sont synonymes de mal".[1] This point is stressed many times in the writings of Aristotle (e.g. <u>Gen.An</u>.770b9, 778b17; <u>Phys</u>.197a14; <u>De An</u>.407b6). The popular suggestion, then, on the happiness of the tyrants, probably rests on ignorance of the nature of freedom.

The discussion of tyrants and happiness may also be understood as a reference to another author with whom this was a favourite theme. In Herodotus' account of the meeting between Solon and Croesus, we find a dialogue on happiness between a philosopher and a tyrant. That happiness does not depend on wealth or power, that the tyrant who can do what he likes is not happy for that reason – this is the theme of the dialogue in Herodotus (I, 29ff.). It is evident that Aristotle had this story in mind when he wrote the present passage. The reference to Solon some pages later (EN 1179a9ff.): "Solon, too, was perhaps sketching well the happy man when he described him as moderately furnished with externals, but as having done the noblest acts, and lived temperately", is apparently a reference to the same story in Herodotus (I, 30). Still the name of Solon is twice mentioned in EN (1100a11, 15) when Aristotle considers if a life has to be finished before you can call it a happy life. This is, again, a reference to Herodotus (I, 33), and it makes it reasonable to suppose that this dialogue not only was well known to Aristotle, but also that he found it a most valuable source for his own account of the best life (cf. §20).

As a problem, the happiness of the tyrant is also found elsewhere in Herodotus. It turns up when Xerxes and Artabanus have their famous dialogue while the Persian Army is crossing the Hellespont (VII, 44ff.), and of course, in the story about the destiny of Polycrates (III, 39ff.). For Herodotus those destinies show the necessity of the <u>nemesis</u> hitting the hybrid characters. There he finds the reason why the Persians were defeated. The meeting between Solon and the tyrant is a picture of the power and authority of little Greece facing the vast Persian empire.[2] In Aristotle the chief ideas of Herodotus are preserved, the claim for moderation and the pride in being a Greek.

The happiness of the tyrant is also a theme in Plato's <u>Gorgias</u>. Polus is confused when Socrates says that power in itself is no good. You cannot tell if a man is happy if you do not know "how he stands in the matter of education and justice" (<u>Gorg</u>.470d), Socrates says, "for where there is great power to do wrong, to live and die justly is a hard thing, and greatly to be praised, and few there are to attain this" (<u>Gorg</u>.526a). The tyrant is neither happy nor unhappy because of his position. Happiness depends on other qualities (cf. <u>Phaedr</u>.248e).

When Aristotle mentions an instance of the supremely powerful tyrant who chooses the wrong path, he reminds the reader of Sardanapallus, the Syrian king, famous for his life of pleasure (EN 1095b21ff.). Sardanapallus is, maybe, picked out because he had given a sort of reason for his style of life. In an epigram he admonishes the reader that he will soon be dead. Therefore, he should take the pleasure he can get (Diodor. II, 23). The passage concerning him in Book I discusses the three forms of life. It is only natural, then, that he appears again here where the life of pleasure is considered anew (cf. EE 1216a16; Pol. 1312a1). In Book I, Aristotle says:

> Now the mass of mankind are evidently quite slavish in their tastes, preferring a life suitable to beasts, but they get some ground for their view from the fact that many of those in high places share the tastes of Sardanapallus (EN 1095b19ff.; cf. EN 1179b15).

For Aristotle happiness depends on the specific human faculties, and the life of pleasure is condemned because it is "a life suitable to beasts" in the literary sense. This objection has been rather common. It is also found in Heraclitus.[3] And Plato says in the Republic:

> Those then who know not wisdom and virtue, and are always busy with gluttony and sensuality, go down and up again as far as the mean; and in this space they move at random throughout life, but they never pass into the true upper world; thither they neither look, nor do they ever find the way, neither are they truly filled with true being, nor do they taste the true and abiding pleasure. Like brute animals with their eyes down and bodies bent to the earth or leaning on the dining-table, they fatten and feed and breed (Rep. 586a ff.).

Heraclitus had no theory about the relation between men and animals. His statements are to be read as mere invectives. But Plato's comparison between the life of pleasure and the life of brute animals takes its point of departure in their chance character.[4] Both are lives lived at random: they lack the fixed point. Neither the beasts nor the man who is busy with sensuality (the ingenious translation of Jowett reproduces the sardonic language of Plato very well) will ever find the way to true being. In Aristotle, however, this comparison gets its meaning from his doctrine of the soul. The human soul has the faculties both of plants and of animals. But to lead a real human life you have to unfold, display, and develop the faculties that you have in addition to those of plants and animals. By this,

Aristotle thinks of the theoretical and practical powers of reason. The life of pleasure is the most spurious candidate for the contents of the best life because it does not activate the specific human powers. The same point is made perfectly clear in EE 1215b30-16a10 with the same ingredients of eastern monarchs, oxes, eating, and sex. But the pleasures that Aristotle is thinking of can also be more refined. In Rhet. I, 11 he mentions things that may be classed as "pleasant amusements", in a chapter full of interest for the historian of Greek culture.[5]

Men in despotic positions, however, have even more problems that obstruct their happiness. It is always difficult for them to find good friends, Aristotle says (EN 1148a27ff.). They live in fear, and distrust good men (Pol. 1313b30). They are, on the contrary, "always fond of bad men, because they love to be flattered ... and the tyrant wants to be alone in his glory" (Pol. 1314a1-7). But a man cannot be happy without friends. Certainly, Aristotle never says that friendship is a condition for happiness. A happy man, however, needs friends to share his happiness. If they are missing, it indicates that something is wrong. The tyrants, having no real friends, because real friendship is only possible between good men, cannot be happy. Something is wrong because "rich men and those in possession of office and of dominating power are thought to need friends most of all" (EN 1155a6ff.)[6]

Friendship may be based on utility or pleasure. But neither of those two forms of friendship is the best one. Tyrants, Aristotle says here, have friends for their pleasure, but on this ground no real friendship can grow up. A friendship is not complete unless two men seek some good together:

> Friendship based on utility is for the commercially minded. People who are supremely happy, too, have no need of useful friends, but do need pleasant friends ... Perhaps they should look out for friends who, being pleasant, are also good, and good for them, too; for so they will have all the characteristics that friends should have (EN 1158a21ff.).

The tyrant's concept of happiness is incomplete, and that can be seen from his incomplete understanding of friendship. His activity is usually not a virtuous one, therefore it excludes the complete virtue of friendship.

From these people, we cannot learn what happiness is, what makes man happy, Aristotle contends. If not from the tyrants, we have, however, to learn it from somewhere. Despotic position is not a condition for happiness and there is no reason to look for the happy man there. As to happiness we can be instructed by the good man who distinguishes himself in perfection of virtue and reason.[7] For these are the two elements from which the good activities flow.

We note that the tyrant plays a role of a negative pattern in Aristotle's ethics, just as he does in his Politics. In EN the tyrant is juxtaposed to the virtuous man, in the Politics to the king, the best ruler.[8] The connection between the two treatises should be noted. The tyrant is a bad ruler because he is a bad man. The account in EN gives the reason for the account in the Politics. The positive pattern of EN is the phronimos or spoudaios. If you cannot be good yourself, you have to imitate the good man, Aristotle says, picking up a statement from Democritus.[9] You are on safe ground if you act like the man who has "practical wisdom" (EN 1143b21-31). This is not valid for the best life. Nobody can acquire the virtue of theōria through imitation of other men. There the idea of imitation applies to the relation between man and God. God relates to the theōrōn as the phronimos relates to the man with mere moral virtue.

The importance of patterns results from the fact that everything is changeable and unsteady in human relations. Therefore, it is so difficult to make abstract rules. Moreover, virtue and happiness are, in Aristotle, primarily found in the life of the individual. This follows from his epistemology, from his doctrine of primary and secondary substances.[10] The concrete exercise is more real than the rule. The individual thing at its proper work is more fundamental than the universal concept. Likewise, the political activity which realises the constitution is more real than the constitution itself (cf. Pol. 1278b10).

This is the reason why the medical analogies are so instructive: health is primarily given in the healthy man (cf. §3), and the good man thus provides a metron: the safest standard is the judgement of the wise and prudent man. This is said repeatedly in Plato's Politicus (284c, 294b, 309c), and it is a main thought in Aristotle. For the acts of the prudent man are a source of pure and noble pleasure, pleasures that are unknown to the brutish tyrant.

§9. THE DISPOSITION DECIDES WHAT IS PLEASANT

<u>1176b21-27.</u> The life of the tyrant can prove neither what is really pleasant nor which activity makes man happy. The positive pattern is the life of the good man, and him we can trust, because "things are both valuable and pleasant which are such to the good man" (76b25). Even Heraclitus knew that men have different pleasures depending on their disposition. Thus some of them are like asses who would prefer sweepings to gold (EN 1176a 2-16). And now Aristotle says:

> For each state of character (<u>hexis</u>) has its own ideas of the noble and the pleasant, and perhaps the good man differs from others most by seeing the truth in each class of things, being, as it were, the norm and measure of them. In most things the error seems to be due to pleasure; for it appears a good when it is not (EN 1113a30ff.).

The good man can be the norm and measure for things noble and pleasant because he, (a) in displaying these qualities, realises them. As was said above, for Aristotle goodness and pleasure are more real in the human being who activates them than in their definition. Therefore virtue is not to be learnt from or found in discussions or distinctions, but in life, which can serve as a pattern because it fulfils the demands on virtue. Here, however, we also have an old idea from the earliest Greek philosophy: (b) that like knows the like. You have to be a really good and noble man to know what is really good and noble. And Aristotle seems to regard pleasure as intermediary between the knowing and the known, emphasising the correspondence between them.[1] The just action is, accordingly, pleasant for the just man and **virtuous** acts are pleasant for him that loves virtue. Aristotle says:

> Now for most men their pleasures are in conflict with one another be-cause these are not by nature pleasant, but the lovers of what is noble find pleasant the things that are so by nature; and virtuous actions are such, so that these are pleasant for such men as well as in their own nature. Their life, therefore, has no further need of pleasure as a sort of adventitious charm, but has its pleasure in itself (EN 1099a12ff., 1166a12, 1170a14ff., 1174a1ff., 1176a15-22).

Thus the third reason to watch the good man is introduced: (c) the actions and emotions of the good man seem to correspond with nature in a certain way. When it is said that he is "norm and measure" of the good and noble, it does not mean that he can freely decide which things are to be valued as good and noble. It only means that the good man is "norm and measure" for us who have not yet attained his level of virtue. In him we can see virtue at work and thereby he is fulfilling nature's ways. Aristotle says in the introduction to his Politics:

> But then we must look for the intentions of nature in things which retain their nature, and not in things which are corrupted. Therefore we must study the man who is in the most perfect state both of body and soul, for in him we shall see the true relation of the two; although in bad and corrupted natures the body will often appear to rule over the soul, because they are in an evil and unnatural condition (Pol. 1254a36ff.).

Tyrants are mostly 'corrupted' in the way mentioned, and good men have 'retained their nature'. They are healthy, as they should be, and that is the reason why they can discern the things which are really good, noble, and pleasant, i.e. the things that are so in their nature. In treating the principle of contradiction in the Metaphysics, Aristotle says:

> For the same thing never appears sweet to some and the contrary to others, unless in the one case the sense-organ which discriminates the aforesaid flavours has been perverted and injured. And if this is so, the one party must be taken to be the measure, and the other must not; and I say the same of good and bad ... (Meta. 1063a1ff.).

Also in his ethics this thought is fundamental for Aristotle.[2] The good man is like a healthy body, and the bad man like a body deformed or injured (EN 1113a27). From this it follows, of course, that we must watch and listen to the good man, for "the same things do not seem sweet to a man in fever and a healthy man" (EN 1176a12).[3]

To feel pleasure at the right moment is a mark of the good man. Because men seek for pleasure also, not only for happiness, these two motives often appear in conflict with each other. But in the good man there is no such conflict because he finds pleasure, and the finest pleasure, in the activities which will make him happy. For the healthy man finds pleasure in fulfilling the demands of virtue and nature. The man who seeks for pleasure will fail to gain virtue, but the man who executes virtuous acts will get pleasure in addition. The good man who has chosen the right path, tends to go right in all

matters, and especially in matters of pleasure (EN 1104b32ff.). This point
is the more important because Aristotle here seems to agree with a statement of Plato: human beings are the puppets of the gods, moved by the
strings of pleasure and pain (Leg.644d). Accordingly, it is a point of great
importance for the education to learn the right emotive response to different
things.[4] Aristotle contends:

> Hence we ought to have been brought up in a particular way from our
> very youth, as Plato says, so as both to delight in and to be pained by
> the things that we ought; for this is the right education (EN 1104b11ff.;
> cf. Top.163b12-16, and Plato's Leg.653a ff.; Rep.401e ff.).

In this way the individual life is actually formed, but man can also be
guided to a good life by these means. And a good life for the state depends
on the goodness and the educational level of the citizens: "Therefore, for
this reason also, the whole concern both of virtue and of political science
is with pleasures and pains; for the man who uses these well, will be good,
he who uses them badly, bad" (EN 1105a10ff.).

§10. HAPPINESS DOES NOT LIE IN AMUSEMENTS

1176b27-77a1. The conclusion in the heading is no surprise. Again and again
Aristotle varies on the same theme to make his thoughts completely clear.
Happiness (eudaimonia) is not the same as pleasure (hēdonē). Amusement
(paidia) is not the same as relaxation (anapausis) or leisure (scholē). Thus
he prepares the ground for the next chapter and for the discussions in the
Politics. The tyrant hopes to find happiness in pleasant amusements, but the
good man knows that virtue and reason are conditions for human happiness.
Aristotle has already banished amusements and pleasure qua exclusive ends
as candidates for the contents of the happy life by associating them with the
life of the tyrant. Moreover, it is asserted here that the life spent in a hunt
for amusements is "silly and utterly childish" (76b32f.). Aristotle finds
that amusements are rather moderate rewards for suffered hardship.
Amusements do not have the final character that we demand from the activity
which should be the aim of life.

In the <u>Politics</u>, Aristotle discusses the use and effects of music,[1] and states the difference between those pleasures and the final aim of human life thus:

> For the end is not eligible for the sake of any future good, nor do the pleasures which we have described exist for the sake of any future good but of the past, that is to say, they are alleviation of past toils and pains (<u>Pol</u>.1339b35ff.).

And shortly before: "Amusement is for the sake of relaxation, and relaxation is of necessity sweet, for it is the remedy of pain caused by toil" (<u>Pol</u>. 1339b15ff.).

Aristotle's teaching is evidently the same in the <u>Politics</u> as in EN. Both treatises take their point of departure in man as he is. Whereas Plato demands a permanent tension of human life, a constant concentration on the Good in itself, Aristotle seems to accept human life as it is lived by imperfect beings. Without complaining he accepts that not all men can become philosophers. He uses sharp expressions against people who devote their lives to pleasure, as can be seen here. But he does not operate with two mutually exclusive alternatives as if the life of the beasts were the only possibility besides the contemplative life. Aristotle operates with a long range of characters, activities, virtues, faculties, and forms of life. He accepts and wants to describe life in its plurality. But he attempts to do it without losing his message of the best life.

It is evident by now that happiness does not lie in amusements. But amusements are not for that reason bad or indifferent. So it may be, but it may also be a good thing.[2] Aristotle says:

> For innocent pleasures are not only in harmony with the perfect end of life, but they also provide relaxation. And whereas men rarely attain the end, but often rest by the way and amuse themselves, not only with a view to a further end, but also for the pleasure's sake, it may be well at times to let them find refreshment in music (<u>Pol</u>.1339b26ff.).

The end is something final, complete, while toil and amusement seem to presuppose each other in the way that if you took trouble and suffered hardship in order to amuse yourself, you would be caught up in a sort of circle. Toil would alternate with amusement and amusement with toil without ever disclosing the path to the final end. Stewart says rightly ad 1176b34: "<u>Paidia</u>

is a necessity imposed upon man by his composite nature. It is a foolish
mistake to make this necessity the end". But, moderately enjoyed, amusements might serve as a sort of medicine and be a good thing as long as they
are not confused with happiness or the end of life.[3] Aristotle says, and we
quote from the Politics again:

> For he who is hard at work has need of relaxation, and amusement gives
> relaxation, whereas occupation is always accompanied with exertion and
> effort, we should introduce amusements only at suitable times, and they
> should be our medicines, for the emotion which they create in the soul
> is a relaxation, and from the pleasure we obtain rest (Pol. 1337b37ff.).

We seek amusement and pleasure for the sake of relaxation and rest.
These, again, fulfil their task as alleviation of former toil and exertion. A
final end is not yet in sight. But, as often, Aristotle has merely presented a
new argument for a conclusion already attained. The definition of happiness
is given, and we know that it is to be an activity. We should think, then, that
it should be sought at the same level with exertion and toil, and not among
amusements, pleasures, and relaxation. But the activity which is the final
end is a thing apart. Aristotle's concept of scholē and theōria will be discussed later (cf. §§14 and 20), but it is an important point of this introduction
to suggest that the final end is a sort of completion, that it includes and integrates both pleasure and activity.

Aristotle takes pains to show that theōria is final not only as the last
link in a long chain of things serving something else, but also final in the
way that it gathers and includes man's different paths to happiness.[4] In
theōria man is freed from the circle of toil-amusement-toil and has come to
a point where everything he always wanted is present at the same time. The
structure of the relation between the three lives is, then, similar to the
relations between the faculties of the human soul, or the different forms of
knowledge as considered in Alpha of the Metaphysics.[5] The higher forms
include the lower. This does not necessarily mean that Aristotle's exposition
is a construction resting on this principle. The inclusion of lower forms in
the higher depends in his ethics apparently on the method. The less valuable
forms of life are also held to be the best by somebody. And the existence of
the opinion has to be explained. Their contentions must at least be partly
right. Opinions held by many or by wise people cannot be completely wrong.

The solution of the problem is to suggest the same principle of hierarchic inclusion as valid for the range of real things as it was for the range of opinions.

§11. THE MORE SERIOUS ACTIONS ARE THE BETTER

1177a1-6. Firstly, Aristotle repeats the conclusion from the passage above: if exertion and amusements alternate, and only one of them is given at a time, and if, further, exertion is what the virtuous life requires, amusement cannot be joined with virtuous life, which is the life thought to be happy.

Then, he goes on to argue from the evidence of the word spoudaios. As we have seen already (cf. §7), it means both 'excellent' and 'serious'. This makes it easy for Aristotle to show that the unserious things connected with amusements are not as good as the more serious things. In the expression meta spoudēs, the construction from the same root means 'with exertion'. Aristotle thus discloses the wisdom of the language. It is, of course, a rather unserious method of philosophy if you mean to say something new, to discover something. But Aristotle believes that he can reconstruct the valuations of the good old days by asking the words what they mean. This is the secret of ēdē in the Greek text (77a6). Ross translates it 'ipso facto', but Burnet's old translation 'ex vi termini' goes more directly to the point. For Aristotle is convinced that old and honourable opinions are conserved in the language (cf. §3).

We have seen that Aristotle was especially fond of the word spoudaios and the connected expressions when naming the good man and his acts as differing from the life of amusements and pleasure. A context of this sort gives him the opportunity to play with words. Here, the meta spoudēs in 77a2 contrasts the meta paidias in 77a4. In this way Aristotle attains two chains of associations. In the first expression: seriousness, hard work, and reliability. In the second expression: amusement, laughter, and easy living. To ask in this way the question where virtue and happiness can be found, is to answer it.

At this point it may be convenient to consider Aristotle's relation to language. We have seen that he analyses traditional opinions and manners of

expression to find a basic point of departure for his argument. The common
opinion, however, for Aristotle does not consist of mere opinions, any more
than language is mere language. The common opinion comprises, as was
said before, a presentiment of what is right and true, and this is reflected
in the everyday use of language.

But there is another reason to consider the contents of the words used
by everybody: language mirrors reality. The value-language reflects the
realm of real values. The common use of words not only comprises the un-
conscious experience of generations, but it is a "guide and signpost to metaphysical knowledge of a structure in reality which parallels that form".[1]
Monan here ignores the fact that Aristotle did not even have a name for
'language'. Thus he could not apprehend it as a thing for itself with 'reality'
juxtaposed as a parallel. Recently, Wicland has given an account of this
problem and offers a new solution from the point of view of modern philosophy
of language: "Die Sprache ist also nicht Gegenstand unter Gegenständen,
sondern sie ist aller Gegenständlichkeit vorgeordnet, alle Gegenständlichkeit
erst ermöglichend".[2] Applied to our context it means that a certain language
makes certain judgements of value possible. The question if an expression
should be 'meaningless' or lack reference in 'reality' does not occupy
Aristotle because the dichotomy of language and reality disappears from his
point of view, although it is not totally unknown to him. In general, then, the
understanding of Wieland is right, but only as adequate as a simplification
can be. He concludes:

> Daher ist auch das Sprachliche für Aristoteles kein Bereich, der noch
> aus etwas ausserhalb seiner verweisen würde. Er überträgt nicht ein-
> fach sprachliche Kategorien auf die Wirklichkeit - weil es phänomenolo-
> gisch ursprünglich eine solche sprachfreie Wirklichkeit ebensowenig gibt
> wie eine gegenständliche Sprache. Indem er sprachliche Formen unter-
> sucht, analysiert er also sogleich die Strukturen der Wirklichkeit - nur
> eben dass es sich bei dieser Wirklichkeit um die Lebenswelt des natür-
> lichen Bewusstseins handelt und nicht um eine bewusstseinstranszendente
> 'Aussenwelt'.[3]

The argument from the evidence of the word spoudaios is, then, no
singular phenomenon, but a regular procedure based on Aristotle's relation
to language. It is, in fact, one of the most common features of his dialectics,
found not only in his ethical treatises, but also in the other writings as well.[4]

§12. HAPPINESS IS NOT FOR ANY CHANCE PERSON

<u>1177a6-11</u>. The argument of this passage is not an attack on the slaves, but on the opinion that bodily pleasures can give happiness. It is the last contribution to defend the contention that happiness does not lie in amusements. Aristotle has argued with the tyrant and the good man as representing the negative and the positive pattern of life. Now, in considering the slave, he repeats the argument from the life of the tyrant and says expressly that he regards bodily pleasures as bad. The tyrant and the slave have, of course, most different social positions, but as to freedom they belong to the same class. To be sure, tyrants can choose freely and the slave cannot, but experience shows that the tyrant mostly misuses his freedom of choice with the result that he is quite as much bound in his body as the slave is imprisoned by his duties.

Aristotle does not contend that the enslaved person is a beast or an inferior being in himself. The slave has no life of his own, and that deprives him of the self-sufficiency demanded from a happy life. But he is not on that score an inferior person. He has, it is true, no part in virtuous activities of the best sort, but that does not mean that he is bad. The virtuous activities are not the morally good actions in the Christian sense of the word. The Greek arete̅ implies fitness and excellence. The judgement on the slave, that he has no part in the virtue that makes men happy, is not an estimation of his person as such, but an evaluation of the conditioned possibilities for his realising his powers and human faculties.[1]

The slave has "no share in happiness" because he is not his own master. He lives as an appendix to another man's life. His functions and freedom are so limited that you can hardly call it a human life at all (77a9). The meaning of the last statement is much discussed. For the different philological interpretations of 77a9, cf. Rodier ad loc. We cannot see any serious problem here because the same statement is repeated in <u>Pol</u>.1280a32ff. There <u>bios</u> is replaced by <u>to ze̅n kata prohairesin</u>: 'a life of free choice'. Stewart is hardly right when he says ad loc.: "<u>Bios</u> is here the life of a citizen, as distinguished from <u>zōe</u>, animal life". But Aristotle never calls the slave a beast or an animal, even though he often compares them and mentions the two classes together. <u>Bios</u> is here rather the full, free life of the citizen who can display his human faculties as distinguished from those who depend

on him: the women, the children, and the slaves (Pol.1259b20ff.).[2]
Aristotle never forgets that the slaves, in spite of everything, "are men and
share in rational principle (logos)" (59b27).

This, however, is only one and the most liberal aspect of Aristotle's
view concerning the slaves. Here he points out the difference between the
slave and the free man as a difference in activities. A slave cannot do
what the free man does, therefore he has no share in human life. But it
seems that if his activities were the same as those of the free man, the
slave could also have a share in happiness. In other words: the enslavement
of the slave depends on his social function and role, not on his nature. In EN
Aristotle discusses friendship and the possibility of a friendly relation between the slave and his master. Here he seems to affirm our account of his
opinion:

> For where there is nothing common to ruler and ruled, there is not
> friendship either, since there is not justice; e.g. between craftsman and
> tool, soul and body, master and slave; the latter in each case is bene-
> fited by that which uses it, but there is no friendship nor justice towards
> lifeless things. But neither is there friendship towards a horse or an ox,
> nor to a slave qua slave. For there is nothing common to the two parties;
> the slave is a living tool and the tool a lifeless slave. Qua slave, then,
> one cannot be friends with him. But qua man one can; for there seems
> to be some justice between any man and any other who can share in a
> system of law or be a party to an agreement; therefore there can also
> be friendship with him so far as he is a man (EN 1161a34ff.).

The slave qua slave, then, is like a tool to a craftsman, or a horse to a
horseman, an ox to a farmer. He is a thing that can be used for ends in other
men's mind. The tool and the draught animal, however, cannot change their
function. They are completely identical with their usefulness. The slave is
of another kind. "As far as he is a man", there may also be friendship with
him. Further, all men are to some extent equals under the law. Aristotle
even includes the slaves in the democracy as sharing the minimum of equality
in this constitution. A master may have his slave as a friend as far as he is
a man; therefore, Aristotle continues, "while in tyrannies friendship and
justice hardly exist, in democracy they exist more fully; for where the
citizens are equal, they have much in common" (EN 1161b8ff.).

In these passages of EN, Aristotle keeps the door open for more liberal
thoughts. But, as is often said, Aristotle was not a liberal. Düring says: "In

seinem politischem Denken blieb er ein laudator temporis acti".[3] And Hardie: "Aristotle was not a democratic liberal, and did not shrink from the idea that happiness, at least in its best form, is for the fortunate few not the meritorious many".[4] In the Politics, Aristotle propounds a more restricted view on the slaves. In the discussions of EN he often treats the slave as an individual, but in the Politics he considers him as a kind of being. There, Aristotle adds that it is the nature of the slave to obey and to be an instrument. His deprivation of happiness depends not only on his job, but also on his nature, on his position not only in society, but in the scale of living beings.[5] What is so by nature, however, cannot be altered, while a man's job and social position can (cf. Pol.1252b9, 1255a24, 1256b25, 1259b18ff.; Poet.1454a20). The reference to the inferior nature of the slave puts him beyond the reach of the invitation to the best life and even to happiness.

Again, the theme in this passage is not the slavery, but the relation between happiness and bodily pleasures. Aristotle suggests that pleasures do not activate human nature. They do not demand freedom or excellence, but can be enjoyed without it. The point for Aristotle, however, is to link happiness with the supposed supreme activity of human nature. If bodily pleasures could give happiness, virtue would be superfluous. For bodily pleasures can be enjoyed by any chance person without any special qualities, without any preparation. If the aim of life was to be attained so easily, education could have no purpose. Who would worry about paideia if they could be happy by means of paidia? By linking happiness to a certain level of education and discipline, Aristotle can depict paideia as the way to happiness and speculate on the final aim of human life.[6] If the slave could be happy, that would mean ruin to philosophy. But theoria is the very thing that must be saved in EN as in the Politics, De Anima, and the Metaphysics.

§13. REASON IS THE BEST THING

<u>1177a12-17.</u> At this point the commentators differ in their notes most openly.
The difference is, however, not so much a difference of opinion as a difference of treatment. Some think that this is the right place to discuss the relation between the psychology of <u>De Anima</u> and the corresponding doctrines of
EN. Others find that the passage can only be understood from the use of the
concept of <u>nous</u> in general, both in Plato and Aristotle. Still others think
that this is the appropriate place to discuss Aristotle's theory of knowledge.
We admit that something can be said in defence of all of them. The problem
of the meaning of <u>nous</u> both in previous Greek philosophy and in Aristotle
has been paid much attention lately, resulting in some useful works.[1] This
treatment will, however, as a startingpoint, try to disclose the meaning of
the passage by considering the peculiar repetition of <u>eite</u> - <u>eite</u>: "whether
it be <u>nous</u> or something else" (77a13-14), "whether it be itself also divine
or only the most divine element in us" (77a15-16). Why does Aristotle let
the possibilities stand side by side in this way without a decision? Here also,
there are many attempts at interpretation.

(a) Stewart thinks (ad loc.) that a reference to Plato can solve the
problem of <u>eite</u> - <u>eite.</u> In the last part of the last pair he finds polemics
against Plato (<u>Meno</u> 99e). This must be a mistake, as can be concluded,
firstly from the lack of analogy to the previous pair: Plato did not call the
best thing in man by another word than <u>nous</u> (cf. <u>Tim.</u> 30b; <u>Soph.</u> 249a; <u>Phil.</u>
30c). Secondly, Stewart regards the passage as a programme for the dis-
cussion in EN X, 7. But it clearly does not anticipate what follows, so this
it cannot be. Moreover, Stewart fails to see its conscious vagueness.

(b) The words as they stand may reflect doubts as to the truth of the contentions. But in other contexts it becomes obvious that Aristotle is able to define the nature of nous precisely, when he wishes to. As Hardie says: "Reason or something else? If these words indicate doubts, the doubts are not further expressed in the EN".[2] On the contrary, the opinion that nous is the best thing in man is the fundamental thesis of EN X, 7. Grant remarks on the use of dokei: "Sometimes it denotes the opinion of others, not of Aristotle himself, but sometimes it is a part of the style, to avoid the appearance of dogmatism'(ad EN I, 1). In the present case, dokei is used in the last sense.

(c) The repetition of eite - eite may also reflect the indifference of the author as to the truth of the statements, or more probably, as to the importance of using the correct names. There is a best thing in man which at its best gives man the best life, Aristotle says, whatever you want to call it. Greenwood and Dirlmeier, who argue for this interpretation, may be partly right. But they cannot explain satisfactorily why Aristotle regards the correct name as unimportant.[3]

(d) The reason for the looseness of expression noted here is, of course, not to be found in the particular origin of the passage either. Gauthier and Verbeke think that the impreciseness of expression is due to Aristotle's immature stage of development.[4] He is still half-Platonic. He is not yet ripe. Consequently, he has not yet taken the step to his own clear-cut doctrine. To this we can only repeat that it is superfluous to suppose that EN X, 6-8 or parts of it originally belonged to the assumed Platonic milieu of the Protrepticus or the Eudemus. Its doctrine is not inconsistent with De Anima or with the rest of EN in such a way that it can be explained by assumptions of stages of development.[5]

(e) The vagueness must, however, be understood. A repetition of the doctrine of nous from Book VI, 6-8 was not necessary. Moreover, in this context it was not desirable. For the vagueness has a certain purpose. Partly, it corresponds to the inclusive, inviting character of the protreptic sermon. The important thing is not to know or use the right words, but to take the decision to realise this virtue. Partly, the mode of expression may be chosen because Aristotle not only tries to defend his own philosophy, but philosophy in general. And he will not tie the justification of this form of life too closely to his own technical terms. He will not convert the reader to Aristotelianism, but to philosophy.

Therefore, we will perhaps not know more about the meaning of this passage merely through the study of the concept of nous. The best thing in man is sought for to determine the best activity, the activity which makes man as happy as he can be. But, and this is an important point, Aristotle does not infer from a fact of psychology to a statement of value. He rather goes the other way. What is most certain to him is that the theoretical activity is the most valuable one: "That this activity is theoretike, we have already said" (77a17-18). From this point of view he apparently shows in-difference as to the proper name of his basic faculty. In every case, the energeia theoretike is the thing to be considered, and nous is, in this con-text, defined as the faculty which makes this activity possible. That this is the sequence of the argument, is shown by the structure of EN X, 7. It starts with a summing up of the characteristics of the energeia theoretike, and it ends with an invitation to the reader to choose "the life of his own self" (cf. §24).

In this introduction nous means neither more nor less than the malista anthropos in 1178a7. Nous here is not primarily the technical term of Aristotle's psychology or his theory of knowledge, but a concept of value comprehending the faculties that first of all makes man a man. It should be noted that the best treatment of nous from the point of view of epistemology recognises the different scope of EN X, 7 by avoiding references to it.[6] This, of course, does not mean that the contents of the concept are totally different in the two cases. On the contrary, a short study of nous in the psychology and epistemology of Aristotle makes it obvious why this faculty is held to be the basic one for philosophy and science. In fact, the value-concept and the technical term converge in a peculiar way (cf. §36).

Greenwood examined the relation between the treatment of the faculties of the soul in EN VI, 6-8 and the account in EN X, 7. He found that the correspondence, if not perfect in details, does not represent any serious problem.[7] The only thing to note is that in EN VI, 6-8, nous is the name of the intellect as a whole, the complete theoretical faculties of man as opposed to the practical ones; whereas the best thing in man is called to epistemonikon or to beltion morion. Far from confining the correspondence between the two books, this observation makes the agreement perfect. When <u>nous</u> is commented on and described in EN X, 7, it is always in contrast to the practical faculties of the soul. Aristotle is here not occupied with the division of work inside the theoretical part of the soul, but only with the superiority of the spiritual eye as compared to practical calculations.

Our passage mentions a couple of features assumed to be distinctive qualities of <u>nous</u>. Firstly, it is said to constitute the "element which is thought to be our natural ruler and guide" (77a14-15). Secondly, he remarks that it takes thought of "things noble and divine". And thirdly, Aristotle touches the question of its divinity. These ideas are worked out elsewhere in the Aristotelian Corpus, and it may be profitable to consider some kindred statements.

<u>Nous</u> is "thought to be our natural ruler and guide". The language suggests an analogy to the political unit, the state or the household, and this metaphor has been used before in EN:

> Metaphorically and in virtue of a certain resemblance there is a justice, not indeed between man and himself, but between certain parts of him; yet not every kind of justice, but that of master and servant or that of husband and wife. For these are the ratios in which the part of the soul that has a rational principle stands to the irrational part; ... there is therefore thought to be a mutual justice between them as between ruler and ruled (EN 1138b5-14).

Both theoretical and practical reason belong to the rational part of the soul, so the quotation cannot be a direct comment on their relation. However, as obviously as in Plato, Aristotle follows what A. Speiser has called the "Gesetz der superponierten Formen".[8] This rule implies that the ratio of the relation between the body and the complete soul also must be valid for the relation between the rational and the irrational part of the soul, and, again, valid for the relation between the practical and theoretical part of the rational soul (cf. <u>Protr.</u>B23; <u>Pol.</u>1334b15). This is apparently the structure of the Simile of the Line in Plato's <u>Republic</u>, and it is employed by Aristotle too in a less complex form. For each relation Aristotle finds the same ratio: means/ end, potentiality/actuality, of which the first part has to obey, the second to command.

The relation between the irrational and rational part of the soul described in Book VI is, then, we may suppose, also valid for the relation between the theoretical and practical reason. Accordingly, there is no contradiction in saying both that practical reason is the "ruling part" (EN 1113a6) and that theoretical reason is "our natural ruler and guide" (EN 1177a14-15). Practical reason rules the deliberation, whereas theoretical reason rules the practical reason. This 'ruling' and 'ordering' should not be understood as an anticipation of Kant's moral philosophy. The metaphor rather stresses the resemblance between the conditions of a well-ordered state and a well-ordered individual. It does not mean that the philosopher should be made a king, but it claims a recognition of his natural superiority (cf. Meta. 982a18, 982b4-7). Nor does it imply that theoretical reason has a force to command, but it surely means that we have to show consideration for its realisation first and foremost (cf. EE 1249b10-12).

The quality of reason implied in the second statement: that it can think of things "noble and divine", will be discussed later (cf. §15). The third statement, however, on its supposed divinity, deserves some consideration here.

The position of nous is mainly described by means of two analogies. Firstly, the analogy between the soul and the household, mentioned above. Secondly, the analogy between the soul and the kosmos. In this last analogy, nous corresponds to God: "As in the universe, so in the soul, God moves everything. For in a sense the divine element in us moves everything" (EE 1248a26; cf. Phys. 252b25; Mot. An. 700a31). Gauthier says ad 1177a15-16: "La divinité de la partie rationelle est une idée chère à l'Aristote de la période platonicienne". But the divinity of nous is not an idea found only in a limited period of Aristotle's thought, quite apart from the fact that the determination of such periods is utterly difficult, if not impossible. However, Gauthier is right in so far as he wishes to underline the resemblance between EN X, 7 and some passages in the Timaeus. In Plato nous is also described as the governing part in us: "We must begin by providing that the governing principle shall be the fairest and the best possible for the purpose of government" (Tim. 89d). Thereafter its divinity is described by an imaginative picture of man as a scion from heaven:

Concerning the highest part of the human soul, we should consider that
God gave this as a genius to each one, which was to dwell at the extre-
mity of the body, and to raise us like plants, not of an earthly but of a
heavenly growth, from earth to our kindred which is in heaven (Tim. 90a).

And, finally, the nourishment of the best part in man is thought to make
him immortal (Tim. 90b-c; cf. §23).

On the other hand, Plato's doctrine of nous is different from that of
Aristotle.[9] The mere use of the word and the stressing of the divinity of
nous is not a sufficient reason for ascribing to him a 'Platonic' period. As
was said above (§2, n.21), the order of the universe is not the only paragon
for human perfection in Aristotle. The idea is not at all strange to him, but
it is the core of Plato's doctrine of nous. In Aristotle nous is divine primarily because its activity is the actualisation of man as a spiritual being, his
perfection. The Platonic idea may, however, still be effective in a way
because, as Léonard has noticed in Aristotle: "Le mot theios n'est jamais
appliqué à d'autres réalités que la pensée et les astres".[10] This problem
will be discussed more fully in §15.

The final reason for the divinity of nous we find in the Metaphysics.
There philosophy is described as "the only free science, for it alone exists
for its own sake" (982b26). And Aristotle continues: "Hence also the possession of it might be regarded as beyond human power; for in many ways human
nature is in bondage" (982b28). Nous is divine, then, because it makes the
most divine knowledge possible. "Most divine" for two reasons: a) it has God
as its mediate or immediate object, and b) it is free and self-sufficient to the
highest degree thinkable, so that Simonides could say: "God alone can have
this privilege" (Meta. 982b30-83a10).

During tries to furnish Aristotle with two gods, the one a cosmic orga-
niser, the other the nous in us.[11] It must be admitted that he can thus explain,
e.g., the final passage of EE more easily than most commentators before him.
The ambiguity of the Greek concept of nous is, of course, known from other
sources as well, e.g. the statement of Socrates in Xenophon's Mem. I, 4, 8, or
in Phil. 22c and 28d. In every case, Aristotle seems perplexed as to the
details of his own theology (cf. the complaint of Cicero, §1, n.5). The only
piece left of Aristotle's dialogue On Prayer says: "God is either nous or
something behind it".[12] Aristotle must have had strong reasons to retain this

doctrine, and its importance is far from superficial. It is closely tied to his
doctrine of philosophy, with the consciousness of his own work as he wishes
to present it. We agree with Düring when he says: "Auf der Frage was der
nous ist, präsentiert er widerspruchsvolle Antworten; die Frage ist seine
pleistē aporia". And later: "In seiner Lehre vom nous tritt sein Dilemma
klar zutage".[13] But we disagree with him in the characterisation of this
dilemma. It is not a psychological one, for Aristotle's doctrine of nous is
not a piece of Platonism, a causal remainder in an otherwise new philosophy.
The doctrine of nous and its ambiguity, as was said above, has grown up
from the philosopher's considerations on the theme of philosophy, from his
attempts to justify his own thought. This could not, of course, be done from
inside as far as the Greeks are concerned. The philosophical problem of
self-consciousness was unknown to them.[14] Accordingly, it is done from
outside, by means of the metaphorical analogy to the complete self-realisation of the gods.

Energeia is the main word in EN, and the most complete energeia is
the final station on man's way to happiness. Eudaimonia was defined as
psychēs energeia tis (EN 1098a17). At other places, Aristotle speaks of the
soul as the actuality of the body, or the soul is the eidos, the particular
faculty and the proper function of man's body. This matrix, however, is
not sufficient to describe the position of nous. Aristotle employs, then, a
more complex structure of analogy:

> Are goods one by being derived from one good or by all contributing to
> one good, or are they rather one by analogy? Certainly, as sight is in
> the body, so is reason (nous) in the soul, and so on in other cases (EN
> 1096b27ff.).

As sight can be said to be the ruler and the energeia of the body, nous
is the ruler and the energeia of the soul. The relation body/soul makes soul
what was called forma informans by the scholastics. As the body is blind
without the faculty of sight, the soul fumbles in the dark without nous. Nous
is, then, not the energeia of the soul's faculties as a whole. It is rather a
forma assistans (as Joachim rightly puts it), "present in man as the pilot is
present in the ship".[15] Nous is the omma tēs psychēs (EN 1096b29, 1144b
10ff.). At one point, Aristotle apparently thinks that the soul has a practical
eye too, namely deinotēs (EN 1144a30), but the thought is not further worked
out.

The metaphor nous = opsis is not uncommon in Aristotle (cf. Protr.
B24; Rhet.1411b12; Top.108a11). Plato, too, uses horan and idein
synonymously with noein.[16] In his still unsurpassed work on Greek Theories
of Elementary Cognition (1906), Beare explains this connection thus:

> The matchless clearness and distinctness of visual impressions, to which
> all perceptions of form are primarily due (Top.113a31), renders these
> peculiary suitable not only for being remembered, but also for being
> arranged, i.e. grouped and classified, under such conceptions.[17]

Both in Plato and Aristotle, however, nous means much more than the
mere faculty of conceptualisation.

Analogies like these should not be brought together to reconstruct a
coherent system. Inconsistent as they may be for the comparing eye of the
collector, they function well in their proper contexts. The analogy between
sight and nous is especially important because Aristotle seems to think that
we find the essence of human life there: "Life seems to be essentially the act
of perceiving or thinking. And life is among the things that are good and
pleasant in themselves" (EN 1170a18ff., 1170b1; cf. Meta.980a20-27; EE
1244b27). The body is an instrument. Most parts of the soul are both instruments and ends. Nous, however, is solely its own end. It is good and
pleasant in itself, and it does not exist for the sake of anything else. On the
contrary, "everything exists for the sake of nous" (Protr.B23,24). Randall
explains it thus:

> The Greeks disliked to use mind instrumentally: they felt mind was to
> be enjoyed rather than merely worked with. So for them the highest
> value of nous was to achieve insight, to see life as a dramatic spectacle,
> in all its shades and colors, with all its complexities and paradoxes;
> to see it as it is, to hold it up, to contemplate it, to see through it.
> Such 'seeing' we enjoy in the theatre at its best; and the Greeks called
> such an intellectual vision theōria, and praised the life of theōria.[18]

Nous is not the form of the body. It is rather described as the "form of
forms" or the "receiver of forms": De An.429a27, topos eidōn; 429a15,
dektikos tōn eidōn; 432a2, eidos eidōn. Nous has, then, two main aspects.
It is a) universal receptivity, and b) the anchoring ground of pure energeia
(cf. De An.III, 5). This fact discloses a principal difference between
Aristotle and Plato. In Plato, as he gives the account of his theory in the

Meno, all possible knowledge is in the human mind already. It merely has
to be made conscious. The nous of Aristotle, on the other hand, is a
pinax agraphos of a certain kind. Nous is the mind that potentially is all
that it can know (De An. 431b17). Caird is probably far from the mark when
he finds the two doctrines fully compatible,[19] but his summary of the nature
of nous is worth considering:

> Reason is capable of apprehending all objects and under all conditions.
> Like pure matter, it is a potentiality for all the forms of things; for it
> has no nature of its own which could come between it and other things
> or prevent it from seeing them as they are. Hence it is not going beyond
> itself in knowing anything else. Rather in all knowledge it is realising
> its own nature and so coming to a consciousness of itself.[20]

EN X, 7 concludes with the contention that nous, above all, is man.
Two of the analogies which we have found that Aristotle employs to distinguish
the position of nous, may be written thus:

a. body: soul = irrational: rational part = practical: theoretical part
b. body: sight = soul: nous

These are ratios of the matrix means/end or ruled/ruler. The ratios not
only represent analogical extrapolations from one field to another. They
turn on divisions inside a whole, and the structure shows a certain ambiguity.
As mere analogies the ratios agree with the general anthropology of Aristotle.
But read as a record of the internal structure of man it is hardly compatible
with the picture of him as a natural species. What we mean by the general
anthropology of Aristotle, Léonard may explain:

> L'homme est, pour Aristote, autre chose et davantage que la somme de
> ses parties: il est une ousia, un ensemble, et donc une totalité unifiée,
> et en tant qu'ensemble, et tant qu'homme, il a une fonction propre, en
> vue de laquelle les autres opèrent. C'est cette fonction qu'il s'agit de
> définir, celle qui, chez l'homme, unifie toutes les autres; il ne s'agit
> nullement des parties: de l'œil, de la main, du pied, mais bien de
> l'homme.[21]

But here we note that the last part of the last ratio in both a and b has an
urge in it to dominate the whole (cf. §36). And this domination is not unifying.
On the contrary, it represents an alternative to the picture of man as one
ousia. Nous is like an appendix which tends to make itself independent, so

superior in relation to man as a natural species that natural man is regarded
as a transition to this other mode of existence. We are not the first to notice
this general tendency in the structure of Aristotle's thought. Commenting on
a problem in the Politics. Newman says:

> The end of a thing is, in his view, as had been said, not the sum of the
> functions discharged by it, but the highest of them only. If that highest
> function can only be discharged by a part of the whole, then that part
> becomes, in fact, the whole. To it all other parts become mere means;
> they exist for it and are merely subsidiary to it.[22]

Newman regards this course as an exception, and so do we. Therefore
one may say that Aristotle in his account of nous makes the highest part of
the soul exclusively dominating in a way that blurs his general anthropology.
It might not be correct to say that Aristotle has two doctrines of man. But
if he has one, it surely falls into two parts. The part concerning man as a
natural species of body and soul presents another picture than the part
concerning man as philosopher and scientist with nous.

Nous grows in importance as Aristotle considers it. Speaking of common
men, nous is respected, but half forgotten. Speaking of the philosopher, nous
dominates the scene completely. This enthusiasm blurs the distinctions too.
It is impossible to give a lucid and simple account of Aristotle's thought on
this point because he himself is not very careful as to proper distinctions.
Defourny says rightly: "Im Verhältnis zu den niedrigeren Seelentätigkeiten
fliessen die Fähigkeit zur Kontemplation, die Schau Gottes und der Gegenstan
der Kontemplation zu dem Bild eines einzigen Zwecks zusammen".[23]

§14. CONTEMPLATION IS THE BEST ACTIVITY

1177a17-19. There is no reason to be puzzled about eiretai (77a18). Grant
admits ad loc. that "it is difficult to point out a precise passage correspondir
to this reference", and Burnet uses nearly the same words. Both of them,
however, think that eiretai may recall the mentioning of the bios theoretikos
in EN 1096a4-5. Dirlmeier,moreover, finds the expression justified by EN
1095b19, 1141a18-b3, 1143b33-44a6, 1145a6-11. This is going too far in the
attempt to make EN a unified whole. The reference found by Grant, Stewart,

and Burnet is the only obvious one. The other correspondences assumed by
Dirlmeier raise systematic problems as well as questions of terminology.

Gauthier, however, tries to make a big thing out of this eirētai: "Cela
n'a certainement pas été dit dans l'EN", he comments ad 1177a17-18. The
word should, then, be a reference to the Protrepticus, to gain an argument
for the hypothesis of the separate origin of EN X, 7. The resemblances
between the Protrepticus and EN X, 6-8 in their contentions on the subject
of philosophy, are striking, but the terminology alone - e.g. the use of
phronēsis in the Protrepticus,[1] - forbids the guess that they are originally
of the same stock. More important is Gauthier's remark that the superiority
of theōria in EN X, 7 is due to the missing distinction between poiēsis and
praxis. He says ad 1177a17-18:

> En somme, le nerf de la démonstration d'Aristote est l'idée de fin:
> l'activité de l'intellect suivant sa vertu propre est la fin de l'homme;
> or, la seule activité qui puisse être une fin, parce qu'lle est la seule
> qui ne soit ordonnée à rien d'autre qu'elle-même, est l'activité con-
> templative; donc l'activité de l'intellect suivant sa vertu propre est une
> activité contemplative. Cette argumentation, irréprochable tant que
> l'on compare l'activité contemplative à l'activité productrice, à la
> poiēsis, ne devient-elle pas caduque si on la compare à l'activité
> morale, à la praxis, dont Aristote nous dit qu'elle aussi elle n'a pas
> d'autre fin qu'elle-même?

This lack of distinction should also mean, then, that our passage was
written close to the Protrepticus. But, if not in its complete form, the
Protrepticus knows the distinction between poiēsis and praxis. Philosophy
is a praxis tōn agathōn, "a doing of good things" (B52), and mere poiēsis
is rejected in B68, 69. On the other hand, it is true that this distinction
plays no great role in the previous eulogy on philosophy. In fact, moral
actions are not spoken of as desirable for their own sake; they are good in
so far philosophy is their indispensable guide (B49).

We should not forget, however, the general character of the Protrepticus.
Its differences from larger parts of EN are not primarily due to some
Platonic spell, but result from the purpose of this sermon. Similarly, the
resemblances between the Protrepticus and EN X, 6-8 are not due to the
peculiar origin of the last named section, but rather to their coincident ends:
the eulogic, adhortative, proselytising, protreptic purpose.[2]

In the next sentence, Aristotle claims that his contention on the best activity is compatible with the rest of EN. That the most happy activity is theōrētikē, then, a) has been said before, b) is compatible with the rest, and c) agrees with truth (77a19). This is a likely introduction to a new treatment. If all of it were put clearly before, the two other qualifications would have been superfluous. As it is, they explain the problem of eirētai (77a18). The theme has been mentioned before, i.e. he has made room for it. He has even reserved it as the highest possibility of human existence (EN 1096a4-5), but here, at first, follows the proper account, which is compatible with the rest and agrees with truth.

The actual extent of the expression homologoumenon ... tois proteron (77a18-19) is difficult to establish. It may refer to the line of discussion beginning with EN X, 6 or possibly to the whole treatise as we have it, or even to the opinions of the philosophers before Aristotle. In the last case, this reference would correspond to the execution in 1179a9-17 (cf. §31), and the reference to truth would correspond to the execution in 1179a17-22 (cf. §32). At any rate, it is curious that no modern translator or commentator has noted the possibility of this last interpretation.

At the end of §2, we formulated the programme for this chapter. Aristotle does not make it clear what he means by the bios theōrētikos. We hear a lot about its merits and superiority, but when asked directly what this life consists of, Aristotle is discreet. Léonard complains: "Sur ce point capitale de sa morale et de sa psychologie, sur le méchanisme intérieur et l'ascèse de vie qui rendent possible la contemplation, le Stagirite s'est tu".[3] It was hardly clearer to his contemporaries or to his readers some generations after him. We have already recorded Cicero's complaint, and Aristotle could probably not even satisfy his closest pupil, Theophrastus.[4] It might have been some help if Theophrastus had drawn a portrait of the sophos, as he did with other characters in EN. But there is none of it.

Aristotle's remarks on theōria are scanty and they point in different directions. As was said above: sometimes this life seems to consist of a) the study of astronomy or b) the study of metaphysical principles. Other times we must think of c) the life of reason in all its forms or d) a blessed recognition of God. Before we discuss these four main possibilities, however, we will take a closer look at the word theōria.[5]

It is conspicuous that even the best commentators only give an immanent account of the meaning of theōria, i.e. that they recur to the terms of Aristotle in their attempts to explain it. Burnet says: "The verb theōrein expresses the energeia of knowledge".[6] And Düring follows the same line:

> Der Begriff theōria bleibt unverändert und so auch ihr Gegenstand. Das Verbum theōrein bedeutet immer 'das Wissen aktualisieren', nicht ein Wissen haben, sondern es wirksam werden lassen. Wissen ist ein Vermögen, eine dynamis, theōria ist immer als ein Tätigsein, als eine energeia dargestellt, und zwar als die beste und lustvollste.[7]

This account is not incorrect. It has, on the contrary, all the support it may need (cf. EN 1146b30ff., 1153a22; Meta.1048a34, 1072b24; Phys.255a 33-b5; De An.412a9-22; Protr.B87; Gen.An.735a9).

But the ratio - epistēmē: theōria = dynamis: energeia - does not tell us more exactly what this actualisation, this activity consists in. Düring tries to move somewhat further. At the same place he says that theōria means "das Wissen wirksam werden lassen". As may be noted, the number of possible interpretations is hardly limited by this contention. We can, however, get a little bit further by comparing this abstract assumption with a general insight stated by Düring in the introduction to his book: "Unser Wissen ist potensiell, solange wir wissen, dass es so etwas wie ein 'a' gibt. Wenn wir einem individuellen 'a' hier und jetzt begegnen, dann aktualisieren wir dieses Wissen. Aktualisiertes Wissen ist immer gegenständlich".[8] If this actualisation is the essence of theōria, in the first quotation Düring constructed two stages although there is only one. The actualisation is not an application of a knowledge acquired, but the acquisition of knowledge is in itself an actualisation, namely of nous, which potentially is all it can know. One of the very best accounts of nous and theōria in the Metaphysics of Aristotle, we find in J. Stenzel. He supports our judgement of the interpretation of Düring:

> Je mehr wir in den Blick bekommen, was theōria heisst, desto schwerer wird es, einen einheitlichen Ausdruck im Deutschen dafür zu finden. Sichtlich bezeichnet es sowohl die psychische Aktualität wie den Einsatz der Erkenntniskraft in die konkrete Situation, also ein nach beiden Richtungen näher zu bestimmendes Evidenzerlebnis. Keinesfalls geht aber die Bedeutung der theōria nach der Richtung blosser beschaulicher Betrachtung.[9]

But it is difficult to see that every knowledge of this sort should be the theōria defended in EN X, 6-8. Granted that this is no bad description of what we have called 'the life of reason in all its forms', there is too much, however, which does not fit in the picture. After all, Aristotle never says that theōria is happiness or happiness theōria. Eudaimonia results from an activity that is theōria tis, 'a sort of contemplation' (1178b8, 32).

The necessity of describing theōria in Aristotle's own terms, which we have noted in Burnet and Düring, indicates that this activity is not a given thing, a simple matter of fact, but rather an ideal constructed on the basic concepts of Aristotelian metaphysics. We will take a closer look at the different lines of his description.

(a) Firstly, theōria points in the direction of the study of astronomy. Thales is recorded to have been studying the stars when he dropped into the well (Theaet. 174b), and the ideal of philosophy in the Pythagoreans as well as in Anaxagoras and Plato has got impressions from this kind of study (cf. Rep. 529c-30c). In EE the author makes Anaxagoras say that the study of the heavenly bodies makes life worth living (EE 1216a11). The references to Plato's Timaeus in the previous chapter, and the account of the 'cosmic religiousness' in §2, all point in the same direction: the task of studying the stars had become a part of the identity of the philosopher.[10] This, of course, does not mean that the philosophers were astronomers too or spent a considerable part of their time on this sort of study. It was rather a matter of ideology. The philosophers derived advantage from the religious feelings of the Greeks to establish and consolidate their business. In this, Aristotle was no exception. The 'theology' of Lambda will be discussed later (cf. §37), but this treatise is the summing up and the culmen of a line of thought in ancient Greek philosophy. In company with some of the discussions in the Physics and the first book of De Caelo, it represents an important line of Aristotelian thought, but it is not the dominating one, nor the only one.

The actual importance of this kind of study in his work can hardly justify the big words Aristotle uses when mentioning it ex professo, as e.g. in Part. An. :

The scanty conceptions to which we can attain of celestial things, give us, from their excellence, more pleasure than all our knowledge of the world in which we live, just as a half-glimpse of persons that we love is

more delightful than a leisurely view of other things, whatever their
number and dimensions. On the other hand, in certitude and in comple-
teness our knowledge of terrestial things has the advantage. Moreover,
their greater nearness and affinity to us balances somewhat the loftier
interest of heavenly things which are the object of the higher philosophy
(Gen.An. 644b31-45a4).

The study of the stars is 'leisurely', i.e. without any practical purpose,
and thus it may represent a pattern of the uselessness of philosophy that
constitutes its freedom.

This eulogy is not a casual one. From the Protrepticus and On Philosophy we know similar passages. The spectator at the theatre or at the
religious feasts was present for the sake of theōria, and Aristotle compares
the contemplation of the cosmos with the activity of the spectator at the feast
(cf. Protr. B44, B19). This activity is a more honourable thing than that
which people find useful, he says. On Philosophy erects a scale of knowledge
from the most necessary to the most noble one. At the top, Aristotle puts the
study of the divine, unchangeable world. Less noble is the physikē theōria,
still less the knowledge of the politician and the lawgiver, etc. [11] Alpha in
the Metaphysics, which ends in a defence of the science that deals with divine
objects (Meta. 983a6-11), will be considered later (cf. §15). In EN we also
learn to know a theōria which is related to the science of astronomy (EN
1141b2).

   (b) The second line of argument connects theōria with the discovery of
the principles of science. With a view to EN 1141a 17ff., Gauthier says:
"Les autres sciences sont pour ainsi dire des corps sans tête. Sur le corps
qu'est la démonstration des conclusions, elle posera, elle, la tête qu'est
l'intuition des principes".[12] This connection is mediated by the concept of
nous, the 'seeing' of the principles (cf. Meta.1051b24, 1059b25, 1060b20;
An.Post. 100b5). Because they are the starting-points of all argumentation,
the principles cannot be found by argument. Burnet explains:

To understand the meaning of the doctrine nous esti tōn archōn, we must
remember that nous and aisthēsis are both 'immediate' (aneu logou).
We cannot give a ground for the principle of contradiction any more than
we can give a ground for our perception of this triangle. This immediate
cognition Aristotle describes in a metaphor taken from sense as a 'contact' (tingein). No error (pseudos) is possible about the archai, we either
apprehend them or we do not, in which case we have, not pseudos or
apatē, but agnoia.[13]

At this point Gauthier believes he has found a touch of the mystic in Aristotle. He compares the ephaptometha in Part.An. 644b32 with the ephaptesthai in Plato's Symposium 212a. It should imply, then, that the world of demonstration and argument border on a world unknown, which is open to intuitive reason only; moreover, that the sciences presuppose a contact with the undemonstrable insights, which are exclusively won through the theōria of nous.[14] But there is nothing mystical about 'seeing' the principles before the demonstration. Also, the geōmetrēs, is a theatēs gar talēthous (EN 1098a32; cf. Protr.B35). That theōria is limited to the discovery of the principles of science must, however, be denied. This is just one line of thought, and there are others (cf. the aporia in Meta.1026a23-25).

Hardie finds that the present line disagrees with (a) above,[15] but his presupposition that theōria is identical with the theoretical sciences is wrong. Theōria is only a very limited, but no less important part of them, their point of departure.

(c) When theōria was presented as the study of the stars or the discovery of the principles of science, it was determined by its subject-matter. The third line is found where Aristotle describes theōria as the proper work of man, when, as it were, he describes it from inside. In this context it does not seem to be tied to special objects. Its worth is rather determined from the supposed constitution of man, as the activity of his best part. This is the main line of thought commented on in the previous chapter (cf. §13).

The basic contention is that every living being has a proper work, an ergon (cf. Plato's Rep.352d-53e), and that he finds his real self in the execution of this task (EN 1097b22ff.; Pol.1253a23; Meta.1035b16; Meteor. 390a10; Gen.An.716a23). In the Protrepticus as in EN this is the main argument in Aristotle's defence of philosophy.[16] Maybe it dominates the scene because it is the most comprehensive characterisation of theōria. If it be the 'seeing' of the stars, the principles of science, or the contemplation of God, in every case the realisation of this faculty is the execution of the proper task of man. Its essence is "the attainment of truth", not more, not less (cf. Protr.B56, B65). Düring thinks that with the expression akribestatē epistēmē in B85-86 Aristotle considers the theoretical life as the knowledge of the principles of science. Be it as it may. If he is right,

all three lines of defence and justification mentioned above are represented
in the Protrepticus as in EN.

(d) The fourth line is closely related to the first. The stars are divine
objects and their admirable, stable movements are, according to Lambda,
due to the One Unmoved Mover. Certain expressions, particularly in EE,
seem to represent a slightly different ideal of theōria. The reading of EE
depends largely on the understanding of its concept of God. For some reason
Jaeger and Gauthier after him try to make Aristotle a religious enthusiast.
The arguments for their judgement they find in the appeal to God or the gods
in EN X, 7-8 and in the final passages of EE. Gauthier particularly sets all
reservations on one side and describes Aristotle as "le métaphysicien en
extase devant la joie du Dieu vivant".[17] Thus he defends an old tradition of
catholic interpretation.

The other extreme is represented by Düring, who, following Dirlmeier,
not only tries to eliminate the religious character of the end of EE, but
also definitely denies that the ideal of the bios theōrētikos is found there at
all:

> Schon hier wird es klar, dass Aristoteles in der EE nicht ein bios
> theōrētikos im Sinne einer vita contemplativa als Ideal aufstellt,
> sondern ein Leben von kalai praxeis; ein Leben in dem die Tugenden
> durch die aus ihnen entspringenden Handlungen verwirklicht werden,
> und zwar um ihrer selbst willen.[18]

Düring interprets the crucial tēn tou theou theōrian (EE 1249b17) as a
subjective genitive and plainly identifies God with the human reason. Even
though the reading is not as artificial and unreasonable as it appears at first
sight, it clearly needs some correction.

The ideal of theōria in EE seems different from the corresponding
doctrines mentioned above. Certainly, it appears closer to the Platonic
theōria as described by Festugière: "La theōria dit plus: elle dit un senti-
ment de présence, un contact avec l'Être saisi dans son existence. Cette
saisie dépasse et le language et l'intellection. L'objet vu ... ne se laisse
circonscrire en nulle définition".[19] It need not concern us further. But if we
accept the traditional objective genitive in EE 1249b17, we get a
doctrine similar to that in EN.[20] The good actions are those which do not
interfere with theōria, but, on the contrary, support it: "God is not an

imperative ruler, but is the end with a view to which prudence issues its commands" (EE 1249b13). Hē tou theou theōria (1249b17) plays, then, the same role for the philosopher as the philosopher for the phronimos and the phronimos for the morally acting man. The self-sufficiency and simplicity of God represent a paragon for the philosopher as he in his turn is a paragon for the men who are not yet victorious in their fight with the passions and bodily disturbances.

Against the religious interpretation of Jaeger and Gauthier, Boll says: "Bios theōrētikos ist nicht eine beschauliche Versunkenheit". And further: "Der reingriechische bios theōrētikos ... ist nichts anders als das Schauen und Sinnen des Denkers und Forschers".[21] This, in our opinion, makes Aristotle too modern and too ancient at the same time. Aristotle stands, as Solmsen has shown, in a post-classical understanding of the relation between the state and the individual. He is not a public man and he hardly understands his work as a public service in the same way as Socrates and Plato did.[22] Accordingly, every reconstruction of the "reingriechische bios theōrētikos" would fail as a characterisation of Aristotle. Therefore, Dirlmeier is also wrong when he says of the happiness of the philosopher: "Es ist nichts anders als die Beherrschung von Welt und Umwelt durch den Geist - im Rahmen der griechischen Polis".[23] It will be shown later (cf. §§20, 21) that Dirlmeier is a little bit off the mark in his description of the atmosphere in which Aristotle works.

At any rate, Aristotle does not accept any short cut to the blessed recognition of God. It is the end of a long road (cf. EN 1105b9ff.). But the idea of homoiōsis tō theō is, maybe, even more important for Aristotle than it was for Heraclitus or Plato (cf. §23; Pol.1325b16-32). The religious interpretation does not make the distinction between the noēsis noēseōs of God and the theōria of the human nous sufficiently sharp, Düring says.[24] This is not an important distinction from the point of view of EN X, 7-8. On the contrary, it is important to see how closely Aristotle considers the contents of the two concepts.   The argument of EN 1178b7-23 (cf. §28) shows the insufficiency of Düring's contention. This does not, of course, mean that Gauthier's "le métaphysicien en extase" is correct, but Aristotle's relation to what he called 'God' was surely not as callous and abstract as Düring assumes. This we can simply infer from the language, which is the language of the mysteries (cf. §4, n.14). To what degree the recognition of God was thought to be immediate and to what degree merely mediate, we are not in the position to answer.

The four main lines in Aristotle's account of theōria are clearly different. It is, then, more than remarkable that he does not choose one of them, but takes pains to bring them together. The uniting impulse and the connecting link form the wish to defend philosophy as the proper fulfilment of man's task. Aristotle has no clear-cut concept of theōria, and he cannot describe the activity which he invites us to share in. What he has is an ideal of philosophy which comprehends most of that which was known as philosophy in his own days, but the different elements are drifting apart. He cannot hold them together any more in one single concept of philosophy which could easily be justified. He stands at the dawn of the Greek quest for truth, and he sees what was partly his own work, that philosophy proper dissolves into different scientific disciplines. What is left are fragments of an ideology which strives to retain philosophy as the head of the sciences and, as we will see, at the head of the society. At this point, as usual, Aristotle was a laudator temporis acti (cf. §12, §31).

In this chapter we have underlined the differences between the concepts of theōria in Aristotle. But he was, of course, too clever a rhetorician to leave the disparate elements side by side like that. In the following chapter and §37 we will consider the possible unit that Aristotle tried to establish.

§15. THE OBJECTS OF REASON ARE THE BEST

1177a19-21. As we have seen, nous in its energeia contemplates the principles of science as well as the heavenly bodies. This may be the thought behind Aristotle's contention that "the objects of reason are the best of knowable objects" (77a21). But to some extent we always use nous in our understanding of the world, because nothing can be understood without principles. Nous may not, then, be directed to God or the stars as special objects, as being different from the other things in the world. Aristotle thinks that there is a particular connection between the superlunary phenomena and the sublunary world. In our knowledge this connection is

mediated by nous, which 'sees' the principles of science and their unity
depending as they are on the eternity and necessity of the superlunary movement. We will take a closer look.

Kratiston is used in connection with nous, Stewart says ad loc., because
"reason is the principle which prevails (kratei) in the world. It has might as wel
right" (cf. 77a13, 19; Meta.1074b33). This presupposes a certain kind of
resemblance between nous and its objects. The nature of this correspondence
however, is hard to determine. Perhaps there is no single, consistent answer
to be found.

The best objects in general, "the things that are highest by nature", are
"the bodies of which the heavens are framed" (EN 1141a34ff.). Those are
much more divine than human beings (cf. Meta.1026a18; Phys.196a33; De
Cael.290a32). They are the objects of sophia (cf. §14). Referring to Thales
and Anaxagoras, Aristotle says: "They know things that are remarkable,
admirable, difficult, and divine, but useless; because it is not human goods
that they seek" (EN 1141b3ff.). The superiority of their objects justifies their
sort of knowledge and their sort of life, Aristotle thinks, for "the highest
(timiotatēn) science must deal with the highest genus" (Meta.1026a21). In
this connection, he calls the highest science 'theology' and adds: "While the
theoretical sciences are more to be desired than the other sciences, this is
more to be desired than the other theoretical sciences". The reason is that
its objects are the best ones (cf. Meta.983a7; Protr.B86).

"Il y a parallélisme entre les facultés du sujet et la valeur ontologique
de l'objet", Rodier says ad 77a21. In fact, at this point Aristotle seems to
hold the old similia similibus theory.[1] Rodier finds support for his thesis in
Rhet.1364b7-12 and especially in EN VI,1:

> For where objects differ in kind the part of the soul answering to each of
> the two is different in kind, since it is in virtue of a certain likeness and
> kinship with their objects that they have the knowledge they have (EN
> 1139a8-11).

We have already noted that the word theios is primarily used to describe
the stars and the highest powers of the intellect. "Like the word 'divine' with
us, theios is used by Aristotle to express the highest kind of admiration,
tinctured with a feeling of enthusiastic joy, but also with some degree of

vagueness", Grant says.[2] Nous is held to be divine because of its divine objects. But here we have a problem.

The study of that which can be objects of sense is inferior to that which can be thought only. In the first case, soul and body work together, in the second case, the intellect works without the support of the body. Thus far, Aristotle follows the track of Plato. The stars may, however, be seen with the eyes too. They are no less objects of opsis than objects of nous. The solution of this difficulty seems to connect philosophy as the study of astronomy or the contemplation of the heavens with philosophy as the discovery of the principles of science. Nous is not the faculty of seeing the stars, but the faculty of seeing what the movement of the heavenly bodies causes and means. As is well known, the circular movement of the heavens is the primary one in Aristotle's representation of the universe. And the sciences in Aristotle are all concerned with movements and changes of different kinds.[3]

For Aristotle, nature is just the eternal change within eternal limits. The source and principle of the movements on earth are the superlunary movement of anthrōpou poly theiotera tēn physin (EN 1141b1) or ta timiōtata (EN 1141a20). Those are thaumasta, chalepa, and daimonia (EN 1141b6), not because of the qualities that can be seen by eye, but because of the qualities that can be seen by the intellect: all events, occurrences, and movements on earth depend on them.[4] Moreover, the circular movement of the heavens is the source of necessity in nature. And all scientific knowledge deals with necessity as well as with movement (EN 1139b23ff.). In this way, the contemplation of the stars is a contemplation of the principle of the principles of science. Nous is divine because it has divine objects, and the objects, the heavenly bodies, are divine because their regular and eternal movement makes generation and corruption on earth follow general, reasonable rules. Thus the changing world becomes understandable for reason and the sciences (Meta.1071a16, 1072a15ff.; and particularly Gen.Corr. 336a32, 336b15ff.; Meteor.346b22).

The circular movement of the heavens is also important for the understanding of the ethics. In the Prótrepticus, the eternal and invariable character of this spectaculum was a pattern for the man of principles in contrast to the incontinence of the weak. Philosophy is the best sort of life because it ignores to tychon and to ou megalēn echon axian (B29). Newman comments thus on the contrast between the irregular occurrences and the eternal ne-cessity: "To Aristotle, at any rate when he speaks scientifically, Accident is an influence arising at the opposite pole of things to the Deity, and inasmuch as it is not directed to an end, bordering close on the non-existent".[5] Because the philosopher has a fixed end, he does not become the victim of tois tycherois (B30): "For the philosopher alone lives with his eye on nature and the divine. Like a good sea-captain he moors his life to that which is eternal and unchanging, drops his anchor there, and lives his own master" (B50). In EN this idea is not that conspicuous, but it is represented by at least one passage (EN 1154b20-30), which will be commented on later (cf. §24).

The sea-captain finds his way by means of the stars. This may add a new meaning to the analogy between ethics and the art of navigation (EN 1104a3-10; cf. §3, n.21). It is obvious, moreover, that the continuity, regularity, and selfsufficiency of the movement super lunam is a paragon for the perfection of human life in EN X, 7. The different ideas are to be considered in the following chapters.

The most important conclusion at this point is that there are connections between the four lines of thought considered in §14. We have seen that there is a relation between the study of the stars and the discovery of the principles of science. More than that: the heavenly movement as a paragon in the ethics makes the authenticity and meaning of the fourth line in §14 obvious and ties it to the rest. The theōria tou theou is the contemplation of the heavens as a pattern of life.[6] But we have also noted a certain tension between the justifi-cation of philosophy as mimēsis and energeia. On the one hand, it is the highest human possibility because it is the realisation of the highest human dynamis. On the other hand, it is the best sort of life because it has an eye for the unchanging pattern of the superlunary life. In some way the faculty of theōria and the objects of mimēsis seem to be related. Nous has, Aristotle contends, an eye for the eternal in the change, for the units in the variety, because of its kinship with "the cause of eternal uniformity" (Meta. 1072a17; cf. §38).

1177a21-22. The first thing to remark on the text is the juxtaposition of theōrein and prattein. Aristotle thus stresses that the quality of theōrein in question does not devolve on prattein or does so to a far smaller degree. The crucial point of the passage, however, is what this quality implies.

At times, synechēs seems to have something to do with temporal durability. At other times, it means more than that. Certainly, the statement in our text implies that theōria satisfies most of the conditions of a perfectly continuous activity. In its pure form, it is the activity of God.[1] As the energeia of the One Unmoved Mover, it has no beginning or end: it is synechestatē. Through the circular movement of the heavens, God mediates a part of his own necessity to nature. This movement is the material aspect of God, but in himself he is pure thought. This theology of Lambda is presupposed in EN X, 7. The heavens and their eternal movement are the horatos theos.[2]

It is, moreover, a problem to understand the 'we' implied in dynametha, because elsewhere the difference between God and man is underlined as to their possible energeiai: "We say therefore that God is a living being, eternal, most good, so that life and duration continuous and eternal (aiōn synechēs kai aidios) belong to God" (Meta. 1072b29-30). The human condition, however, is marked by man being locked up in the body, which claims variation, surprises, new stimuli. As is said in Lambda: "If thought is not the act of thinking (noēsis), but a potency, it would be reasonable to suppose that the continuity (to synechēs) of its thinking is wearisome to it" (Meta. 1074b28). A perfect continuous activity is impossible for a human being (cf. EN 1175a4-6), but we may share in this life for a short time. One has not yet noted the deep, paradoxical irony of Aristotle on this point. A human being may take part in the perfectly continuous life of God, but only for a short time: "And it is a life such as the best we enjoy, and enjoy but for a short time (for it is ever in this state, which we cannot be)" (Meta. 1072b14-15). Rodier concludes ad 77a21:

La contemplation est susceptible d'être continuée longtemps sans fatigue, parce que c'est l'actualisation d'une puissance du plus haut degré, aussi proche que possible de l'acte ... Si, chez l'homme il ne peut toujours durer, c'est précisément à cause de ce qu'il y a dans l'intellect humain de potentiel et d'imparfait.

This, however, does not exhaust the meaning of the passage.

Firstly, Rodier has forgotten the important 'we'. This 'we' implies a promise and corresponds to the inviting character of EN X, 7. Of course, we cannot become completely like God through our theōria, but the eph'hoson endechetai athanatizein (EN 1177b33) would be without any sense if man as man had limits which could not be moved. To put it another way: "It is not in so far as he is man that he will live so, but in so far as something divine is present in him" (EN 1177b26). Aristotle seems to admit that man may partake in the life of another species. A man can behave and feel like a beast, forgetting his humanity. He may also share in the life of God beyond the limits of his merely human possibilities (cf. §§22, 24). But anyway there is a distinction between the human theōria and the divine noēsis noēseōs. It is not described as too great a transition or as an impossible change. Aristotle contends that we cannot share in the life of God entirely because "nothing perishable can forever remain one and the same" (De An. 415b4ff.). We are not invited to change ourselves completely, but, on the contrary, to avoid the incontinuity of the world. The paragon for the unchangeable existence is nature as a whole, which knows no beginning, end, interruption, change, doubts, or weakness: "Das mit sich identische Sein der Weltkugel, dieses Weltgottes, gilt dem griechischen Weisen als das Vorbild, dem er sich angleichen soll".[3] In other words, nature is synechēs and we ought to realise the faculties that can give us the same imperturbability.

This leads to the second point: synechestatē does, then, apply not only to the temporal durability of theōria, but to its contents as well. In Pol. 1279a14, synechēs is used to denote a continuous time. But it may denote a continuous space, too (Pol. 1285b14). Moreover, it is employed metaphorically to denote the connection of thoughts. The proportion A:B = B:C is synechēs, Aristotle says, in contrast to the proportion A:B = C:D (EN 1131a 33, b15). Bonitz records yet another meaning: "continuitatem significat ... qua ipsius rei partes in unitatem coaherunt"[4] (cf. De Cael. 278b15ff.). To synechés is also employed to describe the circular movement of the universe and time in Aristotle's Physics (cf. 222a29-22b7; 231a29ff., 259a15). On

the continuum in Aristotle's Physics we need not comment.[5] But the close
relation between the Physics, Metaphysics, and EN on this point should be
underlined.

It is difficult to decide which and how many of these voices are sounding
in the word as it is used in our passage. But it-is certainly not too far-fetched
to suppose that theōria is synechestatē because it grasps the unity of all
things owing to the resemblance between this activity and the life of the One
Unmoved Mover. "Der Hinweis auf die Stetigkeit der göttlichen energeia ist
nicht zu überhören", Dirlmeier writes ad loc. Nor should the reference to
the power and comprehensiveness of the divine thought be ignored.

Nothing in the sublunary world can move completely by itself (Phys.
257b2). Therefore the One Unmoved Mover is so important for Aristotle's
representation of the world and everything in it. As was said above,
Aristotle's doctrine of nature is a doctrine of its regular movements, and
to explain its regularity, he needs the indestructible superlunary world. The
One Unmoved Mover is, therefore, not only a guarantor of the temporal
eternity of the universe, but he also regulates its exchanges.

The problem of the interpretation of synechēs is analogous to the case
of the bios teleios, the concept of a 'complete life'. It is obvious that the
temporal aspect is important as in the note on the permanence of a virtuous
life (EN 1098a18ff.; cf. 1100b12-20). But we can hardly admit that
Aristotle regarded a 90 years' life more 'complete' than a life that lasted 50
years, for the sake of the number of years only. At times, he even seems to
prefer pleasure to durability (EN 1169a22ff.). The temporal aspect is there,
but it does not dominate the contents of the bios teleios. Similarly, it did
not dominate the concept of synechēs either. The author of EE says: "We
find confirmation also in the common opinion that we cannot ascribe happiness
... to a child or to each of the ages of life ... For nothing incomplete (ateles)
is happy, not being whole (holon)" (EE 1219b4-8). The child is not as happy as
it can be, Aristotle contends. But the reason is not that it has lived for too
short a time. The reason is that it is not yet a complete man. These two
aspects are intermingled in Aristotle's thought. Teleios denotes both the
span and the completion: its contents.[6] The same ambiguity marks the use of
the word synechēs. It means both the continuous time and space, and the
whole which it embodies.

Plato used the sun as a metaphor of the Good in itself in his Simile of the Cave (Rep.514a-517d). With regard to his later theory of heaven and its bodies in the Timaeus, we may ask if the picture was merely a metaphor or perhaps rather an analogy. Plato saw the meaning of the sun in its reference to the guiding principle of the ideas. Aristotle sees the universal nous embodied in the spherical movements. It is obviously not the stars as twinkling dots that he admires, but their continuous movement causing the eternal variety on earth. This regular life can be imitated, and it ought to be our pattern of life. For "those things which are more lasting are better than those things which are more fleeting" (Rhet.1364b30).

§17. PLEASURE AND CONTEMPLATION

1177a22-27. Aristotle's doctrine of hēdonē, pleasure, has already been commented on (cf. §§8-10). Now he finds that theōria fulfils the demands on the happy activity also in the way that it is the most pleasant one. This argument for the bios theōrētikos is already well known from the Protrepticus:

> So too that all men feel at home in philosophy and wish to spend their lives in the pursuit of it, leaving all other cares, is no small evidence that it is pleasant to sit down to it; for no one is willing to work hard (ponein) for a long time (B56).

Both here and in EN, theōria is the most pleasant activity because it is perfect (teleia) and unimpeded (akolytos). Aristotle seems to think that a right action is virtuous if its execution is pleasant. For if it is pleasant, it is voluntary. Moreover, the pleasure of contemplation is identical with the joy of life, although it only belongs to the philosophers, or to them most of all (B87-92). From this we are tempted to infer that the best thing is not contemplation, but the joy of contemplation, the happiness due to the highest activity.

In the Protrepticus philosophy is said to be chosen for the sake of its pleasure. On the other hand, its supreme pleasure is an argument for the contention that it is the best activity, and the other way round: because it is the best, its pleasure is also supreme (cf. EN 1117b15; Pol. 1339b32).

This pleasure is not a bad thing; on the contrary, it makes us "think and learn all the more (theōrein kai manthanein)" (EN 1153a17-23). Pleasure comes when the exercise of the virtue reaches its end (EN 1117b15), and it is reasonable that the most complete virtue should be the most pleasant one, when completed. Seeing, knowing, and the possession of virtue are not, however, chosen for the sake of pleasure, Aristotle says in EN, though they are necessarily attached to pleasures. For "we should choose them even if no pleasure resulted" (EN 1174a5ff.). But, anyway, pleasure is a mark of life. The paramemichthai in 77a23 recalls the symmeichthēs in Plato's Philebus 22a. Hēdonē and phronēsis must be given at the same time, Plato says, for a life that is apathēs would hardly be a life at all (21e).

Aristotle's statement that the pleasure of theōria is 'pure' may have several meanings. The commentators, however, mostly go too far to find the correspondence. The 'pure' pleasure in 77a26 is an answer to the questions raised concerning the tyrant who has never tasted "pure and generous" pleasure (76b20; cf. §8). It means that no pain or appetite is involved in it (EN 1152b36-53a2). Theōria is, moreover, the activity of nous, the eye of the soul. And as sight is the purest sense and gives the purest pleasure, so theōria is the purest activity because it is the sight of the soul (EN 1175b36-76a3).

As to the 'enduringness' of this pleasure, it is simply a reference to the statement in EN 1100b10-22. Its problem cannot perhaps be finitely solved (cf. §16). The 'short time' in Meta. 1072b14, and the 'scanty conceptions' in Part.An. 644b31 may be marks of some part of theōria. Perhaps the rare insights do not constitute the bios theōrētikos as such, though Aristotle would presumably agree with Democritus that the rarest pleasures are the most pleasant ones (DK 68B 232). On the other hand, this sort of pleasure demands permanence and finds its paragon in the eternal and unchanging, whereas the more trivial human pleasures depend on variety and change, surprise and sensation. This must be the reason why Aristotle underlines its 'enduringness'.

The next problem in this passage is the juxtaposition of sophia (77a24) and philosophia (77a25). Greenwood argues that sophia and philosophia here are synonymous.[1] At other places they may be, but here Greenwood misses the point. Certain manuscripts give sophia at both places, the lectio facilior.

Stewart says, however, ad 77a25: "Of course philosophia is right, the argument being - 'if the pursuit of wisdom (philosophia) is so pleasant, how much more pleasant must the possession (sophia) be?'"

This does not mean that sophia is the condition of passively knowing everything. With some possibility for misunderstanding, Stewart has formulated the solution thus:

> The contrast marked by tois eidosi and tōn zētountōn here is not that between the mere hexis of sophia as a treasure ... and the energeia of mathēsis by which that treasure is accumulated ... but that between the energeia kata tēn hexin, and the energeia by which the hexis is formed. The sophos derives more pleasure from the use which his trained faculties make of his accumulated knowledge, than the learner derives from the process by which faculties are trained and knowledge is accumulated ... We must be careful, then, to understand the eidotes here as synechōs energountes, not as merely pōs echontes.

Like Düring above (cf. §14), Stewart seems to think of theōria as a sort of application of accumulated wisdom. This must be wrong. The thinking of nous is in itself an activity, the highest human actualisation possible. The difference between the sophos and philosophos in Aristotle depends on the degree to which theōria is established as an energeia akinēsias (EN 1154b27).

In principle, Aristotle would, of course, agree with Plato that only God may be called 'wise' in the fullest sense (cf. Symp. 199c-204c). God is the only one who "always enjoys a single and simple pleasure; for there is not only an activity of movement, but also an activity of immobility, and pleasure is found more in rest than in movement" (EN 1154b26ff.). In contrast to Plato, however, Aristotle does not underline the chōrismos between man and God. On the contrary, his concept of God is worked out with special regard to the mimēsis of God in the supreme activity of man. This will be discussed later (cf. §37).

The passage at hand on contemplation and pleasure apparently refers to Lambda, like the use of synechestatē treated above. Aristotle says: "Therefore the possession rather than the receptivity is the divine element which thought seems to contain, and the act of contemplation (theōria) is what is most pleasant and best" (Meta. 1072b22ff.). The difference between man and God is not due to the assumption that God can know a lot which we cannot know but to the idea that the simplicity and imperturbability of the divine thought

can never be the experience of mortals except for a short time. Grant notes
Aristotle's lack of modesty regarding the role of the philosopher: "Aristotle
strangely leaves out of account the sense of ignorance which the wisest man
will always retain. His statement is chargeable with philosophic pride, which,
as we have said, Socrates and Plato were free from".[2] Grant's misunderstanding here is very common. God is, however, in Aristotle, not an
intellectus archetypus, a storehouse of all that can be known. And theōria
is not the activity of putting all these things into the human mind. Wisdom is
here not the opposite of ignorance, but the opposite of confusion and bewilder-
ment. Wisdom represents a relief from the variety of sensations in one single
activity and one simple pleasure. It is not the satisfaction of every possible
curiosity, but a conscious enjoyment of one's own powers when resting in
themselves.

Still one word in this passage points to the resemblance between the
bios theōrētikos and the life of God. Diagōgē in 77a27 must certainly be a
reference to the same word in Lambda 1072b14. Ross thinks that the concept
of joy is inherent in diagōgē when it is used about God in the Metaphysics.[3]
Jowett says in Stewart ad 77b4: "The idea of 'culture', implying a use of the
intellect, not for the sake of any further end, but for itself, would so far
correspond to diagōgē"(cf. Pol.1338a10). It means 'life', 'passing time',
'time for private pursuits'. However, it is obvious that Aristotle describes
the life of God in terms used elsewhere to describe the perfection of man:

> On such a principle, then, depend the heavens and the world of nature.
> And it is life (diagōgē) such as the best which we enjoy, and enjoy for
> but a short time (for it is ever in this state, which we cannot be), since
> its actuality is also pleasure. And for this reason are waking, percep-
> tion and thinking most pleasant, and hopes and memories are so on
> account of these (Meta.1072b14-18).

The highest pleasure of man seems to depend, then, on the eternal
realisation of the supreme pleasure in the life of God. In this context,
pleasure is therefore a mark of voluntariness, self-sufficiency, and self-
actualisation, shortly: of freedom.[4]

§18. CONTEMPLATION IS SELF-SUFFICIENT

<u>1177a27-77b1</u>. The explanation of the word <u>legomenē</u> (77a27) is very simple
It is a reference to the discussion of <u>eudaimonia</u> as <u>autarkēs</u> in EN 1097b7-
The discussion there contains a definition of <u>autarkeia</u>: "The self-sufficient
we now define as that which when isolated makes life desirable and lacking in
nothing; and such we think happiness to be" (EN 1097b14-16).

But like <u>synechēs,</u> <u>autarkēs</u> is a word that speaks with many voices.[1]
As was mentioned above, it may mean both 'independent' and 'sufficient' (cf.
§6, n. 8). In Aristotle, <u>autarkēs</u> is employed to describe the life of God, the
ideal of human life, and the integrity of a region or a state. <u>Autarkeia</u> was i
ethical as in political contexts thought to be the primary condition of strength
and freedom to the extent that the words became synonymous. <u>Autarkēs</u>
meant to the Greek, then, 'strong and free through independence and self-
sufficiency'.

Aristotle makes no attempt to restrict its meaning to some technical
import in EN X, 6-8. <u>Autarkēs</u> is that which "when isolated makes life
desirable and lacking in nothing (<u>mēdenos endea</u>)". In <u>Alpha,</u> <u>eleutheros</u> is
used in the same context in a somewhat vaguer sense (<u>Meta.</u>982b25). Like
<u>makaria,</u> the attribute <u>mēdenos endea</u> was originally employed to describe
the state of God or the gods. In this role we know it from Xenophanes (DK
21A 32) and Euripides (<u>Herc.</u>1345f.; <u>Phoen.</u>554; <u>Elect.</u>429f.). In the first
philosophers this attribute is transferred to the universe as a whole, e.g.
in Empedocles' doctrine of <u>sphairos kykloterēs</u> (DK 31B 27,28), and in the
corresponding idea of Parmenides (DK 28B 8,42ff.).

As Pohlenz has shown, the concept of <u>deitai oudenos</u> is the most dominating aspect of the Greek idea of freedom.[2] And Aristotle's definition of
the word is no limitation of its everyday use. It is rather a reminder of the
original comprehensiveness of the concept, and a conscious reference to its
meaning outside the politics where it was a slogan. Gigon says: "<u>Autarkeia</u>
is the path through which man may become like God".[3] This idea makes it
necessary for Aristotle to define happiness by means of an attribute originall
ascribed to the gods or God. The paragon for the way to human freedom is
God, who finds the source of happiness in his own nature (EN 1154b24-28).
The ideal of individual life coincides with the ideal of political life. The deve

opment that ends up with the constitution of the state in the Politics is a
ladder through stages of autarkeia, from the less independent positions to
the more so (Pol.1252b27-53a1).

The Politics, moreover, gives the most informative passage on the
relation between God and the ideal of human life:

> Let us acknowledge, then, that each one has just so much of happiness
> as he has of virtue and wisdom, and of virtuous and wise action. God
> is a witness to us of this truth, for he is happy and blessed, not by
> reason of any external good, but in himself and by reason of his own
> nature (Pol.1323b22-25).

Aristotle does not say that the life of God is completely impossible for
man. On the contrary, the pattern of complete independence is what drives
onwards through the different stages, until at last he is his own master. We
are not invited to be like God in some literary sense, but to make ourselves
analogous to the divine life. Man cannot ever become his pattern, but he
may become more or less like it. The author says: "With us welfare involves
a something beyond us, but the deity is his own well-being" (EE 1245b18).
The difference between man and God cannot be wiped out. It is, moreover,
obvious that the ideal gets its power from the tension between the paragon
and the actual state of things. The freedom and strength of God are not
wholly attainable for a human being, but the path to human strength and freedom goes through the mimēsis of the divine life.

Thus the stages depicted in EN are stages of a progression into freedom.
The man with moral virtue alone is not his own master: he is doing the right
things without knowing from himself what is right. The man of phronēsis
knows from himself what is right and may do it. Thus far he is his own
master. But the realisation of practical wisdom and moral virtue depends
on other men as well (cf. §28). The supreme life, however, is the life that
finds the source of happiness in human nature, in nous, the faculty of
thinking which we have in common with the gods. Aristotle's ethics is not an
invitation to apotheosis, but he knows the secret of the happiness of the gods
and sees no reason why he should not turn this insight to account.

Stewart discusses ad loc. the problem of the relation between man and
his perfection. The bios theōrētikos is an ideal which is often described
without any regard to the possibility of its realisation, he contends:

I take it, then, that when he contrasts the bios theōrētikos and the bios praktikos, Aristotle sometimes thinks especially of the difference between the life of the student or savant and that of the public man – and sometimes (as here, X, 7, §§4-7) wishes rather to call attention to the ti ēn einai, or ousia aneu hylēs, as distinguished from the concrete manifestation, of man's life as a whole. But these two ways of looking at the bios theōrētikos scarcely present themselves to him as two.

And later: "Aristotle, as I have said, looks at the theōrētikos bios from two points of view – as the form of human life, and as the career of the savant; but the two points of view sometimes tend to merge in each other".

Stewart ignores the protreptic character of the passage. Aristotle does not stress the distinction between "the form of human life" and "the career of the savant". On the contrary, the point of the whole section is to show that they are one: that the savant is the human being par excellence.[4] Man finds his ousia aneu hylēs in the life of God. Man, however, is a being with a body and cannot fully realise this form except in the imitation of God as far as possible. In his invitation, as was said above, Aristotle sets no limits to man's possible similarity to God. We guess he knows that human limitations will make themselves felt anyway. They cannot be run away from. It easier to run away from the obligation to exercise one's reason. Accordingly, the invitation starts there.

Theōria is autarkestatē in many ways. Firstly, it is an answer to the demand "to perceive the irrational part of the soul, as such, as little as possible" (EE 1249b22). Secondly, the activity of theōria is most independent of external things. This is already said in the Protrepticus: "The exercise of philosophy differs very much from all other labours; those who practise it need no tools or places for their work, one is able to grasp the truth as if it were actually present everywhere" (B56), and it is repeated here (77a28). The philosopher has the minimum need of ta ektos agatha or chōregia. As Rodier says referring to EN 1153a20: "Les biens extérieurs et même la santé sont, comparés à la sagesse, des choses indifférentes".[5]

Chōregia and the related expressions are favourite words in Aristotle (cf. EN 1099a31ff., 1101a15, 1178a24, 1179a11; Pol.1255a14, 1288b32, 1289a33, 1295a28). Düring gives a short, but complete explanation of the terms ta ektos agatha and chōregia: "Die Aufführung einer Tragödie erfordert eine gewisse äussere Ausstattung, die der Choreg besorgt; diese

Ausstattung ist aber nicht ein Teil der Tragödie selbst ... Im Begriff ektos liegt ektos tēs psychēs'.'[6] One may doubt, however, if chōregia was still a metaphor in Aristotle. Apparently it has replaced paraskeuē in philosophical contexts. A reason for this adoption may be that chōregia more than paraskeuē implies the persons taking part in the play, the persons necessary to perform one's actions rightly.

In 77a30-34, three of the cardinal virtues are contrasted with the fourth one: the dikaios, the sōphrōn, and the andreios, with the sophos.[7] The main difference is, Aristotle says, that the first three mentioned need other people to realise their virtues, while the sophos can contemplate truth alone (cf. Pol.1323b36). Here, the independence of the sophos seems to be an argument in favour of his virtue. In Book V of EN, justice is praised, however, as "the actual exercise of complete virtue" because, and that is really confusing, "he who possesses it can exercise his virtue not only in himself but towards his neighbour also" (EN 1129b30-33; cf. Plato's Rep.343c, 354a). The contradiction seems obvious. But in Book V, justice is described as the opposite of vice. Aristotle says: "Justice in this sense, then, is not part of virtue, but virtue entire, nor is the contrary, injustice, a part of vice, but vice entire" (EN 1130a8ff.).

Theōria never has this position. Theōria is the opposite of bondage, sleep, and inactivity. Thus virtue has two different aspects in EN, for the virtue that is opposite to vice cannot possibly be the same as the virtue that is opposite to inactivity and bluntness. Aretē is both a) the state of man realising his proper ergon, and b) the avoiding of vicious extremes. This distinction does not correspond to the distinction between the moral and intellectual virtues. It rather corresponds to the opposition between the practical and theoretical reason. Apparently, there is a wide gap between virtue as the opposite of vice and virtue as the opposite of unfree, slumbering inactivity. But Aristotle tries to show that the avoidance of vice is a condition for the supreme virtue of activity (cf. §4, n.6). The opposite concepts of virtue, then, correspond to the relation between phronēsis and theōria. In comparison with most accounts this reading implies a disparagement of phronēsis. But it is necessary to repudiate the constructions which try to establish the action of the prudent man as the supreme energeia. When Aristotle names the highest virtue and best activity, he always thinks of theōria.

The passage also raises the old question in Aristotle whether the happy man needs friends. This question he considers in all the ethical treatises attributed to him (cf. EN 1169b3-70b19; EE 1244b1-45b19; MM 1212b24-13b2), without, however, attaining a simple conclusion.[8] The paragon of the life of God seems to exclude the friends in the account of EE. The author says: "So that the happiest man will least need a friend, and only as far as it is impossible for him to be independent" (1244b9-11). But all the same: "We all seek others to share our enjoyment, those whom we may benefit rather than those who will benefit us" (EE 1244b17-19). In EN the need for friends seems to be greater. "For without friends no one would choose to live, though he had all other goods" (EN 1155a5). In fact, it is mentioned as a condition not only for the execution of virtue as opposite to vice, but also for virtue as activity: "With others therefore his activity will be more continuous, and it is in itself pleasant, as it ought to be for the man who is supremely happy" (EN 1170a6ff.).

This tension between community and independence is brought to light in the character of Greek philosophy as dialectics. Burnet explains the ambiguity thus ad 1177a35: "The Greek thinks of scientific inquiry as the give and take of independent minds (dialektikē). But, of course, it is possible for the wise man's soul to commune with itself".

In addition, we note that this passage does not use the word 'friends', but the even stronger word synergoi, i.e. persons sharing in the same work, taking part in the same activity. They are not conditions, then, for the performance of theōria, but standing on their own feet, being their own masters, they find happiness in the same energeia. However, being men they need encouragement from each other.

The section recalls the invitation of Diomedes in the Iliad (X, 223; cf. EN 1155a15). The warriors must fight their own fights although their fellow-warriors may give them mallon thalpōrē (X, 223). That these verses were used in philosophical contexts, we also know from Plato's Symposium (174d), and they are revived in Plato's concept of philosophy: in dialectics as in war, he says, there is only one law, to stand in the line of battle (menein) until the victory is won (Rep. 531c-35a). This concept of community between independent persons is mirrored in Aristotle's remark on the synergoi in the passage at hand.

With us justification normally tries to show that an activity or way of life is useful or based on legitimate interests. Aristotle lets his quest for justification end up by showing how the activity in question rests in itself, how - in this case - human life may be its own reason. Thus it is like nature, and nature needs no further justification. Therefore, the demonstration that theōria is autarkestatē is so important to him.

§19. LOVED FOR ITS OWN SAKE

1177b1-4. Aristotle places his most dubious argument last in this consideration of the advantages of theōria. Philosophy "alone would seem to be loved for its own sake" (77b1-2). It would have been easier if Aristotle had made the distinction between the things actually desired for their own sake and the things justly desired for their own sake. However, he uses many different expressions without making this important distinction. Many things are kath'hautas hairetai (1176b6) or di'hauta hairetai (76b9). Aristotle also employs the expressions ou di'hetera hairountai (76b10); hairetōtatē (1097b16); kath'hauto diōkton (1097a31); di'hauto boulometha (1094a19); and at one place he adds kai mēdepote di'allo (1097a31). The different expressions are used synonymously. However, here we have another expression apparently somewhat stronger: di'hautēn agapasthai (77b1-2). But the expression does not differ in meaning from the rest, as is clearly seen from di'hauta agapatai in 1096a8.

The contention that philosophy is loved actually or justly for its own sake would not have represented a problem. This is compatible with the statements at other places that pleasure, honours, wealth, etc. are actually loved for their own sake. The qualification which makes this passage problematic is the monē in 77b1: that "this activity alone would seem to be loved for its own sake".

Gauthier at once finds support for his guess that EN X, 7 was written earlier than the main part of EN, at a time when Aristotle had not yet made the distinction between poiesis and praxis. We have already seen that this guess leads nowhere because the distinction is also found in the Protrepticus, to which Gauthier tries to ascribe this passage. He says ad loc.: "On remarquera qu'Aristote semble oublier ici le caractère immanent de l'action morale, praxis, et la traiter comme la production, poiēsis ...". The same problem and a corresponding old insertion Gauthier finds in EN 1112b33: hai de praxeis allōn heneka, while EN 1140b7 should give the general doctrine of Aristotle: esti gar autē hē eupraxis telos. Gauthier ignores the fact that the praxeis are not the only things actually or justly loved for their own sake, which seem forgotten in this passage. Pleasures do not serve any further end either (EN 1176b10). Honour and wealth are also "loved for their own sake" (EN 1096a8).

There are three main possibilities: (a) Aristotle presupposes the distinction between things that are actually and things that are justly loved for their own sake, and he contends that philosophy is the only acceptable candidate for the last qualification. This would be at variance with our conclusion in §7 about the position of pleasure. Moreover, the argument is weakened by doxai in 77b1. Whatever this word implies, it does not fit in a statement which should make Aristotle's own opinion clear in contrast to the common opinions or the actual wishes of men.

(b) The other possibility is to regard it as an instance of the well-known formal inaccuracy in Aristotle. It should be, then, an overstatement with no real argument behind it. Greenwood has studied the problem of accuracy and inaccuracy in Book VI of EN and has shown that Aristotle, in spite of his rhetorics, the often unfinished structure of his argument, and the casual use of expression, seldom fails to make his opinion clear when it really matters.[1] There are, however, many passages unimportant to him but important to us, and the other way round. Anyway, this problem cannot be understood as a mark of mere carelessness.

(c) The ratios behind the concept of nous as the best thing in man (cf. §13) showed what we may call the transmission of power to the established end. The position of nous was determined by analogies. We should think, then, that nous could not be more than the analogies let it be. But, once established, this end becomes much more dominating than the argument for it admits. This is a consequence of the structure of the Aristotelian analysis in means and ends. Newman notes as a comment on the considerations of the parts of the soul in Pol.1333a21: "This implies, not only that the worse elements in the individual thing exist for the sake of the better, but also that the thing itself exists for the sake of that which is better than it".[2] Thus the only real end is the supreme end. And if there are many ends, they are all the same considered as mere means from the point of view of the supreme end. This is, however, the perspective of our passage: thēoria is established as the supreme end for man, and compared with it, the advantages of the other candidates for happiness fade away. This does not exclude that pleasure, wealth, and honour may be desired for their own sake, even loved for their own sake actually and to some extent justly, due to the still undiscovered concept of the supreme end. But in the moment when the supreme end is discovered, the previous ends turn out as insufficient.[3]

This quality of philosophy, that it is loved for its own sake, not only recalls the general claims to happiness formulated in Books I, and X, 6 (cf. §6). It is also a part of the description of the ultimate science, theology, in Alpha of the Metaphysics. Aristotle depicts the progress from the necessary arts and crafts to the supreme knowledge, corresponding to the scale presented in the fragment from On Philosophy referred to in §14. He concludes:

> Evidently they were pursuing science in order to know, and not for any utilitarian end. And this is confirmed by the facts; for it was when almost all the necessities of life and the things that make for comfort and recreation had been secured, that such knowledge began to be sought. Evidently, then, we do not seek it for the sake of any other advantage; but as the man is free, we say, who exists for his own sake and not for another's, so we pursue this as the only free science, for it alone (monē) exists for its own sake (Meta. 982b20ff.).

As in the case of the kalai praxeis this does not imply that the science serves no purpose, but it serves no external purpose. The point is that it has its purpose in itself, i.e. that it reproduces its own good, for every telos is a sort of rest. The human telos restores itself through a circular process. As the good man is apt to choose good actions, thus reproducing his goodness, theoretical man reproduces his happiness through his activity.

It is not quite right to say, then, that the telos does not produce anything. In human affairs, the telos is its own condition. Thus Aristotle wants to stress that the telos is not dependent on the permanent support of imperfect fellow men. When attained, it restores its conditions. This is not only the case with <u>theōria</u>, but also with <u>phronēsis</u> because both are telē from certain points of view. Aristotle says in Book VI:

> They do produce something, not as the art of medicine produces health, however, but as health produces health; so does philosophic wisdom (<u>sophia</u>) produce happiness; for, by being a part of virtue entire, by being possessed and by actualizing itself it makes man happy (EN 1144a3ff.).

For Aristotle this does not, however, exclude that the 'health' produced by <u>phronēsis</u> as its own end may be a mere means to supreme happiness from the point of view of <u>theōria</u>.

§20. WE ARE BUSY THAT WE MAY HAVE LEISURE

<u>1177b4-12.</u> The meeting between Solon and Croesus previously considered (cf. §8) was not without effect on the latter. When Croesus is put to the stake by Cyrus and believes that he will soon be dead, he remembers the conversation with the wise Athenian. Saved by a miracle, he admits his mistake and says: "Nobody is so silly that he chooses war instead of peace" (<u>Herod.</u>I, 86-88). The same estimation of peace and war we find in the discussion of Plato in <u>Leg.</u> 628d-e: "Nor will he ever be a sound legislator who orders peace for the sake of war, and not war for the sake of peace". And later: "Every man of us should live the life of peace as long and as well as he can" (803d).

Aristotle uses the relation between peace and war to assert that men prefer leisure to business. More than that: leisure is the better thing because it is the end of business. Business and war are mere means to leisure and peace respectively. The main point is to establish <u>scholē</u> as a state of things desirable in itself, while the alternative occupations, war and business, are shown to be desired for the sake of <u>scholē</u>. The question is, then, what <u>scholē</u> means, what condition it is meant to describe.

If often exaggerated, the Greek contempt for productive work is well known. Plato hardly understands the dictum of Hesiod that "work is no disgrace". At any rate, Plato says, Hesiod cannot have thought of the

production of shoes or the selling of pickles (Charm. 163a). The opposite of
this kind of work is not, however, idleness, but so-called 'noble occupations'.
The Greeks may have had other reasons for their estimation of hard work as
well. Democritus finds that it is base to work as if it were the whole life
(DK 68B 227). There the idea is that life is too short and that the skinflints
(hoi pheidōloi) forget to enjoy it while it is there. The idea of Aristophanes
is more like that of Aristotle. He regards work as compulsion. If there
were no poverty, everybody could "dwell at his ease/ a life without labour
enjoying" (Plut. 514-16). This thought underlies obviously the distinction between the quaestus sordidi and the quaestus liberales in Greek and later
estimation of work. That which is done of necessity, as a mere means to
something else, under compulsion, is not fitting for a free man, nor for a
free state.

The alternative to productive work, however, is not anapausis or
paidia. As was said above (cf. §10), amusements are means as well. Their
primary task is to make us fit for exertion. But scholē is a condition with
its end in itself. Scholē is, then, closely related to the concept of autarkeia
(Pol. 1326b30-32). Thus it may be a condition both of the state and the individual. Mikkola says in a note on Pol. 1269a34-36: "Scholē hat hier die
Bedeutung von Idealzustand, wo das Leben des Staates so gut geordnet ist,
dass der Staat ungestört von inneren und äusseren Streitigkeiten sich gänz-
lich der Verfolgung seines Ziels widmen kann".[1] What is said here of the
state is also valid for the individual.

Amusements are often considered to be the end of life. And Aristotle is
not content to say that they are not. The present note on scholē is, among
other things, meant to clarify how this mistake occurs. Like anapausis and
paidia, scholē is the opposite of compulsory, productive work. Burnet says
ad loc.: "This is the truth which underlies the perverted view that amusement is the end of life". Nor is scholē the same as argia, idleness, though
it was often held to be.[2] In his discussion ad loc., Stewart adopts a conclusion of Jowett's:

> To us leisure means hardly more than the absence of occupation, the
> necessary alternation of play with work. By the Greek, scholē was
> regarded as the condition of a gentleman. In Aristotle the notion is still
> further idealized, for he seems to regard it as an internal state in which

the intellect, free from the cares of practical life, energizes or reposes in the consciousness of truth.

The word is also used in a more general sense (cf. EN 1160a27), while at other places it is employed in an even more particular sense than Jowett indicates. The best thing about Jowett's reading is that he does not presuppose the society of Pericles for the political theory of Aristotle. This is an old mistake, which can be traced in Stewart (cf. his notes ad 77a27-30) and even in Dirlmeier.

In an admirable discussion, F. Solmsen has demonstrated that Aristotle's concept of scholē belongs to the dawn of Hellenism.[3] In the classical age, scholē was the time for political activities, the time when a man could be his own master, not tied up by the need of earning his living. As for Plato and Aristotle, Solmsen asserts a meaning of scholē in addition to this old one: "But the scholē insisted upon by Aristotle in Politics VII and VIII is 'leisure' from private as well as from political obligations - and for the kala".[4] The important thing to note is, of course, that the kalai praxeis are thought to be possible within a limited horizon. In the classical age, ta kala were bound to the service towards the community. In Aristotle, then, we should have scholē both in the sense of 'time for political activities', and in the sense of 'leisure from all obligations'. If this is correct, it is a decisive reason for re-estimating the relation between the bios theōrētikos and the bios politikos in Aristotle, as well as the contents of the life of the philosopher.

The passage at hand reminds us of the close relation between EN and the Politics. Scholē is first of all a social condition for individual display, but it is also thought of as a sort of life:

> The whole life is further divided into two parts, business and leisure, war and peace, and of actions some aim at what is necessary and useful, and some at what is honourable. And the preference given to one or the other class of actions must necessarily be like the preference given to one or other part of the soul and its actions over the other; there must be war for the sake of peace, business for the sake of leisure, things useful and necessary for the sake of things honourable (Pol.1333a30-37).

The account in the Politics is at no point at variance with the account in EN. The analogy with the relation between peace and war is repeated again and again (Pol.1325a5-7; 1334a3; 1334a15). In fact, we could expect a complete instruction on this point from the Politics, and Aristotle promises to describe the contents of the education for leisure (Pol.1338a34), but the book or the chapters are lost.

Solmsen examines in his work the origin and history of the idea of scholē and attempts to determine the original contribution of Aristotle. He finds that "the emotional need for leisure and withdrawal into privacy had developed in reaction to the exhausting worries and tensions of the Peloponnesian War".[5] This extended the meaning of scholē compared to the use of the word in the Periclean Age. Scholē is not only the opposite of productive labour, of the time used for the necessities of life.[6] Scholē was hereafter also thought of as the opposite of polypragmosynē, the business of politics, Solmsen contends.

Scholē was never merely a technical term of philosophy: "What the philosophers did was not to discover the value or necessity of scholē but ... to provide the best contents for a scholē, the need for which was felt by many".[7] And further: "What we must constantly bear in mind is that scholē was exalted by the philosophers but not only by the philosophers. As we have seen, the philosophers 'fell in' with a trend. Their own specific contribution consists in the emphatic association of scholē with the bios theōrētikos".[8] In Plato the concept of scholē is expressed by nearly the same words as in Aristotle. Scholē is the condition for the activities of the soul, whereas ascholia is the condition of the activities of the body, war included: "For wars are occasioned by the love of money, and money has to be acquired for the sake and in the service of the body" (Phaed.66b-d). As we have seen above, this analogy also holds good in Aristotle (cf. Pol. 1333a30):

scholē: ascholia = soul: body = kalai praxeis : anangkaia

But there are different parts of the soul and accordingly there are different kinds of scholē. Both in Plato and Aristotle the term is used to denote leisure for political activities from the work for the necessaries of life, as well as leisure from the political activities for the business of philosophy. This last meaning is obviously the intended one in the famous passage of the Theaetetus on the life of the philosopher (172d-76a). Solmsen thus sums up the evidence of this dialogue:

Here Plato uses the strongest colors to draw a picture of the hurry, restlessness and anxiety that characterize all forms of political and ordinary civic life. The philosopher living his life of sublime aloofness is said to be totally unfamiliar with all varieties of ascholia ... Scholē and ascholia as described in the Theaetetus are no longer two phases of life but two mutually exclusive forms of life. All values – all agatha – are on the side of scholē, which is not only the philtaton but also the timiōtaton.[9]

It is clearly seen that this form of scholē and political commitments are incompatible.

In the state of Plato, the citizens will have "the greatest leisure" (Leg. 832d) for two reasons: (a) they will not be subjects to another, and (b) they must have time to think of other things than money. By making a pause in the struggle for money, scholē is the condition of philosophy, for the bios chrēsmatikos needs no such thing as philosophy: "Every man is ready to learn any branch of knowledge, and to follow any pursuit which tends to this end (i.e. wealth), and he laughs at every other" (Leg. 831c). Especially, we may infer, he laughs at philosophy. Therefore the bios chrēsmatikos must be reduced to make room for the bios theōrētikos. Aristotle did not disagree with Plato on this score, but he went further. Solmsen says: "Aristotle's exaltation of scholē as telos and as skopos of education has no antecedent in the Laws".[10]

As has been said already, the Aristotelian idea of scholē does not imply argia, anapausis, or paidia. On the contrary, it means a free man's work for the community and, on the other hand, his time for self-realisation. Aristotle made no secret out of the dichotomy in his notion of leisure: "Since leisure is necessary both for (a) the development of virtue and for (b) the performance of practical duties ..." (Pol. 1329a1). For Aristotle this is not one and the same thing any more. The leisure for the execution of political duties is not leisure in the strict sense, as used in the passage at hand. In the Aristotelian order of precedence even the listening to music for ethical improvement surpasses the performance of political obligations in worth. Solmsen comments:

> We have seen that the law-giver has to make provisions for the leisure of the citizens because he has to make provisions for their eudaimonia. Leisure is the telos of the citizen's life – but it also seems to be the least political phase of their existence.[11]

In fact, there is a certain depreciation of the politician in Aristotle's writings. He is pessimistic concerning the actual aims of the politician. Already the corruption of democracy shortly after the death of Pericles, makes it rather unreasonable to suppose that Aristotle regarded the politician's task as noble save when he propounds ideals nurtured by the fancies of a noble past.

The introduction of the concept of scholē here does not make Aristotle's idea of philosophy more politically directed. On the contrary, it shows that the virtues of the politician, if he has them, are secondary to the virtues of individual education. We have seen that the other qualities of theōria are related to the nature of the life of God, and so is this one. The man using his reason in theōria is not spending his time arbitrarily. This, from the point of view of Aristotle, may easily be said of the persons spending their time for useful and necessary purposes. The philosopher in the society corresponds to the father in the household and the heavens in the universe. Nature contains its highest good both as something separate and as the order of its parts, Aristotle says in Lambda. Phronēsis may concern the order of the parts, but theōria is surely the highest good as something separate (cf. §26). Solmsen concludes:

> There was a political apathy in the fourth century, and there were lively and indeed fervent manifestations of the civic spirit in the Hellenistic period. Yet in spite of all arguments for continuity, it makes sense and is necessary to define the relations of Aristotle's school and scholē with the spirit of the Hellenistic centuries.[12]

On one point, however, we must reserve our approval of Solmsen's thesis to avoid misunderstanding. Unlike the thinkers of Hellenism, Aristotle had a strong feeling that the Greek was especially qualified for the bios theōretikos. His well-known statement: ou scholē doulois (Pol.1334a20) is a comment on this ineradicable difference. We have seen it in his comments on the dialogue between Solon and Croesus (cf. §8) and on the figure of Sardanapallus, that the non-Greeks are likely to be 'unspirited' or subjects to the tyranny of pleasure. And at the end of the Politics he repeats that only to tōn Hellenōn genos may be virtuous and gifted enough for leisure and happiness in the full sense of the word (Pol.1252b9, 1327b29, 1329a25, 1330a25ff., 1333b5; cf. Plato's Pol.262d). Aristotle admits that he can learn some details from the education of youth in barbarian countries, but his ideal of the bios theōrētikos is clearly reserved for the Greek.

§21. CONTEMPLATION IS BETTER THAN POLITICS

1177b12-26. In Book I, Aristotle mentions the three forms of life: apolaustikos, politikos, and theōrētikos (EN 1095b17). In the course of his considerations, the two first ones are rejected (EN 1095b19ff.), but Aristotle takes pains to demonstrate a) why they have been considered the best life by somebody, and b) how they are parts of the best life (cf. §7).

Here, to politeuesthai (77b13) does not only mean to do the job of administration, the business of ruling the city, but also the life of the citizen as he is absorbed by the life of the city. Bonitz refers to this double, comprehensive meaning of politeuesthai and says that it means partly 'civem esse' and partly 'gerere'.[1] Dirlmeier has probably found the right German translation: "im öffentlichen Leben stehen".[2] To take part in public life is not the best life for man, Aristotle contends. The radicalism of this judgement should not be blurred. The supreme happiness is to be found in privacy, and public life is regarded as a mere means. In the Politics this problem is stated in the form of the question whether the best man and the best citizen are identical. Aristotle answers 'no'. In this 'no' there might be hidden a 'not yet', but surely it also comprises the nostalgic 'no more'. Burnet sums up the idea of Aristotle thus: "The good man and the good citizen are not the same except in the case of the man who is leading the highest life in the ideal state".[3]

In the actual conditions, the best man is not the best citizen. On the contrary, the best activity is found in privacy. It consists of an execution of the best activities of man, and these activities cannot yet, or no more, or not at all, be realised in public life. The best life is not a quality of the life of the citizen, but a thing beside it. This is said here, and it seems to be compatible with the account of the relation between phronēsis and theōria given in §4. Greenwood comments: "Just as at the end of VI phronēsis is said to be a means to the production of sophia ... so the politikos bios is

said to be a means to the production of eudaimonia (1177b12-15), which is
only another way of stating the same fact".[4] The point of Aristotle in the
passage at hand is not only to make clear the main difference between the
bios theōrētikos and the bios politikos, that the first one has its end in itself while the last one serves some further end, but, moreover, that the
further end which the bios politikos serves, at its best, is the bios
theōrētikos. Sophia and theōria are at one with the happiness they produce.
To the energeia politikē, however, happiness is a foreign end (EN 1144a3ff.).

As has been said above, politics for Plato was a theoretical science.
For Aristotle it is a practical science and this makes the politician and the
philosopher fall apart. Themistius, then, is probably quoting Aristotle
rightly when he says:

> We should do honour to Aristotle who slightly altered Plato's words and
> made his counsel truer; he said that it was not merely unnecessary for
> a king to be a philosopher, but even a disadvantage; what he should do
> was to listen to and take the advice of true philosophers, since then he
> filled his reign with good deeds, not with good words.5

Thus, after all, Aristotle thinks that philosophy may be good for something. In the Protrepticus he even mentions some ways in which philosophy
can serve politics (B8, 44-46, 49, 51-52, 70, 72-73). There is no contradiction here. For while the politician fulfils his proper task by serving the
happiness of theōria, the philosopher may or may not be a support for the
life of the city: the value of his activity does not depend on its effect, whereas the activity of the politician does (cf. EN 1145a5, 1141a20). Moreover, it
seems that the politician carries the responsibility both for his own actions
and for the effects on the city of the activity of the philosopher.

In his defence of philosophy, Aristotle has no scruples about mentioning
its accidental usefulness (cf. Pol. 1325b14ff.). Greenwood's statement of the
politician par excellence and the contemplative philosopher par excellence,
may be just what Aristotle thought of:

> Pericles knew what true happiness was: he did not realise it by his own
> life, as Anaxagoras did, but he knew, better than Anaxagoras, the
> external means to it: he could anthrōpeuesthai better, though he could
> not athanatizein so well. It is only in complete isolation from the ideal
> of the theōrētikos bios that the politikos bios becomes irrational.6

Philosophy integrates the work of the politician by giving it the aim. The theōria of the philosopher orders the state in much the same way as the One Unmoved Mover orders the universe: hōs erōmenon (Meta.1072b3). For the life of the philosopher is the ideal of human freedom and perfection. Of course, the politician has other tasks than promoting theōria, but this task gives him the principle of his decisions. EE concludes with the statement that the good and bad actions are those which respectively promote and impede the theōria tou theou (1249b17). Political and moral actions serve theōria by supporting its conditions. On the other hand, theōria serves politics by being its essential end and goal. In the analogy of Aristotle: medicine serves health, and indifference concerning health would leave medicine without a proper task (cf. EN 1145a6ff.).

This order reflects the Aristotelian range of values. It is based on the idea that theōria is the only activity in which man can exclusively and perfectly be himself, free and unimpeded, essentially depending on nobody else. Philosophy is not only the principle of political action, it is also the scope and principle for the considerations of practical thought. The statements concerning the virtues bound to the body and the actions with external aims, are more likely and reasonable than necessary and true (cf. §3). But in his account of philosophy, Aristotle attempts to establish a point of departure, a principle based on the unchangeable nature of man. He is well aware of the difficulties, because individual men differ more than any other species (EN 1176a10; cf. Part.An.687a23). However, Aristotle seems to think that man betrays his true nature more clearly when he is on his own than when he lives among other men. Caird has formulated the collision between the inward and the outward necessities thus:

> With Aristotle, on the other hand, moral practice is the hampered activity of reason, working with a matter which can never be perfectly subdued or determined by it, exercising itself in a medium which is exposed to the inroads of a necessity that comes not from within but from without, not from itself, but from nature and circumstance.[7]

The necessity from within is the main feature of theōria. In this it is related to the noēsis noēseōs of the God. This activity is not leisure, but the contents of leisure. We may refer to the curious passage on the ordering power of the principle of the universe in Meta.1075a12-25. Here the universe, as was said above, is considered analogous to the state and the household. The sun and the stars are the paterfamilias and the philosopher. They are not at liberty to do what they please, whereas the other members of the universe, the state, and the household may "follow their own fancies" (75a22). Translated into modern language this implies that for the philosopher freedom and necessity coincide, in contrast to common men, who must overcome the difficulties which impede the realisation of liberty in the bios politikos and the bios apolaustikos. The philosopher has made himself independent of external means as far as possible so that he may follow the compulsion of his own nature all the more.

The second thing to note in this passage is the apparent reservations as to the possibility of attaining the ideal life thus depicted. Three times Aristotle reminds us of the limitation of mere human nature: (a) hōs anthrōpō (77b22), (b) labousa mēkos biou teleion (77b25), and finally (c) kreittōn ē kat' anthrōpon (77b26). It is important to note that these reservations are not his last words on the subject. On the contrary, Aristotle says explicitly that this does not prevent us from aspiring to immortality (cf. §23).

The structure of the argument is similar to the argument in Meta. I, 2. Firstly, Aristotle establishes the nature of the supreme science (Meta. 982b10-27). Then, he states the possible reservations (Meta. 982b27-83a3). And finally he maintains his invitation in spite of everything that can be said against it (Meta. 983a3-10). In the Metaphysics, Aristotle contends that the reservations are due to a false opinion of the nature of God. In EN the reservations are due to a false idea of the limits of man (cf. §22). It is obviously wrong to read a resignation into this hōs anthrōpō (77b22). For man is not merely human. He alone may transcend the limits of his natural species. And Aristotle, in his treatment of philosophy, sees the end and essence of man in this going-beyond rather than in his actual state, which is only thought of as a point of departure.

Lastly, we encounter here again the problem of the 'complete' life, if it is to be understood as a quantity or as a quality (cf. §16). The demand for a 'complete' life is the same as the demand for 'complete' virtue (EN 1098a 16ff., 1100a4ff.). The mere temporal solution of MM 1185a4 surely depends on a false interpretation, whereas EE 1219b6 discloses the same ambiguity as the passages of EN. Nor is the understanding of teleion as a mere quality right.[8] Rodier hits the point ad loc.:

> Le chronos teleios ou le mēkos biou teleion est le temps nécessaire pour assurer le développement de ces facultés, l'acquisition de ces biens et aussi la possibilité de goûter pleinement de bonheur ... Ce temps est dit teleios non par soi, mais dans le même sens que l'éducation, par exemple, parce qu'il sert à produire quelque chose de teleion.

This fits perfectly with the explanation given in Meta. 1021b30ff.

§22. HAPPINESS AND THE NATURE OF MAN

1177b26-31. That the bios theōrētikos would be too high for man is not the final conclusion of Aristotle. It is rather a hypothetical objection held to be inconclusive. In one way it is true, in another way not. Aristotle raises an aporia and solves it by means of a qualification. This is the normal procedure of his argument. To see this better, we may take a closer look at his concept of the 'human' and the 'divine'.

In Aristotle it is not the complete truth about man to say that he is 'human' The paradoxical contention is that man is more than 'human'. The extension of the anthrōpinos is limited to one aspect of the life of man only. And even this is not the most important one. Burnet has seen it clearly: "Anthrōpikos is used like the latin humanus with special reference to the weakness of mere human nature".[1] In Aristotle it is used like the word anthrōpeia in Democritu when he says that the soul and its goods are "divine", while the body and its goods are "human" (DK 68B 37). The use of anthrōpos in 77b30 is significant There it means 'man without his nous'.

That the humanity of man is only one aspect of his life is seen from the expression "in-so-far-as" (77b26-27). Likewise, the concrete enslaved person is both man and slave. "In-so-far-as" he is a slave, he has certain limitations (cf. §12). But "in-so-far-as" he is a man, he has a minimum of rationality (EN 1161b5ff.). Aristotle does not deny that a man may be a slave or a slave a man. The concrete particular seems to belong to two different species, here as in our text. A man may also be considered both 'human' and 'divine'.[2] This intermediate position between the heavenly and sublunary region is expressed in the introduction to the Politics: Man neither belongs fully to the heavenly nor fully to the sublunary region. His realm is the city constructed for happiness (Pol.1253a1-29). Actually, he is synthetos, i.e. his parts cannot be defined, but his life may be described from different points of view (Meta.1043b29ff.). This may be the technical meaning of synthetos here (cf. EN 1154b20). This term is an obscure point of Aristotle's ethics. Surely, it denotes a sort of composition, but the question is what this composition comprises. The associations with Plato's Phaedo are more blurring than illuminating. For a solution of this old problem, see §26.

Ad EN 1094b10, Grant mentions the varieties of the meaning of the term theios as used by Aristotle:

> It is specially appropriated by him to the various manifestations of Reason (nous) in the universe: (1) to the substance of the heavens ... (2) to the heavenly bodies ... (3) to the intellect of man ... (4) to the life of contemplation ... (5) to happiness in general .... (6) to superhuman virtue, consisting in unalloyed reason ... and (7) to the instinct of the bees.

In the passage at hand, theios recalls the expression in EN 1102a4 that happiness is something "prized and divine". This predicate does not exclude man from attaining the object thus qualified. On the contrary, all living beings may partake in the divine. More than that: in their partaking in the divine "as far as their nature allows" they are realising their own nature (De An.415a26-b7). Here Aristotle apparently presupposes the doctrine of God as the intrinsic order and the ordering principle of the universe. Moreover, he presupposes the picture of God as the only fully and necessarily realised energeia from Lambda of the Metaphysics.[3] There is no reason to read reminiscences from the Eudemus or Aristotle's 'Platonic' youth into these passages.

On the one hand, Aristotle lets all creatures share in the divine. On the other hand, he reserves happiness for man. A horse, bird, or fish cannot be happy, he says, because their species do not imply any share in the divine (EE 1217a26). There must not be a contradiction here. If the divine order of the universe is intended to comprise all living beings, Aristotle makes no secret of man's unique position:

> Of all animals man alone stands erect, in accordance with his godlike nature and essence. For it is the function of the godlike to think and to be wise; and no easy task were this under the burden of a heavy body (Part.An.686a28; Pol.1254b25ff.).

The same duality we find in Plato. On the one hand, he says that there is some theion in all creatures (Leg.950b). On the other hand, he gives man a position of exclusive preference (cf. Rep.611d; Apol.38a; Gorg.512ab; Theaet.176ab; Leg.875c). The assumption that nous is the most divine thing in us has been discussed already (cf. § 13). The announcement of a divine element in man gives Aristotle the reason for his invitation to share in the divine life. The idea of homoiōsis tō theō is already efficient in Aristotle's first invitation to philosophy (cf. Protr. B28, 108-110) and it dominates the account in EN.

§23. MAKE YOURSELF IMMORTAL

1177b31-34. We have already noted the correspondence between the structure of the argument at hand and the argument in Meta.I, 2 (cf. §21). Both there and here the reservations are introduced as objections from traditional Greek religion (cf. Meta.982b27ff.). Sayings like the verse quoted in Rhet. 1394b24: "Mortal creatures ought to cherish mortal, not immortal thoughts", were obviously proverbial, as Stewart notes ad loc. The best commentators refer to parallels in Pindar, Epicharmus, Sophocles, Euripides and Aristophanes. The list could easily be prolonged by including the passages in Greek literature where this advice is presupposed as a firm conviction on the nature of the relation between man and God.

It is often said and well known that the gods of Homer are like men in some respects. But likeness in shape and passions is there only to underline the difference: the gods are immortal and happy, whereas human beings are not. One aspect of the earliest Greek philosophy may be described as a revolt against the privileges of the gods. The sayings of Empedocles with a bearing on this subject are well known (DK 31B 112, 132, 146-47). His negligence of the prohibition of _hybris_ gave him a terrible death, if Diogenes Laertius is right (8, 67ff.). But this did not scare other thinkers out of doing the same. G. Müller has examined this break with the Homeric religion and found it related to the ideas and the language of the Mysteries (cf. §4, n.14).

On this point, the distance between Aristotle and Empedocles is perhaps not too great. Elsewhere in Aristotle we often meet the demand to avoid _pleonexia_, but not here. On the contrary, Aristotle has obviously decided to break with the consciousness of Homeric religion as to the relation between the human and the divine. Dirlmeier says: "Hier wird die Ethik des Maases für Augenblicke gleichsam aufgehoben, es fällt jede Schranke, die doch seit uralten Zeiten zu den Grundforderungen hellenischer Selbstbescheidung gehört hatte".[1] If it is true that these positions reflect two different religious trends, Aristotle includes them both. The Homeric religion is preserved in his claim for moderation and temperance; the religion of the Mysteries in his invitation to immortality.[2]

The originality of Aristotle is, as a rule, described in contrast to Plato. To see his proper contribution in the right perspective, however, Aristotle must be compared with the pre-Platonic philosophers as well. For when he diverges from the thoughts of Plato, he mostly rehabilitates previous Greek thought. In Plato, the absolute difference between the realm of the gods and the realm of men was expressed in the _chorismos_ between the idea and the concrete thing. Aristotle denies this _chorismos_ emphatically. Thus he prepares for the renewal of the pre-Platonic idea of immortality related to the Mysteries.

In Plato, the relation between God and man is mediated through _mimesis_, the imitation of the unique paragon. This idea is also effective in Aristotle, but the relation of his _sophos_ to the gods is at any rate closer. The idea of _energeia_, that God and man can share in the same activity, is foreign to Plato. But in Aristotle, the supreme activity is no mere _mimesis_, but an assimilation to the imperturbability of the superlunary region. This assimilation comprises both the realisation of the best human faculty and the imitation of the divine life, both _energeia_ and _mimesis_. We may repeat, however, that Aristotle had no convulsive redemption in mind, but a simple life of thought, a life never lost in accidental circumstances.

The concept is not that of the philosopher/king, as Dirlmeier presumes. In the meantime, this idea disappeared also from the dialogues of Plato. What Aristotle had in mind was a private form of life which, in spite of its private character, might inspire the politician and the morally acting person and thus be a principle of order in things human. "Dieser Philosophe@ könig arbeitet sich empor bis zur Schau der Gottheit", Dirlmeier says.[3] Firstly, this is a wrong description of theōria. It is not a sudden initiation. Secondly, the idea of the philosopher/king is not to be found in Aristotle at all. The connection between the person of Themison and the invitation to philosophy in the Protrepticus is not of this kind. As to the Politics, even the shortest course of examination will show the falsity of this interpretation (cf. §35).

G. Müller, who gives the reading of Empedocles recorded above is misled by the language and finds too many similarities between Aristotle and Empedocles:

> Wenn das alles richtig ist, so finden sich wesentliche Charakteristika der von Aristoteles im K der EN beschriebenen Eudaimonie schon bei Empedokles, nämlich der Aufschwung des denkenden Geistes zum höchsten, göttlichen Sein, darin die letzte Erfüllung des Menschseins, zusammenhängend mit der Verähnlichung des erkennenden Organs zu dem zu erkennenden Gegenstand. Diese Erfüllung erreichen nicht alle Menschen, mögen auch alle wesensmässig dazu berufen sein.[4]

Müller forgets that the revolt of Empedocles was incomparably more conspicuous in his century than the corresponding idea of Aristotle in his. Moreover, Empedocles is guided by the desire for redemption whereas Aristotle seeks for freedom and simplicity.

In Plato the proverbial wisdom of thnēta phronein also has a very low reputation (cf. Tim. 90b-c; Leg. 713e). In attaining truth, man is attaining immortality, because truth in Plato is the appearance of the eternal and permanent ideas. There is not only a simile similibus-theory of knowledge behind this. Plato thinks that the human soul may attain the same character as its objects. It may become immortal in some way by contemplating immortal things. It is, in fact, hard to find any difference between EN X, 7 on this point and some striking utterances of Plato. Whereas the Aristotelian sophos shares in the same energeia as God, the Platonic philosophos imitates the divine being in attaining truth. However, an explanation of these obscurities is apt to end in a reproduction of their own phrases. The correspondence between the two manners of expression may hide serious differences in meaning, and the other way round: they may, in spite of their differences, cover the same experience. The one cherishes his mortal part, Plato says

> but he who has been earnest in the love of knowledge and true wisdom, and has been trained to think that these are the immortal and divine things of man, if he attains truth, must of necessity, as far as human nature is capable of attaining immortality, be all immortal, as he is ever serving the divine power; and having the genius residing in him in the most perfect order, he must be preeminently happy (Tim. 90b–c).

We find, then, the same close relationship between happiness, contemplation of truth, and immortality in the Timaeus as in EN. The Laws give another reason to cherish our nous. Here the idea of anamnēsis is still alive. In the Phaedo and the Meno, where this idea dominates the account of human knowledge, immortality is attributed to the human soul without any distinctions. In the Laws, however, nous alone is the reminiscence of the divine order of the past in the time of Cronos. Our nous must be cherished, then, for the sake of the renewal of this happy and well-ordered age:

> Still we must do all that we can to imitate the life which is said to have existed in the days of Cronos, and, as far as the principle of immortality dwells in us, to that we must hearken, both in private and public life (Leg. 713e).

The principle of immortality is, then, at the same time the principle of happiness and good political order. Here the difference between Aristotle and Plato is striking enough. In Plato, nous is the faculty connecting us with an ideal order of the past. In Aristotle the life of nous has political effects for quite other reasons: its realisation is the formal ideal of human freedom and perfection which should be the aim of the state.

Plato's invitation to immortality in the Timaeus and the Laws is re-echoed in the Epinomis. There, the author rejects the thnēta phronein in behalf of astronomy. The heavens replace the old idea of the envious gods (Epin. 987d–88b), and the rituals of science are praised as both more true and more benign than the old veneration.[5]

Concerning wisdom, beauty, and everything else the wise man relates to God as a monkey to man, Heraclitus says (DK 22B 83). He certainly did not say this because he was impressed by the points of resemblance between monkeys and men. On the contrary, Heraclitus wishes to underline the invincible distance. Aristotle would perhaps not disagree with him on this statement, but he rather stresses the possibility of man to partake in the life of God in one way or another. As is often mentioned, the position of man in the range of beings is that between the animals and God (Pol. 1253a27, 1287a28; Part.An. 656a8; De Somn. 463b12).

Virtue as the opposite of vice belongs to this intermediate position, "for a brute has no vice or virtue. So neither has a god" (EN 1145a25). But everything is not therewith said about man. Aristotle reminds his reader of the existence of a superhuman virtue in the tales of the past, "a heroic and divine kind of virtue" (EN 1145a19; cf. Pol. 1332b16). As they say: "men may become gods by excess of virtue" (EN 1145a23). The instance of a theios aner given is Hector, but the point of Aristotle is not to set off the bravery of Hector or his faithfulness to his family or his city. What Aristotle wishes to stress is that a transgression of mere human limitations was though of as possible even in Homer. The transgression Aristotle no longer finds in bravery or faithfulness. With this reference he tries to make room for the possibility of attaining the superhuman virtue of theoria. And his witness is Homer, who elsewhere proclaims the absolute difference between mortals and immortals. One may well compare this note on Hector with the end of the conversation in the Meno. Different sorts of men are called 'divine': poets, diviners, prophets. "Yes, and statesmen above all may be said to be divine and illuminated, being inspired and possessed of God, in which condition they say many grand things, not knowing what they say", Socrates remarks ironically. The point of the conversation is that only one sort of man fully deserves the name 'divine', namely "the educators of statesmen", i.e. the philosophers (Meno 99a-d).

The intermediate position of man is also expressed in the Protrepticus. Thanks to phronēsis our lives can be like the life of the gods compared to other living beings (B109). And again: if nous in man were removed, he would be like a plant. If it could reign alone, man would be like God (B28).

Now man has his <u>nous</u> and may do a lot to secure its dominating position, although it is perhaps impossible to escape the irrational powers of the body and its soul in full measure.

The commentaries on the passage at hand have often discussed the question whether the psychology of Aristotle reckons with an indestructible part of the soul, and thus whether Aristotle argues for the possibility of a sort of life after death or not.[6] There is no reason whatsoever to make a serious problem out of this question. The question was not unknown to Aristotle, but of no special importance to him either. The problem of immortality in the <u>Phaedo</u> or in Aristotle's own <u>Eudemus</u> does not propound a Christian solution. Taking the risk of being too general we may say that Christian thought is primarily interested in immortality as the possibility of resurrection and future life, whereas Plato and Aristotle are primarily concerned with immortality as an actual mode of present life. Randall says rightly:

> For the Greek, immortality was a quality of being. <u>Athanatos</u> is an
> attribute of the gods: they are always 'deathless and divine'. Justice
> is deathless, Beauty is deathless, and the soul of man can put on such
> deathlessness.[7]

In the <u>Phaedo,</u> none of the arguments for a future life is decisive. If the theme of the dialogue is immortality, then it is not concerned with the final destiny of Socrates, but with the unshakeable firmness in his quest for truth and with his indifference as to the phenomenon of his own death. The sources of the fragments of the <u>Eudemus</u> are too bad to allow a conclusion on this point. Admitted, there are not a few references in the Aristotelian Corpus concerning the indestructibility of the human soul or parts of it (e.g. <u>De An.</u> 408b27, 413a4-27, 430a17-25; <u>Meta.</u> 1070a24-26). But this metaphor of immortality is employed to underline the exceptional position of <u>nous</u>. All other parts of the soul correspond to some function and organ of the body. Only <u>nous</u> is a thing apart (cf. §§13, 26, 36). Rodier says ad loc.: "L'intellect seul paraît être éternel et impérissable; lui seul est, sans doute, non seulement séparable, mais encore actuellement séparé du corps". One would think, then, that man may be immortal by virtue of this remarkable part of the soul. That <u>this</u> is the part of him that will have eternal life. It may be so, but Aristotle is obviously more occupied with immortality as a mode of life than as a mode of survival. Nous is not there to secure the permanence of human consciousness beyond death. This it can in no way produce.[8] Nous is there as the faculty which makes it possible to transcend the limitations of man as a species among species and partake in the life of the thinking God who has ordered these species or, at least, secures their immutability.

To know more exactly what athanatizein (77b33) means here, we must know more about the nature of the participation in the divine life. Firstly, athanatizein is a negation of the thnēta phronein. Dirlmeier comments on the expression ad loc.: "Das a privativum hat seine volle Kraft". This means that athanatizein is employed to express the counterpart of the mere anthrōpeuesthai (78b7). Metaschein athanasias (Tim. 90c; cf. Xenoph. Mem. IV, 3, 14) says the same thing, hits the same point: not to think of 'mortal' things (cf. DK 68B 189). The positive counterpart of this negation must be the short glimpses of divine beauty and order mentioned in Part.An. 644b22-36, Meta. 1072b15, 25 and Pol. 1339b27-31. But the nearer we come to the real answer, the more vague are the expressions of Aristotle. The partaking in the divine life is never described so that we can agree on its contents or even get a clear idea of what he is thinking of. Aristotle clearly adopts the Platonic idea of homoiōsis tō theō (Theaet. 176b), but Plato is not lucid either "To become like God as far as possible, i.e. to become just and holy with thought accompanying". The expressions reflect obviously a hope and an ideal but it is left obscure even though each author probably regards it as attained in his own case.

This idea has many forms in Aristotle. In the Protrepticus, the imitation of God is thought to consist in the use of reason which is "the god in us" (B110). In De Anima, we are "partaking in the eternal and divine" by producing living beings like ourselves (415a26-b7; cf. Gen.An. 731b24-32a1). In Gen.Corr. we partake in the divine continuum, in the perpetual coming-to-be and passing-away which is the closest material approximation to eternal being (336b26-37a17). A difficult passage that may have a bearing on this point is Mot.An. 700b30-1a25. Here Aristotle maintains that the immovable objects of science and the standards of ethical choice are analogous to the Prime Mover. Presumably, we may, then, partake in the divine both through research and moral action. On the other hand, it is surely wrong to look for a lucid doctrine on the subject. Aristotle does not describe a matter of fact. He propounds ideals, and ideals may be even more ambiguous than facts.

Both Plato and Aristotle use the qualification "as far as possible" when discussing the problem of attaining immortality. To become fully immortal is apparently impossible (cf. EE 1225b33) both in the sense that we should live consciously beyond death and in the sense that we should partake in the divine life for a long time. But Aristotle seems to promote the wish even if it cannot be completely fulfilled. To explain this difficulty, Stewart refers to Kant and EE 1249b6ff., saying:

> The theōrētikos bios is an ideal; it cannot be realised by man, for he is concrete. But the effort to realise it, as far as possible, is all-important in human life. The effort to realise it coordinates man's powers, and exalts their vitality - it gives him élan, and carries him on to the attainment of many things within his reach, which he otherwise would not aspire to. Perhaps we may venture to translate the doctrine of this section into the language of modern philosophy, and say that Aristotle makes 'the Idea of God' the 'regulative principle' in man's life (ad 77b31-34).

To some extent this may be true, but it should be possible to reformulate Aristotle's position without any help from Kant. Firstly, Stewart does not make the distinction between the setting of the ideal and the realisation of it. It seems to us that the problem here is to set the ideal, to determine what should be sought for in human life. The question is just what makes man happy and not how and to what extent he may be happy. Stewart explains, then, a problem which is not advanced by Aristotle yet. Moreover, his explanation reads a resignation into the text. But this is not the last word of Aristotle. We have seen his treatment of the objections from common sense (cf. the end of §21). Those are not objections as to the possibility of the realisation of this ideal, but objections even to the setting of such an ideal! Stewart's modesty in regard to the bios theōrētikos, then is not the modesty of Aristotle.

Even less to the point is Léonard's description of Aristotle's tragic resignation:

Aussi la contemplation aristotélicienne, orientée vers un objet trop
noble pour les seules forces humaines, vers le seul objet poutant qui
puisse satisfaire, est-elle finalement un échec. Échec glorieux, car il
est beau de ne pas aboutir là où il est humain d'échouer; mais échec
quand même.[9]

Aristotle does not set any limit for the immortalisation of man, nor does
he say that it has no limits. His perspective is somewhat different. He
does not propound erotics in the same sense as Plato in the Symposium, the
Phaedrus, the Lysis or the Republic.[10] The homoiōsis in Aristotle is
thought to be won through concentration and discipline rather than through
transgression or ascension. We must be aware, however, that Aristotle here
propounds an ideal that he has taken pains to establish. He is depicting philoso
in the way which could most easily justify it rather than describing the actual
business of thinking. The difficulty to point out clear differences between
Aristotle and Plato on this point does not mean that they actually agree on the
condition of man and philosophy. It only means that they put on much the
same face while justifying their business. Their account of philosophy is a
matter of ideology, not a matter of analytical description.

As was said above, there is no reason to remind men of their limits of
perfection. They will make themselves felt anyway. Aristotle is more afraid
that man will let his chance to be immortal and happy go, than that he should
be too divine. Greenwood concludes his examination of this passage with a
question:

> How far should a man in practice athanatizein and how far anthrōpeuesth
> (1177b31, 1178b7)? Casuistry could present countless cases in which a
> conflict of duties would arise, where anthrōpeuesthai could hinder
> athanatizein and athanatizein would hinder anthrōpeuesthai. But Aristot
> takes no account of the possibility of this.[11]

The answer is not that difficult. The two perspectives of human life are
not both ends or both means. Accordingly, they cannot be compared in the
way Greenwood attempts. Athanatizein is an end, and anthrōpeuesthai is not
only a means, but obviously a means to athanatizein. There can be no confli
then, because their scopes are different. The panta poiein (77b33f.) underlines that anthrōpeuesthai is a mere means. From this point of view, the
mere human life of man is not desirable in itself, because man as a whole

does not exist for his own sake. On the contrary, the mere human faculties and gifts of man have to be mobilised for a superhuman end. The activity of nous is this superhuman end, for nous does not belong to man as such. To make oneself immortal means, then, to serve to kratiston en autō (77a13, 78a5-6), i.e. to escape the destructible realm of means and find rest in the indestructible realm of ends.

§24. MAN MUST CHOOSE THE LIFE OF HIS SELF

1177b34-78a8. The first question raised and answered in this passage is the question of what makes man a man - "ce qui fait que l'homme est homme", as Rodier says ad loc.. Here Aristotle identifies man with his highest faculty, not only with reason and thinking, but apparently with reason in its theoretical use. As we have seen, this is at variance with the general anthropology of Aristotle as well as with his doctrine of definition. Adkins says:

> The last point (i.e. that man is his best part) is a fallacy in terms of Aristotle's own philosophy: anything should be defined per genus et differentiam, and both are constitutive of that thing. Man is not only his divine spark, but all his other elements also.[1]

The curious thing is that man is sometimes referred to as the natural species without his nous - which is something divine - and here is referred to as his nous only.

Aristotle has apparently gone a step further from the account of human soul in Book I. In the introductory course on psychology he makes it clear that the particular life of man does not consist in "nutrition and growth", nor in "perception":

> There remains, then, an active life of the element that has a rational principle (praktikē tis tou logon echontos); of this, one part has such a principle in the sense of being obedient to one, the other in the sense of possessing one and exercising thought. And as 'life of the rational element' also has two meanings, we must state that life in the sense of activity is what we mean; for this seems to be the more proper sense of the term (EN 1098a3ff.).

So far, phronēsis could be the core of the best life. Logos here probably means the same as in Pol.1253a9-18, rationality in all its forms
comprising the faculty of judgement of good and bad, just and unjust, as
well as the faculty of accounting for one's decisions and feelings in words.
Bröcker understands the expression logon echōn thus:

> Der Mensch sieht seine Aufgabe als Aufgabe. Und nur so vermag sie
> ihn zu bestimmen. Dies verstehende Sehen von etwas als das was es ist,
> und die Möglichkeit, dadurch sich bestimmen zu lassen, ist aber gerade
> das, was Aristoteles als "Wort" bezeichnet.[2]

Thus man is identified with his particular gifts and with the execution of
his proper task. This he has from his nature no less than all other natural
species. As far as phronēsis is concerned, it is easy to show that it makes
the specific form of human life possible, namely the life in the city. In moral
choice man cannot ignore his body and its desires. He rather shapes them,
thus making himself a whole in each choice when his rationality overcomes
his irrationality. At any rate, this is Aristotle's general picture of moral
man. If he agrees with the opinion that "the irrational passions are not less
human than reason is" (EN 1111b1), phronēsis represents a sort of compromise: it is the specific human difference in relation to other living beings,
but it does not ignore the fact that man cannot escape his body and the life in
the community. All the same, phronēsis and its life represent but a seconda:
ideal of life in Aristotle. Moral man taking part in the community cannot
attain supreme happiness. This conviction urges Aristotle to justify the life
of theōria, which, at least in principle, is a life consistent with privacy.

The dilemma is clearly seen above in the examination of nous. This is
at the same time both the most human thing and a thing which does not belong
to man as such. Aristotle defines man out of the community. Compared to
man, the state is another thing, like the body. He says: "If he were to choose
not the life of his self, but that of something else" (78a2). "Something else"
can only refer to the body and the claims of the society, which are the origins
of the two other forms of life challenging the supremacy of the bios theōrētikc
or, as it is named here, ho kata ton noun bios (78a6-7).

There is a possibility that nous in the passage at hand is used in a wider
sense than in the introduction to EN X, 7. But, firstly, such a change in termi

nology seems rather unlikely, and secondly it would rather have confirmed our indications of his dilemma if it were the case. For the identification of man with his supreme faculty is not restricted to EN X, 7. The expressions here are in full agreement with the more elaborate discussions in Book VI. There Aristotle says in a remarkable passage:

> And the element that thinks would seem to be the individual man, or to be so more than any other element in him. And such a man wishes to live with himself; for he does so with pleasure, since the memories of his past acts are delightful and his hope for the future is good, and therefore pleasant. His mind is well stored too with subjects of contemplation. And he grieves and rejoices, more than any other, with himself; for the same thing is always painful and the same thing is always pleasant, and not one thing at one time and another at another; he has, so to speak, nothing to repent of (EN 1166a22ff.).

We note the quietism of this passage and the curious use of theōria denoting introspection. The thinking element contemplates the memories of past acts and the hopes for the future, but it does not partake in the struggle for life. The best man is self-sufficient because he has his head full of thoughts which are most pleasant to dwell upon. His sorrows and joys are not caused by others. They take place inside his own mind. Whatever this means, it is not an appeal to accept moral and political obligations.

Shortly afterwards, the thinking element is apparently represented as a more active thing. The philautos, Aristotle says,

> gratifies the most authoritative element in himself and in all things obey this; and just as a city or any other systematic whole is most properly identified with the most authoritative element in it, so is a man (EN 1168b30-33).

Gauthier finds that reason thus issues duties to be done, but this assumption depends on a false reading of to kyriōtaton and peithetai (1168b31).[3] The thinking element in man is what man is most properly identified with. For its activity is his end, and "each thing is defined by its end" (EN 1115b22).

This element is to kyriōtaton just because it is the end which all the other faculties 'serve' (peithetai). Kyriōtaton has this main sense in Aristotle (cf. Pol.1282b14; Meta.1048a10ff.). It is the best thing which exists for its own sake, whereas all other things exist for the sake of it. Burnet comments ad 1098a6 on this term:

The reason is that the ergon is the end of the hexis and therefore better
Where there is an ergon para tēn energeian, that is better than the
energeia (1094a5); but, when the end is the energeia itself, it is the
final cause, and the hexis is only a dynamis in relation to it. Now the
dynamis is referable to the energeia (1170a16) as that which determines
it and makes it what it is (to kyrion).

This part, then, is not authoritative in the sense that it issues commands
or demands obedience. It is authoritative for us in the way that we always
have to aim at it and serve it because it is the best thing. The strong collo-
cation of timiōtata and kyriōtata affirms this supposition (cf. Protr. B61;
Meta. 1074b14ff.), and it may be understood synonymously with the beltista
kai timiōtata in Protr. B16. The best thing in us, then, is kyriōtaton, not
because it decides what we must do, but because it fixes the direction of our
decisions.

The best thing in us is a small but powerful ongkos, Aristotle says,
(78a1). Why does Aristotle call nous a mikros ongkos? There is probably
more than one right answer to the question. The expression is, of course,
a metaphor because nous cannot be big or small in any sense relating to
space (cf. Meta. 1073a5). The question remains, however, what the metaphor
means.

(a) F. Brentano (quoted by Gauthier ad loc.) thinks, that it refers to its
public esteem. In support of this assumption, we may refer to the dictum of
Anaxagoras treated below (cf. §31): "He would not be surprised if the happy
man were to seem to most people a strange person; for they judge by
externals, since these are all they perceive" (EN 1179a13–15). Although this
is not the most obvious reading, it need not be wrong. Authors speaking
metaphorically often wish to say many things at the same time, i.e. by one
expression.

(b) Rodier follows Ramsauer in thinking that nous is called 'small'
because it can only fully realise itself for a 'short time', whereas God can
do the same thing perpetually. The mikros ongkos (78a1) should, then,
recall the mikros chronos in Meta. 1072b15. There is no reason to reject
this guess even if it should not be the whole answer.

(c) Arleth finds the most striking parallel in Soph. Elench. 183b22,
where it is said that the principle is smallest in compass, but most potent in
influence.[4] So nous is the apparently insignificant thing, which, nevertheless

has the most comprehensive power because it is the archē of thought and of human life. This solution seems at any rate more far-fetched than the two mentioned above, due to the ambiguity of the text referred to as the main witness.

(d) According to Gauthier ad loc. Thomas Aquinas thought that Aristotle wanted to underline the immateriality of nous by means of this metaphor. If this is the case, Aristotle has rather called it immensely great, like Peri-ander, who, when he was asked: "What is the greatest thing in the smallest?" answered: "A strong mind (phrenes agathai) in a human body".[5]

(e) The last theory refers to Plato's Republic 442a-c, where he states the analogy between the ideal city and the soul. The leading group in the state is small related to the whole, and so is the leading principle in the soul. This analogy is repeated in EN 1168b31ff.. What it means, then, should be: in spite of its simple nature, it steers a complex whole. To say that it is small is to say that it has surprising power. It seems impossible to bypass the metaphors in this case and state the thought of Aristotle in plain words.[6]

At any rate, this best thing is what is the essential characteristic of humans. The malista anthrōpos (78a7) corresponds to the expression malista hēmeis in the Protrepticus (B62, 85-86; cf. EN 1169a2) and the to en hēmin theion in EE 1248a27. This 'man at his most' enjoys the greatest pleasure. For pleasure is not becoming (cf. Plato's Phil. 53c), but an activity (EN 1152b13). And the greatest pleasure originates from the execu-tion of the proper ergon (EN 1099a7-21, 1169b31-33, 1176b24-27). Now theōria is thought to be the particular activity of man and therefore the most pleasant one (cf. §17). But this is not the only reason for regarding theōria as the most pleasant activity. Besides the reason related to the concept of energeia, we get a reason related to the concept of mimēsis.

We have already noted what we called the 'quietism' of Book VI. In Book VII we also discover the same trend in Aristotle's treatment of pleasure. Aristotle here appears as one who requires rest and concentration. He detests the demands for novelties and contemplates the simplicity and unity of the divine pleasure as the supreme pattern of life. He dissociates himself not only from the stupid desires of the vicious body, but therein he also dissociates himself from the limitations of human life and its conditions.

EN X, 6-8 is not a sudden intrusion in an otherwise common-sensical frame.
This supposed framework is broken more than once by passages like this
one:

> There is no one thing that is always pleasant, because our nature is not
> simple, but there is another element in us as well, in as much as we
> are perishable creatures, so that if the one element does something,
> this is unnatural to the other nature, and when the two elements are
> evenly balanced, what is done seems neither painful nor pleasant;
> for if the nature of anything were simple, the same action would always
> be most pleasant to it. This is why God always enjoys a single and
> simple pleasure; for there is not only an activity of movement but an
> activity of immobility, and the pleasure is found more in rest than in
> movement. But 'change in all things is sweet', as the poet says,
> because of some vice; for it is the vicious man that is changeable, so
> the nature that needs change is vicious; for it is not simple nor good
> (EN 1154b20ff.).

As was mentioned above, Burnet strongly emphasizes the idea of
philautia and its importance for the unity of EN (cf. §4, n.10). In many
publications, Dirlmeier has renewed his thesis. The words philautia and
philautos are not used in EN X, 6-8, but all the same Burnet and Dirlmeier
have undoubtedly found a main correspondence between X, 6-8 and the rest
of EN beyond the well-known similarities between Books I, VI, and X. The
first thing to note is that this correspondence is yet another argument for
the unitarian hypothesis: that EN was conceived by the author mainly as we
have it. The 'quietism' pointed out in Books VI and VII cannot be interpreted
in disfavour of this assumption.

Burnet's definition of the nature of philautia, however, needs some
correction. He says ad loc.: "For philautia in its highest form is the love
of the higher self, and it is good, as proved above 1170a13 sqq., for it is
just the self-consciousness of the activity of thought (noēsis noēseōs)". No,
philautia is nowhere depicted as a noēsis noēseōs. The problem of self-
consciousness was moreover not known to the Greeks in this form.[7]
Aristotle is too well aware of the border-line between men and God to use
this expression indiscriminately of them both. His concept of athanatizein
presupposes a tension between the human and the divine (77b33). Aristotle,
then, does not remove the border-line, if he invites us to transgress it.

The lover of his self is rather the man who directs all impulses and
actions so that his reason may thus take advantage of them. The philautos
is an integrated individual being, his own master, because his supreme
faculty reigns and directs his lower faculties as their intrinsic end (cf. EE
1249b6-11). The lover of his self must, however, be a good man. In the
vicious, philautia is, of course, improper. But if a man is good, his
goodness may become permanent through his self-love (EN 1168b28-69b1).
C.W. Müller expresses the essence of the concept thus:

> ... und auch die Freundschaft der 'Gleichen' deren vollkommene Form
> (teleia philia) die Freundschaft der kat'areten homoioi (EN 1156b7) ist,
> beruht letztlich auf dem Willen zur Selbstverwirklichung und gipfelt in
> der sublimierten philautia des Guten. In diesem Zusammenhang ordnen
> sich bei Aristoteles auch die homoiosis theo sowie die theophilia ein.[8]

This doctrine is more suggested than worked out, but already the
suggestions make some points clear.

The most curious part of this doctrine is the way Aristotle connects
solitude and friendship, privacy and moral education: "But he (i.e. the
philautos) may even give up actions to his friend; it may be nobler to become
the cause of his friend's acting than to act himself" (EN 1169a33). Aristotle
apparently says: the highest act of friendship is to love oneself, to become
an integrated individual to the extent that you may be a paragon for others.
You may do your friends favours more directly, but the best favour you can
do them is to make yourself perfectly free so that they can have a pattern to
aim at. In this most noble way the philautos may become the cause of his
friend's acting.

Thus the doctrine of friendship also seems to defend the solitary privacy
of the philosopher. Aristotle does not only defend the bios theoretikos among
other things. He awards it a position which makes it the aim and fulfilment
of all things human: moral actions, friendship, education, politics. The
transition to the love of the real self is at the same time a transition of
society into privacy, an abandonment of external responsibility in favour of
the single obligation to make one's self immortal as far as possible. This
does not mean, however, that Aristotle forgets society or his fellow human
beings. But the best thing a man can do, not only for himself, but also with
regard to his friends and the community, is to serve as the paradeigma of

the fully realised man, i.e. to be a philosopher (cf. Pol. 1325b15-32). In this sense, the supreme good for the individual and for the state is identical. Not so that all citizens may become philosophers (cf. EN 1105b9ff.); but all citizens, Aristotle contends, need the fully realised man as a paragon in all parts of their life.

Düring sums up his interpretation of Aristotle's account of philosophy in this way: "Das Hauptanliegen des Aristoteles war also, den sokratischen Satz ho anexetastos bios ou biōtos anthrōpō (Apol. 38a) zu verteidigen und mit neuen Argumenten aus seiner eigenen Lebensanschauung zu erhärten".[9] This is the least that can be said. Düring is certainly not overstating Aristotle's conviction regarding the value of sophia. From the point of view of this knowledge of the 'main concern' of Aristotle, his considerations of ta anthrōpina must be understood. This motive is effective not only in EN X, 6-8 but in his constructions of psychology, politics, and metaphysics as well. It is not only a question of realising the best life among many sorts possible. Man must try to find his life, which is the possibility to be himself. For no one would choose to be someone else, even if he gets the whole world in exchange (EN 1166a19ff.). Maybe Aristotle writes thus thinking of his own relation to Alexander the Great and the parallel story about Solon and Croesus. At any rate, even the virtue of the best politician is secondary to that of the philosopher, as can be seen from the juxtaposition of Pericles and Anaxagoras (cf. §21, n.6; §31).

§25. THE VIRTUES OF ACTION ARE SECONDARY

<u>1178a9-14</u>. Life in accordance with other virtues than the best activity of man's best part is merely happy in a secondary sense: <u>deuterōs</u> (78a9). This devaluation is underlined by putting <u>deuterōs</u> first in the sentence. <u>Deuterōs</u> here recalls and develops the theme suggested by <u>deuterōs kai pollostōs</u>, "in a secondary and even far lower degree" in 1176a29. The relation between the intensity and purity of their respective pleasures corresponds to the relation of value between the different virtuous actions (cf. §17).

<u>Deuterōs</u> and what follows must not be understood as a concession to <u>to syntheton.</u> On the contrary, through <u>deuterōs</u> the invitation to immortality retains its power in spite of its exclusive position. What Aristotle said positively in X, 7, he now says negatively in the definition of the practical virtues as different from and secondary to the supreme virtue and its happiness. The morally acting man may also be happy, Aristotle admits, but not in the same sense as the <u>sophos</u>. The happiness of the politician and of the man observing his civic duties is a sort of reward for their contribution to the happiness of the <u>sophos</u>. That also other men than the philosophers may be happy does not mean, then, an admissive plurality in Aristotle's doctrine of happiness. The <u>eudaimonia</u> of the philosopher is and remains the happiness of man. But as the <u>bios theōrētikos</u> to some extent depends on social cooperation and interaction, the moderate and prudent man will be rewarded for their contribution. Stewart says in a paraphrase ad 78a10:

> The exhortation <u>chrē de</u> ... <u>eph'hoson endechetai athanatizein</u> is addressed to the bulk of mankind, because it is open to every man who is not <u>pepērōmenos pros aretēn</u> to contribute - if not in some

brilliant way, as politician, or soldier, or leader of fashion, or athlete – at least as honest man, to the eudaimonia of a city in which savants are produced and held in honour (cf. EN 1099b18ff.; §6, n.4).

The same point is better put by Gauthier ad loc. who refers to the notes on health and medicine in Book VI (1144a3-6, 1145a7-9). Practical virtues are 'secondary' to theōria in the same sense as medicine is 'secondary' to health. Irrespective of the utility of this art, health is its end for whose sake it exists.

This grading of value is reflected in the structure of EN X, 8. It opens with the admission that other men can also be happy in their way, other men than the sophoi. But it closes with the makarismos of the philosopher as theophilestatos. And if the sophos in X, 7 is opposed to the politician, here he is clearly opposed to the ordinary, law-abiding citizen.

Ad deuterōs in 78a9, Düring says:

> Gauthier bemerkt: 'Ce n'est qu'à titre secondaire qu'est heureuse la vie selon les autres vertus'. Stewart und Dirlmeier halten mit Recht daran fest, dass Aristoteles eine Hierarchie konstruiert; die Höchst-form schliesst in sich die anderen Formen ein.[1]

We have already discussed this contention in §10, n.4. From our point of view both Gauthier and Stewart need some correction. The principal statements on the relation between phronēsis and theōria given in §4 are valid here. As to the quotation from Düring, it must be said, firstly, that the sentence from Gauthier is not a note, but his translation of 78a9-10. Secondly, Gauthier cannot be interpreted as propounding an alternative to the hierarchic understanding of the relation between the faculties and the forms of life. He says:

> Il ne s'agit pas pour lui de distinguer deux types de bonheur séparables, le bonheur parfait du philosophe et le bonheur secondaire du politique, mais de hiérarchiser les deux types de vie que mène conjointement le même homme, a la fois philosophe et homme politique. L'idéal d'Aristote, c'est en effet l'idéal de la vie mixte.[2]

Gauthier also reads a hierarchic structure out of the account of the different lives, but his concept of 'la vie mixte' is simply wrong. It is an attempt to find the philosopher/kings of Plato's Republic in the text of Aristotle, as Dirlmeier does.[3]

Gauthier is right in speaking of two sorts of life rather than two sorts of men. He is also right in presupposing the demand that the sophos also must be phronimos to a certain extent. But when he maintains that the ideal of Aristotle is the mixture and not the best life, he has lost the track in sheer apologetic dexterity. Thus an opinion is assigned to Aristotle, i.e. as the core of his ethics and his concept of philosophy, which he unfortunately never expresses. If Aristotle ever propounds a 'vie mixte' in any sense, it certainly also comprises pleasure, as Düring has seen rightly.[4] But the mixture can in no case be understood as a mixture of equally valuable elements. The 'mixture' is produced in the way that the bios theōrētikos is both the most pleasant life and the most virtuous life because it is the real end of both the bios apolaustikos and the bios politikos. We are not sure if it is right to call this a 'mixture' at all; in every case this use of the word would differ clearly from the use of it in Gauthier. For the other lives are not only parts of the bios theōrētikos but distinctive possibilities as well.

The bios theōrētikos comprises the sorts of life in the same manner as Aristotle's opinion comprises and modifies the opinions of previous thought (cf. §31), as God is the final cause of all the movements on earth (cf. §37), as the highest faculty of the soul presupposes and uses the other faculties as instruments (cf. §36), and as the philosopher is present in every single action in the state, in the capacity of being the ideal of human freedom and perfection (cf. §35). One may judge this view as somewhat highly strung, but it is the opinion of Aristotle.

There is a difference between the interpretation of Gauthier and that of Stewart, if not the difference that Düring points out. Stewart's note ad loc. reflects serious confusion. He is forced to introduce some auxiliary hypotheses to save the main point of his interpretation already criticised in §18. Stewart's distinction between the concrete man (to syntheton with phronēsis) and the form of man (the abstract ideal of theōria) is not even Platonic (cf. §4, n.2), but only a bad Kantian construction. Moreover, it produces contradictions. On the one hand, theōria is - for Stewart - only the abstract form of man, a regulative idea. On the other hand, it may be realised by a small group. Stewart should have chosen, but it is a bad position because both possibilities seem to be wrong. Aristotle does not use the distinction few/many in this context, and of course not the distinction between concrete and formal man. The point of the notion of to syntheton is different. It is rather introduced to prepare for the fight for immortality than as a request for resignation (cf. §22). A final account of the meaning of this concept will be given in the next chapter.

Is there, then, one or two forms of happiness? The manner of expression is, perhaps, not that important, but even among the best commentators there are renderings which need to be corrected. Seidl says:

> Als praktischer ist der Intellekt mit den sinnlichen Seelenvermögen verbunden und erreicht die 'zweite' Eudaimonie, als theoretischer trennt er sich von ihnen ab und erreicht (wenigstens für Augenblicke des Lebens) die 'erste', 'abgetrennte Eudaimonie'.[5]

One can hardly accuse Aristotle of this sort of shamanism. There is a remarkable difference between the happiness of phronēsis and that of theōria, but there is also a connection. The different phases are not like the route of Parmenides before and after the meeting with the goddess.[6]

Theōria gives phronēsis its aim and phronēsis contributes to theōria as a means. Greenwood is even further off the mark in his consideration of the problem:

> It thus appears that the relation of sophia to eudaimonia is far more direct than the relation of phronēsis to eudaimonia. For whereas the activity that arises from sophia is either eudaimonia itself or the best and most important part of eudaimonia, the activity that arises from phronēsis is only one element in that complex activity (orthē prohairesis) which itself must be combined with praxis to make a still more complex activity (theōria kai praxis kata tēn allēn aretēn) which is either not eudaimonia at all or is at best an inferior and less important part of eudaimonia.[7]

But sophia cannot be realised without regard to the character and the prudence of the man in question. More than that: even if the man himself is phronimos, he needs in addition a well-ordered society that can give him his leisure. He needs the phronēsis of others as well. Greenwood says elsewhere (cf. §4, n.4) that phronēsis is both an external and component means to theōria. The connection is, then, not so complex and indirect as he maintains here.

The analogy between the phronimos and the sophos as to self-sufficiency is decisive. The phronimos is his own master because he knows the end of action from his own thought. This freedom is related to the freedom of the sophos, and we may infer that it is just the freedom from compulsion and external directions which is the source of happiness and pleasure in the two cases (cf. §18). The phronimos is, of course, not free to the same extent as the sophos, but their respective sorts of freedom depend on one another. It would be unreasonable, then, to ascribe happiness to the second and not to the first one, even though the phronimos is only happy deuterōs. On the other hand, the difference of value should not be obliterated as in Léonard, who ignores the protreptic character of this juxtaposition and – like Seidl above – regards it as a mere classification of forms at hand.[8]

Although it should be elementary, it must be underlined that Aristotle is not speaking here as a natural scientist making distinctions and definitions to discover the structure of the reality at hand. Maybe he preserves some traits of his usual handicraft. At any rate, most commentators ignore the invitation in these passages and treat them as mere statements of opinion. Thus they hold EN X, 6-8 to be an overstatement of the superiority of sophia. It must be repeated that this is a sermon which defends and justifies philosophy. If the classifications and definitions are not as lucid as usual in Aristotle, this is not a work of his juvenile Platonic enthusiasm. This enthusiasm is as Aristotelian as anything in the Corpus. It is the enthusiasm of a barrister defending his own case. EN X, 6-8 is among other things an apologia pro vita sua.

The main features of the virtue described here are: (1) that it is 'human' in contrast to the 'divine' virtue of theōria. But the distinction between to theion and to anthrōpikon does not imply an appeal to concentrate on the latter (cf. §22); (2) these 'human' virtues are concerned with what we do in relation to each other (pros allelous, 78a11); (3) it takes the passions into account (78a13), and – most important – (4) its main rule is to prepon hekastō (78a13). These four features are not found in the virtue of theōria. It is 'divine', concerns the relation of man to himself, disregards the passions and the demand for moderation.

Gauthier and Ramsauer discover the three other cardinal virtues in this summing up (cf. §18, n. 7). But that is not the point of this representation of practical virtue. Its score is the counterpoint relation to the invitation to immortality above, i.e. its stressing of to prepon. Dirlmeier finds its point in the juxtaposition of the irrationality here to the demand for rationality above: "Damit sind alle Situationen zusammengefasst, in denen Lust und Unlust eine entscheidende Rolle spielen", he says (cf. EN 1106b16). But the ideal of the bios theoretikos is not indifferent to pleasure. Dirlmeier note fits the following passage better than this one. In our opinion, the main contrast between the virtue described here and the virtue of theoria is the indifference of the latter as to the demand for moderation.

Strictly speaking, not only theoria and phronesis are confronted here. From the point of view of theoria, phronesis is put together with the moral virtues. The happiness of doing to prepon is not described as dependent on the condition that the person himself is the source of the standard, as the phronimos is. This may be due to the condensed character of the passage, but it may also be an effect of the tendency found in §14: the urge of the end to dominate the whole. The differences between the lower parts of the structure are not noted when the whole is considered from the summit.

Sophia is dependent on the practical virtues and the serious decisions of the individual. One becomes just through just acts, and temperate through temperate acts, he says, and continues:

> But most people do not do these, but take refuge in theory and think they are being philosophers and will become good in this way, behaving some- what like patients who listen attentively to their doctors, but do none of the things they are ordered to do. As the latter will not be made well in body by such a treatment, the former will not be made well in soul by such a course of philosophy (EN 1105b9ff.).

There is no way to avoid or skip the difficult process through the education of character and moral consciousness. Philosophy proper is impossible without this preparation.

The rest of EN X, 8 considers the theme of the previous chapter once more. If X, 7 is apodictic, X, 8 is rather argumentative. But the conclusion is the same. Unfortunately, the argument is not less rhetorical, and it hard- ly represents an advance in clarity. The main purpose is the development of the thought behind deuteros in 78a9. It is supported by a distinction between the essential and accidental implication of theoria, by the analogy to the life of the gods, by the difference between man and animal, and by a general retrospective glance at the previous opinions of religion and thought.

§26. THE EXCELLENCE OF REASON IS A THING APART

<u>1178a14-23.</u> There are three kinds of virtue mentioned here that directly or indirectly relate to the body and its passions. The virtue arising from the body must be the 'natural virtue' considered in EN 1144b3ff. Then comes <u>hē tou ethous aretē</u> (78a16-17), the virtue of character, which results from habituation (EN 1104b9-31; cf. Plato's <u>Rep.</u> 518e). And the last one is <u>phronēsis,</u> which, then, is classed among the virtues concerned with bodily passions, if more indirectly than the natural virtue and the virtue of character (cf. EN II44a11-b7). So the passage at hand corresponds perfectly to <u>Pol.</u> 1332a38ff.: "There are three things which render men good and worthy: nature, habituation, and rational principle".

Unlike Grant ad loc. we find nothing mysterious about the account of <u>phronēsis</u> here. <u>Phronēsis</u> belongs to man as a unity, and the close connection and cooperation between the elements of this unity are expressed and underlined by the five different words in this passage beginning with <u>syn-</u>. <u>Nous,</u> however, does not belong to this unity. As Gauthier rightly says ad loc., the use of <u>to syntheton</u> here is not a reference to Plato. The unity and diversity of soul and body called <u>to synthcton</u> in the <u>Phaedo</u> (78b-c; 86a), do not occupy Aristotle. The elements of <u>to syntheton</u>, Gauthier interprets, are rather man with his soul on the one hand and <u>nous</u> on the other (cf. <u>Rep.</u> 518d-e). He is clearly wrong in the last contention. The point of Aristotle is just that <u>to syntheton</u> excludes <u>nous</u>. <u>To syntheton</u> is man as far as he can be described as an organic unity. But <u>nous</u> is a thing apart. It must be considered as a particular case. It is not an element of the human soul at the same level as the faculties that are concerned with the body. <u>To syntheton</u> is, then, man without his <u>nous</u>. The question of its elements and how they work together is not important here. The point of Aristotle is to show that <u>nous</u> is "separable, impassable, and unmixed" (<u>De An.</u> 430a17) in contrast to all the other faculties of the soul, which belong to <u>to syntheton</u> and cannot be separated from it. <u>To syntheton</u> is not the whole man, but only man as far as he is a unity.[1]

This leads ut to the problem of understanding the full meaning of <u>kechōrismenē</u>. Düring says: "Den <u>nous</u> betrachtete Aristoteles als <u>chōriston,</u> 'transzendent'".[2] Even if this should be right, it is hardly a

complete or a good explanation. That nous is something particular we have
already seen. It does not belong to man considered as a unity (to syntheton),
but is rather regarded as an appendix to his natural faculties. In Heraclitus
we find a related thought with the same manner of expression: to sophon is
kechōrismenon (DK 22B 108). To explain the word as used in our text,
however, we have to go to the psychology of De Anima. As to the question
of the separability of nous in its relation to the body, the different sources
of Aristotelian psychology agree perfectly (cf. Post.An.100b5ff.; De Sensu
445b16; Gen.An.737a10; De An.403a8, 408b18ff.). In contrast to the other
functions of the soul, nous is not bound to any single organ of the body. It
is independent of the body (De An.429a24ff.). But kechōrismenē means
more than that. Nous is thought to be free and unimpeded, whereas the
faculties that are bound to the body all have a special job to do. Further,
nous does not decay with the body. It is stimulated, not worn out, in case
of intensive use (429a31-b5). Reason is, as it were, coming into us from
outside, thyraten (Gen.An.736b28). Accordingly, there are good reasons
for using the word kechōrismenē about nous. But we may still note some
peculiarities.

Chōriston is used about ousia in the Metaphysics. One of the
characteristics of a real thing is that it is chōriston, i.e. that it can be
discerned as something for itself (Meta.1017b23-25, 1028b30). But the
word is also the key to Aristotle's criticism of Plato's theory of ideas.[3]
He is never tired of repeating that Plato considers the idea to be something
beyond the thing at hand which it should make understandable. This tmēsis
between the concrete thing and the form under which it can be comprehended,
Aristotle obviously rejects, as in the case of the Good in itself (cf. EN I, 6).
Nevertheless, Aristotle uses the same cue to describe the position of nous
in man. The word reappears - this is remarkable - in his description of
God's relation to nature in Lambda. God is the eternal and unmovable
substance which is 'separate (kechōrismenē) from sensible things' (Meta.
1073a4). The same thought is repeated in Meta.1075a11-19, when he asks if hē to
holou physis has its good as kechōrismenon ti or as the intrinsic order of its par
Both are right, Aristotle says. This ambiguous character of the good in nature co
responds to the ambiguity of the good for man. Phronēsis represents the good as
order of the parts and theōria the good as something separate. This parallel

is the more obvious because Aristotle often says that nature behaves like a man with phronēsis.[4]

The problem of nous poiētikos in De An.430a10-18 cannot and should not be treated here.[5] All that might be said about it is that Aristotle here through his method of qualification makes a distinction which reserves the position of kechōrismene to a mere part of nous. Why he does it, we will probably never know for sure. The general doctrine is that the whole nous "seems to be born in us as an independent substance, which is beyond decay and death" (De An.408b19). Hardie puts the problem in its proper light:

> Aristotle, it might be said, is feeling his way towards a position in which he could both claim a special status for reason and maintain his entelechy doctrine as an account of intellectual activity as well as of perception, imagination, pleasure and pain, and emotional states (De An. 403a3-16). I suggest, therefore, that the distinction between active and passive reason, although it gives rise to new problems in the interpretation of Aristotle, might, if developed, help us to make better sense than we can without it of the doctrine of theoretical reason in EN X. But it is another question whether the perplexities in the relation to which we find the doctrine interesting were among the considerations which suggested it to Aristotle.[6]

The distinction between active and passive nous is not found elsewhere in the Corpus.

We have not yet discussed which is the property of nous that is treated in the passage at hand. Gauthier and Dirlmeier insert aretē, as the headline to this paragraph does. Joachim inserts eudaimonia, considering that the passage treats the happiness of nous as a thing apart. Both interpretations are possible and both are in correspondence with the doctrine of Aristotle on this point. He had, then, perhaps, both possibilities in mind, and we can see no reason to make a problem where there is none.

The entelechy theory of the soul and the doctrine of nous as a 'thing apart' are not incompatible. They serve two different purposes, belong to two different dimensions of thought. There is, therefore, no reason to regard the one or the other as a survival from an earlier stage of Aristotle's development. The constructions of Jaeger and Gauthier are often based on a correct description of the ambiguity of the texts: They read them rightly, but their interpretations are wrong.[7] Formal deviations from the exposition in _De Anima_ do not justify a developmental hypothesis. Still worse, the developmental constructions ignore the most importunate problem raised in this passage. Caird saw this problem once, but after Jaeger the commentators have been blind to it. We will return to Caird in a moment. Let it suffice to say that the apparent discrepancies between _De Anima_ and EN may be due to the perspectives of the two treatises. Gauthier here represents the vain acuteness that looks for inconsistencies with an eye so sharp that it ignores what the passage is all about (cf. his note to 78a22). The only commentator we have found who indirectly confirms our interpretation of to syntheton and the position of nous is De Corte. He says:

> On ne peut exciper de la phrase célèbre qui termine l'argumentation d'Aristote: peri de tou theōrētikou nou heteros logos (415a11) pour alléguer que l'intellect échappe à cette loi de l'unité sérielle (to ephexes) de l'ame humaine, pour constituer une forme supérieure surajoutée et comme plaquée du dehors. Le contexte dit uniquement que les êtres périssables (tōn phthartōn) qui possedent la raison et la faculté dianoétique, possèdent aussi toutes les autres facultés, sans que la réciproque se vérifie. Si le cas du nous theōrētikos est different, c'est simplement parce que l'intellect peut exister a part de toute autre faculté chez les êtres incorruptibles, tels les dieux.[8]

It should, however, be added to this interpretation that the particular position of nous cannot be explained as a function of Aristotle's enthusiasm for the gods or immortality in any semi-Christian sense. He is engaged in constructing an ideology around his invitation to philosophy, and his doctrine of nous is a part of the preparation for the conviction that philosophy is something particularly important. We will return to this problem (cf. §36).

Caird wrongly shares the common opinion that the idea of to syntheton is at variance with the idea of organism:

> The organic idea which he seems to accept, especially in his conception of life in all its forms, is continually traversed by another idea which is essentially alien to it - the idea that all finite existence is a combination of elements which are not essentially related.[9]

The observation is right, but it does not apply to the idea of to syntheton. As was said above, the idea of to syntheton agrees well with the idea of organism. To syntheton does not denote 'a combination of elements which are not essentially related'. On the contrary, it denotes everything that belongs to the unity of man in contrast to <u>nous,</u> which is a thing apart. The organic idea is not traversed by the idea of <u>to syntheton,</u> but by the concept of <u>nous</u>. This is apparently also the opinion of Caird when he says:

> Thus a deep line of division is drawn between the intuitive and the discursive intelligence, between the pure reason and the passions and interests of mortal life. And the organic idea, which is already strained to the utmost by Aristotle in his conception of the relation between the soul and body of plants and animals, is once for all set aside as regards the rational life of man.[10]

In this dilemma the hypothesis of Jaeger simply does not work. For a similar pheonomenon is also found in the <u>Metaphysics</u> and the <u>Politics</u>: the organic idea is broken by the constitution of a supreme principle. Caird has seen – in this he follows Zeller – the omnipresent importance of this problem and ends up with ascribing to Aristotle a dualism which he cannot explain:

> As such, God is the first mover and the final end of the universe; yet, as we shall see, Aristotle has great difficulty in connecting him with the finite at all, and only succeed in doing so by a metaphysical <u>tour de force</u> ... the ultimate result of his system is even more decidedly dualistic than that of his master.[11]

We too, in fact, find it mysterious that a clever rhetorician like Aristotle could use the expression <u>kechōrismenē</u> at the core of his own doctrine, when it was the cue for his polemics against his master.

<u>Diakribōsai gar</u> ... (78a23) is a genuine Aristotelian way out of difficulties, and remarkably often he breaks off when he is about to consider the theme of the <u>bios theōrētikos</u>. The instance given by De Corte quoted above is instructive. This breaking off was not only a question of relevance. It is not only determined by the demand to exclude superfluous thoughts in a process of strict argumentation. Besides, we know few authors who are more fond of appendixes and excursions than Aristotle. This reserve must have some particular reason behind it, and we may suppose that it marks the doubt of Aristotle himself as to the feasibility of his project. But he was not willing to give it up for that reason. Undoubtedly he was held up in a genuine dilemma.

§27.CONTEMPLATION AND EXTERNAL EQUIPMENT

1178a24-78b7. The passage at hand cannot be suspected of being a later intrusion merely because of the repetitions of the ideas from the chapter above. EN X, 8 is as a whole a repetition of EN X, 7. Aristotle, as usual, states the same point in another way. It is his normal procedure to start from the beginning once again when the idea is left obscure from one point of view. Here we have a certain correspondence with the passage treated in §18. Firstly, he underlines the self-sufficiency of the supreme activity. Secondly, he contrasts in both passages the sophos with the practical virtues. But the passage at hand expresses some new ideas as well.

The first thing to note is the use of ho politikos (78a27). Here it indicates the man who is pursuing the whole class of practical virtues. The politikos embraces the eleutherios, dikaios, andreios, and sōphrōn. Then we understand the importance of the treatment of the 'politician' above (cf. §§20-21). The life of the philosopher is juxtaposed to the life of the ordinary citizen, the man absorbed by the duties of the community, and not only to the political leaders. It is impossible to understand why certain commentators attempt   to show that there is no difference or conflict between the two forms of life. For Aristotle is inviting the reader to keep himself aloof from the world of civic duties, and he is equally eager to show that this aloofness serves the city to a greater extent than the mere execution of the practical virtues. By 'practical virtues' we mean, then, the moral virtues and the intellectual virtue of phronēsis. We will return to the problem at the end of this chapter.

The main thought here is that the sophos qua sophos is self-sufficient. He does not need, as far as his proper activity is concerned, external equipment. The politikos, on the other hand, needs the anangkaia and the ektos chorēgia not only as being a man, but for the execution of his virtues. Even in the case of the politikos, however, prosperity and happiness are cautiously discerned. Léonard says:

> La prospérité extérieure n'est jamais désignée, chez Aristote, par le mot eudaimonia; dans l'EN, le mot euēmeria est employé deux fois en ce sens: 1099b7 et 1178b33; euetēria deux fois également: 1098b26 et 1155a8; euzōia en 1098b21. Eutychia ajoute, à l'idée de prospérité, l'idée de bonne chance: 1099b8, 1124a14, 1153b21.[1]

And we may infer that the distance between supreme happiness and wordly goods is even greater. For when Aristotle elsewhere speaks of happiness and prosperity, he first and foremost thinks of the happiness that here is called so deuterōs (cf. EN 1099b2-10, 1100b5ff.). The relation of ta ektos agatha to the supreme eudaimonia is both more indirect and more complex.

In the Protrepticus the self-sufficiency and the needlessness of the philosopher are underlined (B56). But the assumed beginning of the treatise is just a reference to the external goods of Themison as a splendid starting-point for philosophy. He is rich and has a good reputation as well (B1). Happiness, however, is to be found in to pōs tēn psychēn (B2), but wealth gives leisure and leisure makes room for philosophy. It is curious that Aristotle is much more reserved on this point when he treats the conditions of the sophos abstractly. He apparently refuses to see that the supreme freedom of speculation is built on the work of other men whom he blames for their dependence. A reason for this is that he regards the state with its classes as a natural fact, but at the same time considers the destinies of individual men as if they had a free choice.[2] To meet the objection that the sophoi are dependent on other men's work, he propounds the thesis that the sophos, as to his proper activity (pros tēn energeian, 78b4), needs nothing. It is, however, remarkable that scholē is not counted as an external good.[3] On the one hand, scholē is thought of as an empty time which should be filled with valuable activities. On the other hand, Aristotle appeals to simple citizens to act in such a way as to make room for scholē. Without this blind spot, it would be difficult to argue for the independence of the sophos. Aristotle likes to mention what the ordinary citizen owes the thinkers who make most of their scholē. But he seldom mentions what the thinkers owe the citizen. However, to chide Aristotle for the flaws in his political consciousness is too easy to be interesting.[4]

The juxtaposition of praxis and prohairesis here (78a35) is never sufficiently commented on. Virtue needs both, Aristotle says, and we may infer from the continuation that whereas praxis is the more essential to the secondary virtue, prohairesis is the more essential to the supreme virtue. This corresponds with the general doctrine, too. The moral virtues do not originate from a prohairesis in the full sense. Praxis and prohairesis are first equated in the act of the phronimos.[5] If we are right, Aristotle further says that prohairesis is more essential to theōria than praxis, i.e. its execution. The reason he gives for this differentiation is that the execution needs external goods, as in the case of the practical virtues, whereas consideration and act of choice do not. Gauthier refers correctly to 1111b5-6 "Choice (prohairesis) is thought to be most closely bound up with virtue and to discriminate characters better than actions do" (cf. DK 68B 68). The reason Aristotle gives is that choice is more free, more voluntary, than the form of the execution of the acts. But Gauthier and the other commentators ignore the importance of this statement for the understanding of Aristotle's invitation to immortality. It apparently throws light on the problem of the realisation of the bios theōrētikos. Because it is an aretē, theōria can also be said to consist of both praxis and prohairesis. But as the phronimos must reckon with the hindrances of the external conditions for the execution of his virtue, the sophos must fight with the hindrances placed upon him through his nature, as being a man. If he cannot execute theōria always, he is still a sophos, thanks to his choice. This simple observation, if it is correct, makes superfluous most of the previous theories on the problem of to what extent the bios theōrētikos can be realised.

Empodia should be read in its proper context (78b4). Dirlmeier says: "Hier hätte ich kein Bedenken, in W. Jaegers Sinn von einem Nachklang platonischer Motive zu sprechen ... Aber es ist kein Zweifel dass Aristotele was die Sache selbst betrifft, nie anders dachte als Platon". Dirlmeier ignores the fact that the statement on external goods as empodia is only a part of a more complex statement. External goods are 'hindrances' in the same abstract sense, i.e. pros tēn energeian, that the sophos needs nothing of it. But of course the sophos needs external goods, and does so to the same extent as the politikos, for even he is a man. He is, however, both a man and a sophos, and this requires a sort of balance. The result of this tension fits well in the general doctrine of Aristotle. Gauthier was the first to note it: "L'abondance des biens extérieurs est une entrave pour la contemplation, mais leur absence serait elle aussi une entrave: il nous en faut l'exacte mesure qui favorise la contemplation sans la gêner" (ad 78b4-5). This observation confirms the unity of EN. We can see how the rule of to meson in this case is an instrument for the supreme happiness. A minimum of practical virtue is, then, necessary for the realisation of the supreme virtue.

Rodier finds a problem in the contrast between the sophos and the politikos here. Of all the commentators he has perhaps the sharpest eye for confusion:

> On ne voit guère comment le sage qui se live à l'intellection pure, pourra être affranchi des conditions nécessaires au bonheur et à la vertu politiques. Ne faut-il pas, pour être souverainement heureux, qu'il soit courageux, juste et libéral? Pour qu'il put se passer du concours de ses semblables et de la société, il faudrait que se fût une bête ou un Dieu (Pol. 1253a29). Mais, s'il vit en société, pourrat-il atteindre le bonheur souverain sans avoir les vertus sociales? Il eût été plus conséquent, peut-être, de déclarer que la sagesse supreme s'ajoute à la vertu politique ... et de se résigner à admettre, par suite, qu'elle est soumise aux mêmes conditions (ad loc.).

Firstly, Rodier ignores the fact that Aristotle expressly invites us to transcend the life of the citizen. The sophos is neither a beast, nor a mere citizen, nor God. The citizen may live like a beast or like Sardanapallus (cf. §8), but he is not a beast for that reason. He may also share in the life of God without, of course, ever becoming a god himself. Rodier fails to see the tension, the fleeting world of possibilities in which Aristotle puts man. And without this picture of man Aristotle's protreptics has no sense. Secondly, Rodier fails to see that the relation between the citizen and the sophos is mediated by the concept of scholē. Aristotle is not classifying things actually at hand, nor is he busy planning a great future order of the state. He attempts to give philosophy a position in the invisible order of things, an irrefutable ontological status, to save it from the attacks of a society in which its presence is no longer a matter of course. Rodier's charge of inconsistencies, then, leads nowhere. But the blind spots in the arguments of Aristotle may give us some hints at that which lies behind his considerations.

As was said above, anthrōpeuesthai (78b7) is the counterpoint to athanatizein (77b33). This juxtaposition corresponds to that between the politikos and the sophos. Anthrōpeuesthai is a hapax in the Corpus. The word becomes more frequent in the centuries afterwards. Pros to anthrō-peuesthai should be translated: 'to play our parts as men'.[6] It obviously reflects a certain distance from mere human life as if it were not the only possibility. Gauthier says ad 78b7: "Aristote pas plus que Platon n'a voulu faire du philosophe un solitaire, ni même un émigré à l'interieur de la cité: il veut qu'il reste un citoyen et prenne sa part de la vie publique". This is hardly a right description either of the position of Plato or of that of Aristotle (cf. §2). At any rate it is ill-placed here. Aristotle apparently wants two things at the same time: a self-sufficient sort of life which none the less is important for the state (cf. §35). If his ideal of the bios theorētikos also comprises political virtues, it does so accidentally. The direct engagement in the life of the city is not the best life, and, we may add: either for the city, or for the individual. This is the opinion of Aristotle. The best friend is the self-sufficient one who can serve as a pattern for his friends, and not the man who does friendly deeds (cf. §24). Analogically, the best man in the city is thought of, not as the man who is busy with civic duties, but as the man who can serve as a pattern of the fully realised human life. Aristotle's defence of philosophy is as paradoxical as his account of friendship. He prefers the indirect service for the direct one, thus making room for the sophos as 'un reclus' (cf. Festugière in §2, n.19) without taking him out of the society. Being a man, the sophos must also have some political virtues in the direct sense, but to the least extent possible. And Aristotle will have us believe that he is not less useful to the state for that reason.

In our opinion, haireitai (78b6) reflects the same distance from the business of the citizen as anthrōpeuesthai. Stewart, however, reads just the opposite:

> The words haireitai etc. are to be carefully noted, as stating explicitly the inherence of the theōrētikos bios in the praktikos bios. The theōrōn is a man and chooses to live a social life. Aristotle's theōrētikos bios was travestied by those who afterwards made it a life of actual withdrawal from the flesh. Aristotle's ideal of theōria is a 'regulative idea' of which the Neo-aristotelians made a 'constitutive use' (ad loc.).

But Aristotle does not say that the theōrōn "chooses to live the social life". He says that "he chooses to do virtuous acts" (78b6), and that is something quite different. We have here the same tension as between the thnēta phronein and the athanatizein above (cf. §23). But this time it is considered

from the summit, not from the natural state of man. We have treated the
tension between the two poles as mutually exclusive: the more immortality,
the less human business; the more human business, the less immortality.[7]
And this interpretation stands firm. Stewart obviously thinks that the act of
athanatizein can be executed as a kind of addition to the thneta phronein
without reducing the importance of the latter. But theoria is not described
as an additional engagement. It is repeatedly considered as a particular
form of life in contrast to the social life of the citizen (cf. §§20-21). The
sophos 'chooses' to do virtuous acts just because it it not the part of the
bios theoretikos as such. It is something outside the core of this form of
life. If the sophos serves the polis, he does it as a pattern of human freedom and perfection. All the same, his engagement in civic duties is
necessary to a certain extent because the purity of the bios theoretikos is
only possible for him to a certain extent, being a man after all.

§28. THE GODS ARE HAPPY IN THEIR CONTEMPLATION

1178b7-23. Aristotle's method of elimination in this passage deserves some
comments. To make the old point, that theoria is the supreme activity,
perfectly clear, he now refers to the gods. For the gods are undoubtedly
blessed and happy (makarious kai eudaimonas, 78b9). In this discussion,
Aristotle mentions exactly the same alternatives to theoria as in the
passage treated above (cf. §27). God is neither dikaios, eleutherios,
andreios, nor sophron. These are virtues that belong to man as to
syntheton and not functions of his nous.[1] Then, God must be sophos or
theoron, which for Aristotle is the same thing. He still gives one argument
of elimination and ties it to the first one: to live is to be active, zen is
energein (78b18-19). And there are three sorts of energein: a) prattein,
b) poiein, and c) theorein (78b20f.). As was seen above (cf. §4,n.11),
prattein is often used synonymously with energein, excluding poiein.
The terminology of Aristotle is not fixed once and for all. Here the distinction between praxis and poiēsis is not the important one. Aristotle needs
to underline the difference between moral action and productive work, on the
one hand, and contemplation on the other. Therefore new distinctions appear.

The gods must live in some sort of energein, he argues. This cannot be prattein or poiein: ti leipetai plēn theōria? (78b21). This kind of argument we also find elsewhere in Aristotle, and particularly in connection with related matters of discussion. Scholē as the purpose of music is found in a similar argument of elimination in Pol.1338a15ff., and Gauthier refers justly to the Protrepticus B43:

> Best of all one would see the truth of what we are saying, if someone carried us in thought to the Isles of the Blest. There there would be need of nothing, no profit from anything: there remain only thought and philosophical speculation (to dianoeisthai kai theōrein), which even now we describe as the free life (cf. Pol.1334b30ff.; Cicero's De Nat.Deor. III,15).

This is one of the most striking parallels between EN and this early work. The exclusion of sleep as a possible pastime for the gods, we have treated above (cf. §5), and it is also found in Plato.[2]

Grant comments ad loc.:

> If it be conceded that the life of God is only analogous to the life of the philosopher; we might then ask, why not also analogous to the life of the good man? Plato, by placing the 'idea of justice' in the suprasensible world, allowed a more than mortal interest to morality, and he speaks of the just man, by the practice of virtue, being 'made like to God' (Rep. 613a).

This argument in Aristotle cannot, however, be properly interpreted as a mere argument from analogy. The analogy holds good so far as the philosopher in the human world and the nous in the order of the soul correspond to the position of God in the universe. But the analogous structures are bound together by the assumption that the philosopher and his nous are really god-like in their essences. The key word is syngenestatē (78b23; 79a26; cf. Rep. 611e). In this contention the argument from analogy is transcended. As to nous, this kinship was already hinted at in §13, and the passage treated in §§33-34, below shows that the philosopher is thought to be akin to the gods in more than mere analogy.

There is no reason to be surprised by the change between 'God' and 'the gods' in this passage. Tous theous (78b8) and hē tou theou energeia (78b20-21) do not represent a contradiction. Hoi theoi, ho theos and to theion are used indiscriminately, not only in Aristotle, but in Plato as well.[3] In the Republic, Plato once changes from plural to singular within the same sentence (Rep. 380c). Aristotle's representation of the divine is both polytheistic and monotheistic, depending on the point of view. This phenomenon is, of course, prefigured in the history of Greek religion, where there are many gods, but Zeus is nevertheless 'father of gods and men' (e.g. Il. I, 507ff.). The same structure we find in Lambda of the Metaphysics: there is One eternal Unmoved Mover, and there are many. Obviously, Aristotle does not find it necessary to make a decision.

In the text at hand, however, the change between singular and plural might have a special motivation. Aristotle refers to the usual opinion of men, and the 'polytheistic' point of view was undoubtedly nearer to the common Greek than the 'purified' concept of the one God in the poets and philosophers.[4] The easy change between the singular and plural may have the positive meaning that there is no unbridgeable gap between the common assumptions and the ideas of the philosophers concerning the gods. Further, this indecisive change may have been carried out to save the analogy between the philosopher in the state and God in the universe. There might be more than one philosopher in the state, and their number should not be fixed by an artificial analogy to the number of the gods. But whether this was what Aristotle had in mind we will probably never know for sure.

The activity of the philosopher is, then, akin to the activity of God. But we note here that the interpretations of this activity offered, seldom do more than paraphrase Aristotle's own words. We have already noted the impossibility of putting the contents of theōria in another language than that of Aristotle himself. This was said about the human variety of it, but it is hardly less conspicuous in the attempts to explain the divine activity. Joachim says:

> If, however, our thought - or any thought - were engaged upon a reality which was pure form, then the whole and complete reality would be self-manifest as the thought: the contents of the thinking - the form - would be precisely and completely the reality to be known. Thought and the real are one and the same actuality when the real is without matter (aneu hylēs) ... This intuitive apprehension of a real, in which the grasping is what is grasped and the real is self-manifest, is theōria: the highest level to which man's thinking can attain, the spiritual activity which God timelessly is. For God is a continuous and timeless

self-revelation – a thinking is self-conditioned and self-contained, a grasp of the real which is the real which is grasps – a no$\bar{e}$sis no$\bar{e}$se$\bar{o}$s (thinking of thinking).[5]

We do not deny the correctness of this explanation. We rather doubt if it is an explanation at all. As far as the natural movements are concerned, Aristotle's God has an obvious function in the representation of the universe. God, as the ideal of perfection, gives rise to the eternal, circular movement of the heavens on which natural generation and corruption depend. Aristotle could have let it go at that. But his idea of God is more comprehensive. God is the point in which all his hierarchical structures converge. He is not only the source of the eternity and necessity of the natural world. God is also the ideal of excellence, freedom, and perfection in the human world. It is not easy to make these different functions fit together, and Aristotle's concept of God carries all the marks of being constructed. The historical background of this construction Solmsen has treated brilliantly in his book on Plato's Theolo (1942). There he discloses the different sources of the theological ideas of Aristotle. Here, however, we will rather concentrate on the purpose of these constructions.

Düring thinks that 'God' and 'nature' are used synonymously in the early Aristotle (ad Protr. B18). He says, however, on his later thoughts:

Der Gott des Aristoteles ist also nicht Weltschöpfer und greift nicht in das Naturgeschehen oder Menschenleben ein; er hat die Ewigkeit dadurch verwirklicht, dass er die Entstehung zu einem ewigen Kreislauf machte.[6]

There are, of course, passages in Aristotle which point in this direction, passages which can hardly be confined to some limited 'period' of his development (cf. Protr. B18, B50; De Cael. 271a33; Meta. 1072b29, 1074a38-b14). But the identification of God with nature is never complete. He may be understood as 'the order of the troops', but he may also be understood as 'the general' (cf. Lambda 10). As something outside nature, God lives a life of his own, and he is happy, supremely happy in that way.

God neither acts nor produces. He thinks. But this does not imply a lower degree of activity, Aristotle says. The human being who thinks is also more active than the person who merely acts or produces. For 'activity' is at the same time 'actualisation'. Aristotle often uses _energeia_ and _entelecheia_ in the same sense.[7] The most active, then, the most actual, is the one who thinks, and thinking is the supreme actualisation of man (cf. Pol.1325b15-32). God is, therefore, thought of both as nature in its eternal necessity and as the paragon of human perfection. As far as he is considered in the last function, he is regarded as the transcendent source of natural necessity rather than identified with the necessity itself.

The history of this idea of God, as is well known, goes back at least to Xenophanes, who figured out a god who _oulos de noei_ and who _kinoumenos ouden_ (DK 21B 23-26). Jaeger and others have written the history of Greek theology, and there is no reason to repeat it here.[8] It is easy to discover, however, that Xenophanes' criticism of religion may be used against his own concept of God. Xenophanes was not a Thracian, therefore his god has not red hair and blue eyes (cf. DK 21B 16). He was, however, a thinker. Accordingly, his god is "all eye, all thought, all ear" (DK 21B 24). It is obvious that the philosophers in their new concept of God idealise the essence of their own unstable happiness. The warriors have the even more furious Ares. The citizens have the even more industrious and patriotic Athene. For the sailor, Poseidon is all sea. For the businessman, Hermes is all trickery. Why should not the philosophers have a god who is "all thought", even more permanently thinking than the most devoted _sophos_? This is elementary, but it has to be said to make the ideological character of Aristotle's construction obvious. The concepts of God in Heraclitus (e.g. DK 22B 32), Empedocles (e.g. DK 31B 134), Anaxagoras (e.g. DK 59B 12), Socrates (e.g. Apol.23a), and Plato (e.g. Rep.381b), all illustrate the same point: God is as much the protector of philosophy in these thinkers as Artemis is the protector of the stock game for the hunters.

This, however, does not mean that the philosophers do not take the internal problems of their constructions seriously. For Xenophanes as for Aristotle the external interest behind their theological constructions is only present in the constructions themselves. It may, all the same, be justifiable for the interpreter to distinguish between the constructions and their internal problems, on the one hand, and the concern behind them, on the other. In the case of Plato, Solmsen has shown that the concept of God is taken seriously enough and develops a logic of its own. Nevertheless, it may be read as re-flecting interests of justification.

Dirlmeier records a development in the 'purification' of the concept of God. He says:

> In dem Kampf gegen den Anthropomorphismus der homerischen Götter, oder anders ausgedrückt: um die Läuterung des Gottesbildes, sind zwei Etappen sichtbar: 1) der Kampf gegen die Immoralität der Götter ... 2) der Kampf gegen die Moralität der Götter. Wenn Platon und Aristoteles 'populär' sprechen (z.B. Rep.352a10; Gorg.507e6-8a7; EN 1134b28), so schreiben sie den Göttern Gerechtigkeit zu; hier aber in der EN denkt Aristoteles systematisch (ad loc.).

There is, of course, no mysterious process of purification at work in this history. Nor is there any opposition between 'popular' and 'systematic' exposition in Plato and Aristotle which can be employed in this way by the interpreter. The two steps of 'purification' correspond neatly to the retreatment of the philosopher from political affairs. The concept of God in the later Plato and Aristotle is 'purified' of political virtues because the consciousness of the philosopher concerning his own business had changed. Neither in the later Plato nor in Aristotle does this mean that the sophos is thought of as a useless or superfluous member of the society. But he serves it as a paragon of freedom and perfection rather than by means of direct commitment, and so does God.

The change between the two steps in the development of this concept, however, did not happen at a traceable moment in history. From Xenophanes to Aristotle the two concepts of the theos, as the wise and the morally blameless, intermingle. But in Plato, the conflict between the bios theoretikos and the bios politikos became an obtrusive problem. It is the main theme of his Seventh Letter, and we have made an attempt to trace the development of the conflict in §2. The simple point here is that the concept of God reflects the ideal of life. We may, then, well presuppose that the ideal of the bios theoretikos is present where we find a corresponding concept of God, and, further, that the relative importance of this ideal corresponds to the extent to which God is imagined as thinking. The contrast between what Dirlmeier calls the 'popular' and the 'systematic' exposition of the idea of God in Plato and Aristotle is at least partly due to the protreptics. In both God is thought of as the representative of supreme justice and moral perfection, but only in so far as these virtues are conditions for the life of pure thought.

Whatever this speculation is, it is not religion. Düring does not even want to call it 'theology'.[9] Because Greek religion was always closely identified with the cult and the feasts, the speculation on the theme of the gods was surprisingly free. When reading Euripides we understand that even the strangest idea of the gods was hardly ever apprehended as a sacrilege.[10] As is well known, the processes against Protagoras, Anaxagoras, Socrates, and Aristotle had other reasons. If we look for the religion of Aristotle, we should not, then, read his books, but ask if and how he took part in the cults of Greece.

The 'theology' of Aristotle has an instrumental character even at the height of its enthusiasm. The thought is not foreign to him that man may be even wiser than the gods. Owing, perhaps, to its lack of lucidity he only mentions this idea of Empedocles, but he mentions it twice without scorn or angry refutation (Meta. 1000b3; De An. 410b4). If Aristotle was pious, it is hardly reflected except in his wonder facing the ways of nature and the stars. His 'theology' is exploited in the attempt to defend the business of the sophos, and its apparent piety is an effect of his method: to express his thoughts as a complete picture of nature and human life not only as they are, but in correspondence with the thoughts of his predecessors. Aristotle regards his discussions as final solutions of old problems in which the previous attempts of solution are included. The hybris of Empedocles in his statement of the gods is not turned down because of its impiety, but because its revolutionary character needs a particular revelation for its justification. Aristotle knew no such way to truth. He believed in the successive discovery of truth through the history of thought. He regards himself as the trustee of an estate, and his enthusiasm for philosophy is mingled with a presentiment that it is an estate doomed to bankruptcy. But he will not give it up.

§29. MEN AND ANIMALS

1178b24-32. After the account of the possible analogy to the gods, there follows naturally a delimitation of the correspondence between men and animals. The dialectics that places man between the two poles of his existence, we find elsewhere both in EN and in the Politics (EN 1145a17-27; Pol. 1253a1-18). As in the passage at hand, the possible likeness with the gods is underlined, whereas the relationship between man and animal is described by stressing their actual differences. Aristotle could have expressed the relation otherwise, and he often does. But his anthropology from the biological point of view does not seem to fit in very well with his anthropology from the theological point of view. At any rate, there is some apparent conflict here, as was mentioned above (cf. §§4, 36). In his treatment of man from the biological viewpoint, Aristotle also considers his 'animal component' (Pol. 1287a30). And at other times he suggests that at least some animals may have some sort of reason (cf. EN 1141a27; Gen.An. 753a7ff.; Hist.An. 488b15; Meta. 980b21). Here, however, the argument ignores the kinship between men and animals. The decisive point is that animals have no share in theōria, and happiness "extends just so far as contemplation does" (78b28-29).

The argument is dubious. Happiness is identified with the supreme happiness through an argument which might include the secondary happiness as well. For animals cannot be said to act morally either. They have no praxis, Aristotle says elsewhere, because they have no prohairesis (EN 1111b12, 1159a20, 1139a20; cf. EE 1225a28). Therefore they cannot be happy (EN 1099b32-1100a1; Phys. 197b4f.). The thought here is, then: without praxis, no happiness, and without prohairesis, no praxis (EN 1139a31). Accordingly, the argument used in the passage at hand to distinguish theōria might also be used in defence of the candidacy of phronēsis. One could argue that theōria is the only thing which is common in the relation between man and the gods and a property which clearly distinguishes men from animals. But in this case the last argument is superfluous, unless one supposes that the gods and animals possibly have some faculties in common.

Aristotle tries to hide the impreciseness of this idea by means of an additional argument: theōria is essentially identical with happiness. It does not produce it kata symbebēkos (78b30-31). This must be understood as still one argument to reduce the position of phronēsis. But as such it is an exaggeration. It is true that phronēsis elsewhere is thought to produce supreme happiness as medicine produces health, and the activity of phronēsis may fail to produce supreme happiness as the work of medicine may fail to produce health. But the connection between phronēsis and happiness is not for that reason accidental. Happiness is the one and only end of phronēsis, and thanks to this strong connection, the phronimos is also said to be happy, if only in a secondary degree (cf. §25). Here, this is simply ignored by Aristotle.

The Platonic element in the language of this passage should not be concealed.[1] We have seen already that the excellence of nous is called kechōrismenē (cf. §26), a predicate that Aristotle otherwise uses about the idea in Plato. The possibility to attain the happiness of this excellence is described in this passage by means of three different expressions which are among the favourite words of Plato to denote the relation between the idea and the concrete thing: metechein (78b24), homoiōma ti (78b27), and koinonei (78b28).[2] Dirlmeier ad loc. notes the Platonic character of homoiōma, but the correspondence with the language of Plato extends further. We note that in the crucial passage in Theaet. 176b Plato uses homoiōsis, whereas Aristotle here uses homoiōma. The first expression denotes an action, Léonard says, but the last one a result.[3] The relation seems, then, to correspond with the relation between the philosophos and the sophos.

After the discussion of the opinions that happiness should be pleasure, honour, and wealth in Book I, 5, Aristotle apparently restricts himself to a short reference to the bios theōrētikos as something which will be treated later. But he immediately goes on to discuss the Platonic Idea of Good.[4] Gauthier has argued that this is done to prepare for the later treatment of the bios theōrētikos, but he has found very few scholars of the same opinion.[5] We think that the passage at hand confirms his thesis. Through Book I, Aristotle establishes what he later will be looking for, and he works out the notions of the finality and the self-sufficiency of the Good immediately after the treatment of the Idea of Good in Plato. His own notion of the Good is the concept of the best life, not of a transcendent idea. But this concept of the best life is thought to replace the Platonic Idea of Good and make it super-fluous. The Platonic mood of expression here may not mean that Aristotle is not yet free from the Platonic fetters. On the contrary, the expression may have been chosen just to indicate the importance of the concept of the best life by hinting at the concept in Plato which it was thought to replace. The probability of this guess depends on the nature of the connection between EN X, 6-8 and Book I. That there is in fact an exceptionally close connection here, has been established by Margueritte long ago. His final conclusion we have already discounted, but he irrefutably certifies the kinship between the beginning and the end of EN.[6]

§30. THE VIRTUOUS MAN WILL BE HAPPY

<u>1178b33-79a9.</u> This passage apparently represents mere repetitions (cf. §§18, 27). But the repetitions have an obvious purpose and do not indicate that the text is in a bad condition. Particularly EN X, 8 is a sort of balance between extreme thrusts and reservations, corrections, admonitions. From the stressing of the exceptional position of theōria, the pendulum now swings back again: "our nature is not self-sufficient for the purpose of contemplation" (78b33-34). From the rhetorical indentification of happiness with supreme happiness, and of virtue with supreme virtue, the account now turns back to a provisional rest in commonplaces: "for the life of the man who is active in accordance with virtue, will be happy" (79a8-9). Aristotle apparently wants to regain the trust of sceptical readers or listeners who might have been repelled by the exaggerations in his eulogy on philosophy. But this rest only prepares for still one thrust forward. In §§33-34 he again sets all reservations on one side and praises the bios theōrētikos in a manner which also made his contemporaries and fellow students sceptical.

We have already commented on the main points related to our problem in this passage. We note, however, the explicit delimitation of the relation between political power and happiness. The power of the potentate does not imply that he is more fitted for virtuous acts than the simple citizen (cf. §8). Grant says ad loc.: "Aristotle seems to lose no opportunity in expressing his contempt for great potentates", and refers to EN 1176b18. But the passage may mean more than that. The juxtaposition of idiotēs and dynastēs (79a6-7) is striking. If we ask which of them is the politikos in 78a26-27, the answer must be: none of them. The political life is not considered a possibility of compris both power and virtue any more. Unlike the passage commented on in §21,

the political scene as a background for ethical choice is represented as
power without virtue on the one hand, and virtue without power on the other.
This is of course not an explicit statement of opinion, but the passage reflects
the political pessimism of Aristotle and confirms the interpretation of scholē
in §20. This pessimism should not be ignored, even if it does not exhaust
Aristotle's thoughts about politics and its possibilities.

The simple citizen is "thought to do worthy acts" no less or even more
than the potentate. Ta epieikē prattein (79a7) refers probably first and
foremost to the moral virtues of the individual. It reminds us that the
politikos (78a26-27) is no more a citizen of the Periclean days, but a being
who - in spite of everything and after all - lives in a city and accordingly
has some duties to perform, even if he has no power.

§31. THE WISE MEN AGREE WITH US

1179a9-17. In the chapter on Aristotle's method of dialectics, we treated his
manner of discussion with previous philosophers and the reason behind his
respect for previous and common opinions. The passage at hand is an
instance of this sort of argument and offers an opportunity for some further
comments.

The purpose of this reference to Solon and Anaxagoras is to show that
the account of virtue and happiness given does not break with the tradition,
but, on the contrary, 'harmonises' with it, symphōnein (79a16-17). Stewart
misses the point ad 79a16:

> The opinions of men like Anaxagoras and Solon are probably true; but
> we must verify them by direct reference to the facts of human life, as
> given in our experience; if they do not agree with these facts, they may
> be set down as mere theories - logous a.22.

The opinions of Anaxagoras and Solon differ considerably and cannot both
be verified directly. Aristotle tries through this argument to make room for
his own opinion, which is meant to comprehend what is true in the opinions of
his predecessors.[1] With these references he attempts to establish his own
doctrine as the fulfilment of a searching and hesitant tradition. Rodier says
rightly ad 79a11-12:

Aristote n'approuve pas, en effet, la façon dont Solon comprenait to
kalliston. Il refuse d'admettre, notamment, que oudena anthrōpōn
eudaimonisteon heōs an zē (EN 1100a11), et il n'aurait probablement
pas choisi comme exemple de vie bienheureuse celle de Tellus
d'Athènes.

Tellus, the simple Athenian, was happy, Solon thought (cf. Herod. I, 30
and its treatment in §8), because he lived to see his children's children
and died in battle for the city, honoured by his countrymen. This was not the
supreme ideal of life for Aristotle, but it points to it and prepares for it:
"En réalité, les "actions" les plus belles, ce sont les pensées du
philosophe" (Gauthier ad 79a9-13). Like the life of Tellus, the bios
theōrētikos was a) a simple life, b) determined by an inner necessity, and
c) not depending on power or externals. Further, d) it was something
atopos to the rich and mighty one. So far the ideal of Solon was right, but
it was not yet complete, Aristotle contends.

"Aristoteles ist der erste, der sich selbst historisch als Glied in einer
Entwicklung gesehen hat", von Fritz says.[2] But there are many possible
attitudes to the past. Aristotle is seldom content with a mere repetition of
previous thought. Verdenius comments:

> Accordingly, the only thing Aristotle holds himself entitled to add to the
> views handed down by tradition is some co-ordination. This co-ordina-
> tion should not be regarded as something entirely new, but rather as the
> clarification of a meaning already inherent in tradition itself.[3]

Aristotle uses previous thinkers as witnesses and advisers, but he
defends his own case as well. This can be clearly seen from the discussion
of ethical institutions in the Politics. This account is firmly conservative,
but seldom reactionary. Ritter makes an important point:

> So werden Tradition und Alter von Aristoteles als Prinzip der Legitimität
> für ethische Institutionen zurückgewiesen ... Es gehört zur Philosophie,
> das sie sich dem zuwendet, was 'von Alters und jetzt und immer gesucht
> worden ist'" (Meta. 1028b2). Aber das bedeutet nicht, dass damit für
> Aristoteles die Wahrheit im Anfänglichen und Ursprünglichen noch die
> ganze Wahrheit sei ... Demgegenüber besteht für Aristoteles die
> Kontinuität des Geistes darin, dass das Alte und Anfängliche erst im
> Fortgang positiv zu seiner Entfaltung kommt.[4]

This reading has sufficient support (cf. Pol.1268b27ff., 1269a2-7, 1280a8; Meta.993a15). The treatment of ancient institutions corresponds perfectly with Aristotle's treatment of ancient and reputed opinions. They should not be ignored, nor do they represent the whole truth.

The analogy between ta legomena and ta hyparchonta implies that both need a theory to make a sensible whole. Le Blond says:

> Ces appels à l'opinion des sages et de la multitude ne constituent pas seulement, ni même principalement, un procédé éristique ou persuasif, ad hominem, mais ils sont réellement pour lui, une sorte d'expérience, une expérience indirecte, qui prolonge et amplifie l'expérience personelle dans le temps aussi bien que dans l'espace.[5]

It should be added, however, that experience for Aristotle is not yet the same as truth. A doctrine which goes against opinions too much (cf. EN 1101a22) can hardly be true. Truth is found when the contradictions between previous opinions have been solved in a new theory. Or, at any rate, that is what truth looks like.

In his otherwise admirable discussion, Verdenius does not distinguish sufficiently clearly between the different sources of Aristotle's dialectics. Aristotle appeals partly to (1) the opinions of wise men, as he does here and often elsewhere, e.g. in the introduction to the Metaphysics and De Anima. Further he appeals to (2) the opinions of the many (Rhet.1355a15; EE 1216b31; Pol.1281a4; EN 1153b27). And lastly he thinks that (3) the age of the opinions is a good reason for considering them twice (Meta.1074a38; Rhet. 1387a16; Pol.1264a2; EN 1098b16). Often the many do not mean the same as the wise (EN 1095a17ff.). Accordingly, there is a need for reconciliation. But this is found in the actual solutions of the aporiai and not in a coherent philosophy of history, as Verdenius seems to think. The truth is not found in history at all, but in the interpretation of its contradictory advices. The analogy to the use of myth in Plato's dialogues may be somewhat far-fetched, but it is surely illustrative.[6]

Anaxagoras is the main witness in Aristotle for the happiness of the bios theōrētikos (cf. Protr.B19, B110). The stories told in EE (1215b6, 1216a10) correspond with the use of Anaxagoras in Book VI. There the contrast between the political and the contemplative life is illustrated by references to Pericles and Anaxagoras/Thales respectively (EN 1140b8;

1141b4). Here, in the immediate presence of Aristotle's own ideal, the contribution of Anaxagoras is toned down. His remark on the happiest man as an _atopos tis_ (79a15) is interpreted as an anticipation of the Aristotelian ideal, and the expression is obviously thought of as fitting well for the purpose of appeasing the sceptics among his fellows. It refers to the common enemy: the people's mocking view of the absent-minded scholar (cf. §2).

The juxtaposition of Anaxagoras and Solon corresponds to the juxtaposition of Anaxagoras and Pericles in Book VI. But Margueritte is not right in the contention that Solon here is regarded as "le type du politique".[7] Gauthier is, however, equally wrong in rejecting this opinion without any ceremony (ad 79a9). In Book VI, the persons of Anaxagoras and Pericles are contrasted. Here the ideals of Solon and Anaxagoras are contrasted. In this sense, Solon is a representative of the _bios politikos,_ whereas Anaxagoras, as always, represents the _bios theōrētikos._ Aristotle not only tries to show that his ideal agrees with that of the two wise men, but also attempts to show that his ideal of life makes the two contradictory opinions compatible, by giving both their fair share in truth.

§32. THE THEORY DEFENDED BY 'THE FACTS OF LIFE'

<u>1179a17-22.</u> The reference to tradition cannot prove anything. What it has to offer is merely a _pistin tina_ (79a17-18). The decisive thing is 'the facts of life' (Ross). A similar claim is often found in Aristotle: the theories must correspond with _ta hyparchonta._[1] Otherwise they are mere _kenoi logoi_ (cf. EN 1098b9, 1172a34ff.; _De An._402b26; _Gen.An._ 760b27-33; _Pol._ 1333b16, 1334a2).

A short look through the commentaries discloses that the passage is ambiguous, the first question being: what is it that should be tested against 'the facts of life'? In our opinion, it cannot be the contentions of Anaxagoras and Solon. The reference to the wise men was already a sort of test, namely of the Aristotelian account of the best life. The passage at hand, then points back to the complete account of the _bios theōrētikos_ in EN X, 6-8. So far, Dirlmeier is right, and Stewart is clearly wrong in the quotation given above (cf. §31).

But there is another problem here, the next question being: how should the ideal of the contemplative life be tested against 'the facts of life', and where is this test given? We may expect some sort of empirical control of the ideal propounded, but what immediately follows is merely some apparently dogmatic statements on the supreme happiness of the philosopher. Aristotle, however, is not accustomed to veil the problems with enthusiastic talk. This means that our expectations are wrong.

All the previous commentators fail here, mostly by ignoring the problem. Thus the rest of X, 8 also escapes the understanding. Rodier is closest to a real solution when he says:

> Il s'agit ici, non pas de montrer l'accord des résultats obtenus avec les faits - quels autres faits pourrait-on invoquer que les opinions des sages ou de la multitude? - mais de prouver la possibilité d'appliquer à la pratique les données théoriques qui précèdent, et de déterminer les conditions de cette application.

We find, however, no attempt in the last section of EN to determine the conditions of the application of the theory.

Theories of the natural world may be tested and must be tested against ta hyparchonta. But ethics is not a natural science. The ideals may find some support in the correspondence with ta legomena, but the real test is ek tōn ergōn kai tou biou (79a19), i.e. not in the 'facts of life', but in the works and life of the individual who, at first, provisionally accepts this instruction on moral choice and the best activity, and then finds in his own experience that the logos given is true. There is no way, Aristotle contends, besides the individual choice of staking one's own life on the promise of happiness. This passage reveals, then, the deeply reflected difference between ethics and psychology in Aristotle.[2] The methodological remark in the introduction: that we cannot listen rightly to a lecture on ethics unless we are willing to change our lives, to become better men (EN 1103b26, 1095a5, 1179a35), is repeated here in a different way.

The following passages try to make it probable that the attempt will succeed, by references to common religious convictions. Interpreted in this way, the passage at hand is the core of Aristotle's protreptics or quasi-protreptics (cf. §35). If a serious attempt fails to attain the happiness considered, Aristotle says, the construction may be regarded as mere talk.

§ 33. THE GODS DO CARE FOR HUMAN AFFAIRS

1179a22-29. This passage was for a long time regarded as spurious. Stewart followed Ramsauer in the belief that these remarks on the care of the gods for human affairs were an insertion from a later source. But Grant already knew the dialectical practice of Aristotle. He says ad loc.:

> Aristotle expresses here no opinion, one way or the other, as to the reality of a Divine Providence. Dokei merely indicates that an opinion is held; the word is frequently used to indicate a false opinion or a fancy.

The passage then, should not be excluded for the sake of its contents.

Burnet made this reference to the dialectical character of EN his favourite key of interpretation. He supports Grant in a paradoxical way of expression:

> It has been objected to this passage (1) that it breaks with the connection of ideas, (2) that it is inconsistent with Aristotle's view of the relation between God and Man. Both objections are true, but neither a sign of spuriousness. The words dokei and eulogon show that it is merely a new endoxon (ad loc.).

Dirlmeier, who first[1] accepted the argument of Ramsauer, has lately marked his agreement with Burnet. The contents of the passage should be, then, "die übliche Einbeziehung von Traditionellem" (Dirlmeier ad loc.). But the reading of Burnet is wrong here, and so is his interpretation. It is wrong because it is too easy: it ignores the positive meaning Aristotle always attached to the common opinion.

Aristotle does not refer to these ideas because they are wrong or superficial, but because he finds some sort of truth in them. Verdenius represents the other extreme in the treatment of this passage. He says that Aristotle "accepts, for instance, divine providence without any discussion". And later, more carefully: "But the fact that he connects this tradition with his own conception of human reason as the element of man which is most akin to God, shows that he attached real value to it"[2]. We should seek a proper balance here. The truth of a reference was never indifferent to Aristotle, even if he often considered common opinions dubious. Rodier, whose commentary now seems forgotten, hits the point exactly when he says ad loc.:

Mais il lui arrive souvent, et particulièrement dans l'Éthique, d'exposer des idées qu'il ne partage pas, et qu'il juge exotériques ou même inexactes, en ayant l'air de les approuver, soit parce qu'elles peuvent, comme ici, confirmer d'une certaine façon ses propres théories, soit parce qu'elles expriment l'opinion du plus grand nombre, et qu'on peut, à la rigeur, les admettre à titre de métaphores.

Aristotle freely uses old bottles for new wine. The suspicion against this passage overlooks its possible metaphorical meaning. This we will try to work out in this paragraph and the next.

But for the problematic parallel in Plato (Tim. 90a-b), we can see no good reason why therapeuein here or in the renowned conclusion of EE (1249b20) should mean 'cultivate' (Ross, Dirlmeier). Probably it simply means 'serve'.[3] Aristotle tries, then, also to involve the virtues that serve the supreme virtue of ho kata noun energon (79a22-23). The passage has the character of a conclusion, like the passage at the end of EE. Aristotle is, we believe, not likely to forget the virtues of actions completely, even if they are merely mentioned in an additional manner.[4] The virtues of action are also supposed to be found in the supremely virtuous man. He, of course, cares for the things that are dear to the gods, i.e. using his nous (cf. the idea of philautia §24), but he is also "acting both rightly and nobly" (79a27-29). This ambiguity clearly supports a revaluation of the meaning of therapeuein above.

Dirlmeier, who made this passage the subject of a comprehensive study, gives references to parallels for the idea that the gods care for human affairs. We know it from Plato (cf. Rep. 364a), from Xenophon (Mem. I, 1, 19) and, of course, from the tragedy (e.g. Agam. 370). But Aristotle not only defends the idea of epimeleia, he also refers to the opinion that the gods 'reward' (anteupoiein, 79a28) their friends. Dirlmeier regards this as a sublimation of the principle of do ut des.[5] This is an exaggeration, and it does not explain anything.

Aristotle has a problem, or strictly speaking, two problems and he accepts tradition as a metaphorical expression of these problems, if not as their final solution. He has to explain (1) why somebody is happy whereas others are not, even when they both are virtuous or try to be. And he has to make it probable that (2) a certain form of life means a reasonable prospect of happiness. This corresponds to the ambiguous character of individual responsibility for human success. On the one hand, success is never certain But on the other hand, we do everything to secure it.

Who makes us happy, then, if we are not the architects of our own fortune? In EE the author mentions among other possibilities that happiness may come "through a sort of divine influence" (1214a25). This is never rejected. On the contrary, the author supports this possibility in the later discussions of EE (1246b37-47a3, 1248a16-b7). This reflects, of course, the contentions of Plato in Tim. 68e-69a. In EN the remarks on the subject are vague, but sufficient. The work of the divine influence is made room for both in the introduction (EN 1099b11-18) and the conclusion (EN 1179b20ff.). Aristotle obviously tries to kill two birds with one stone in his doctrine of the bios theoretikos: in this sort of life success is secured because the source of uncertainty, i.e. the influence of the gods, in this case surely favours the candidate. The metaphorical meaning of the reference to the common opinion is not only compatible with the views elsewhere propounded, but must be understood as an attempt to inspire the confidence of the individual, whom he incited to stake his life on the bios theoretikos above (cf. §32)

§34. THE PHILOSOPHER IS DEAREST TO THE GODS

1179a29-32. The word theophilia is cautiously studied by Dirlmeier, and we will restrict ourselves to some additions and corrections.[1] In Greek tradition theophiles is used almost synonymously with eudaimon. Both words denote the person who profits from a particular providence that guarantees success. But this providence he has often procured by his own merits (cf. Phil. 39e). The connection between do and des, however, always included room for surprise.

The history of the concept shows that theophiles was at first the rich and honoured individual. Then, perhaps with Simonides (cf. Dirlmeier 232, 15), it became the virtuous one who acts rightly and nobly. Lastly, in Aristotle, the theophiles is the blessed philosopher. This concept follows, then, the history of the concepts of 'virtue' and 'happiness'. The turn from the righteous man to the thinker is taken in Plato, corresponding to his renunciation of the bios politikos for the sake of the bios theōrētikos (cf. Rep. 352b, 613a with Tim. 90c).

From this short discourse on the history of the theophilēs, we may conclude, then, that Aristotle here does not attempt to say something new about the happy man. He only states the opinion that if the just and righteous man can be said to be theophilēs, this must apply to the philosopher even more. Aristotle does not speculate on what the gods have in mind. He is making a point by means of the traditional language. The word, he thinks, reflects a knowledge of reality, and the language is in itself, however, a limited source of truth.[2] But at the same time, Aristotle shares Plato's rejection of the idea that God should be jealous (Tim. 29e), and he believes that he will recognise his true soldiers (Meta. 982b32-83a5). Probably this idea is as old as the ideal of the bios theōrētikos itself. At any rate it is supported by the thought that reason is something divine (cf. §§13, 22, 23, 36).

There are, however, some remarks in Aristotle's discussions on friendship which at first do not seem to fit in very well with the idea of the friendly gods. He says:

> But when one party is removed to a great distance, as God is, the possibility of friendship ceases. This is in fact the origin of the question whether friends really wish for their friends the greatest goods, e.g. that of being gods; since in that case their friends will no longer be friends to them (EN 1159a4ff.).

God does not need anything, not even men (EE 1244b5ff.; 1245b14-19). Obviously, this excludes the possibility that God and man can be friends in the same way as men between themselves can.[3]

But, firstly, philoi can denote many degrees of closeness in Greek. It can mean a) the relation of intimacy, b) the relation of familiarity, and c) the relation of belonging to something or somebody. Then, if we take a closer look at the crucial passage in EN 1158b33ff. partly quoted above, it does not categorically deny the possibility of any sort of friendship between gods and men. The rhetorical 'us' is transcended in all good things by three sorts of persons: gods, kings, and "the best or wisest men" (59a2). If 'we' cannot be friends with them, it is not said that, e.g., the best and wisest men cannot be friends with the gods. Admittedly, the relation to God is thought of as a particular case. But even if gods and men cannot be philoi in the usual sense, this does not exclude the concept of the sophos as theophilestatos. It is often, if not always, ignored that theophilestatos is not so strong as the expression theophilēs. Aristotle's use of the superlative very often denotes the highest degree possible where no completion is ever found. And so it is used here in syngenestatos (79a26), theophilestatos (79a24, 30), and eudaimonestaton (79a31). The superlative here rather underlines the relativity and incompleteness of the predicates.

The account in EE corresponds surprisingly well to this interpretation of EN 1158b33ff. The author says: "For it would be ridiculous to accuse God because the love one receives in return from him is not equal to the love given him, or for the subject to make the same complaint against his ruler" (EE 1238b27). Also here, God, the king, and the philosopher are present through some sort of analogy. In a brilliant refutation of Dirlmeier, Verdenius gives an interpretation which supports our understanding of EN on this point:

> Aristotle expressly admits the possibility of philia between God and man (EE 1238b18), and only adds (b27): geloion gar ... Dirlmeier, p.521, comments on this as follows: "Der Gebrauch von lächerlich zeigt eben, dass die anthropomorphe Vorstellung einer wechselseitigen Freundschaft mit Gott abstrus ist". But Aristotle does not exclude antiphilein, but only homoiōs antiphilein (cf. EN 1163b1-5). The only remarkable thing is that Aristotle mentions the fact that God is too perfect to think of anything else beside himself as showing that the self-sufficient man cannot be completely like God (EE 1245b16), but not as proving that God cannot philein.[4]

This interpretation is probably right, but Verdenius overlooks the metaphorical character of the conclusion.

Aristotle in fact attaches some value to the argument in the passage at hand. This can be seen from kan houtōs (79a31), which implies that once again he has reached the same conclusion, that ho sophos malist' eudaimōn, through a new approach (79a32).

Most commentators hesitate facing this eulogy on philosophy. It is marked by some unreality, even by Greek standards. Grant says: "Aristotle, on the contrary, rather over-represents the strength of philosophy. And in his picture of the happiness of the philosopher we cannot but feel that there is over-much elation, and something that requires toning down".[5] As an explanation it is not enough to refer to a "general defect of Greek thought"[6] or to the individual enthusiasm of Aristotle. There is nothing unreal about enthusiasm.

Aristotle stands at the dawn of the great tradition of Greek thought. But his eulogy is more than a dream of the past. He obviously has a problem which he tries to solve by means of a tour de force, but this vigorous pull leads nowhere. He could not even make Theophrastus, his closest pupil, accept this effort (cf. §14, n.4).

The general suspicion of ideological reasons behind this attempt should not be stressed. The criticism of ideology may hit the work of Aristotle at a number of points. Of course, here the framing of an ideology is especially conspicuous, but we should look for a more particular explanation of these difficulties as well.

To shape a piece of ideology does not need to be difficult at all. But here we cannot but feel a sort of compassion with Aristotle because he is urged to make a point which he probably suspects himself. The argument in EN X, 6-8, however, is not a casual solution. It corresponds, we think, to the structure of his Politics, his psychology, and his Metaphysics. What is recognised here as unreal and artificial lies hidden in those other treatises as well. It is the purpose of the concluding paragraphs to make some short references to this structure and propose an explanation of the dilemma of Aristotle.

PART FOUR: THE PROBLEM OF THE LIFE OF THE PHILOSOPHER IN ARISTOTLE

§35. THE PHILOSOPHER AND THE LAWGIVER

The following treatments of the pragmateiai on politics, psychology, and metaphysics are intended to be summaries. The purpose is to show the readings which underlie the scattered references to them in the commentary above. The points of view are mostly well-known. The attempt to establish that the ambiguity in the considerations on the bios theōrētikos in EN corresponds to similar ambiguities in the Politics, De Anima, and the Metaphysics is new. Moreover, we will try to give grounds for the suspicion that these ambiguities are related through a common origin. In our opinion they cannot be explained in isolation. A valid explanation must apply to all of them.

In the commentary above, we have considered different political aspects of Aristotle's picture of the best life (cf. §§ 12, 20, 21, 24) and there is no need to repeat it here. Our theme is not the political thought of Aristotle, but the role of the best life and the philosopher in his account of the state and its conditions. In EN it is said that politics is an art which includes all other arts and sciences by determining their goal, the anthrōpinon agathon (EN 1094b7, 94a26). Aristotle also contends that it must be finer and more godlike (theioteron) to attain this end for a nation or for city–states than merely for one man (EN 1094b7ff.). We should think, then, that the difficulties noted in the account of ethics would be solved from the supreme viewpoint of politics, if they can be solved at all. But this does not happen. In our opinion, the Politics repeats and reflects a similar tension as regards the best life, as we have found in EN.

Political wisdom and practical wisdom are the same hexis (EN 1141b23), but their relation is not of the kind that the one sort of consideration could answer the questions of the other. In the treatment of both political and practical wisdom, the bios theōrētikos is present in a particular way. It is like a boundary value which determines the worth of them both. We will examine the nature of this determination in the state.

It is easy to see and easy to show that there is a problem here. Jaeger speaks in general terms about the discrepancy of 'idealism' and 'empiricism' in the Politics:

> We must begin by observing the peculiar Janus-face that the Politics presents as a whole, gazing on the idealists as if it were a Platonic Utopia and on the realists as if a sober and empirical science, and yet obviously being really both at once.[1]

More concretely this Janus-face is represented in the problematic relation between the sophos and the political man. The 'idealism' of Aristotle may be interpreted as an attempt to integrate his ideal of the best life and the supreme happiness in an otherwise commonsensical frame. And his 'empiricism' may be understood as a function of phronēsis, prudent and realistic comments on the conditions of human community. The problem arises from Aristotle's wish to do both: establish the structure of political life and its virtues and justify the bios theōrētikos. The question which life is the best one is also here left in a remarkable vagueness owing to the contradictory interests. Newman has observed this difficulty in Aristotle's representation of the citizen:

> The view of the Third Book that a 'good man', and therefore a full citizen of the best State, must be capable of ruling (1278b3f.) can also perhaps be reconciled with the permission apparently given him in the Fourth Book (c.3) to live a contemplative life, but Aristotle does not notice the discrepancy, and we are left to harmonize the two doctrines as best we can.[2]

There is no reason to harmonise the two doctrines "as best we can". On the contrary, the discrepancy should be treated as such. Otherwise the reader must add an element of his own thought or ignore one of the interests concerned. As could be expected, Newman ignores the importance of philosophy for the Aristotelian concept of the state: "A habit of intellectual

inquiry, if so we may translate philosophia, must be present in its citizens,
if only to give them occupation in leisure and to save them from rusting at
such times".[3] This is not a correct description of the notion of philosophy in
the Politics. Aristotle regards it as much more than a pastime for the
leisure-class. As will be seen, Newman is later even apt to accept the
rhetorical harmonisation of Aristotle without question.[4]

From a systematic point of view, philosophy is of as crucial importance
to the Politics, as it is to EN. But the examination of the work and effect of
the philosopher is even more scanty in the Politics than in EN. The best
life and the supreme happiness are like vanishing points. The state is
constituted by the concept of the supreme good for man. It is there to serve
this end, but that is nearly all Aristotle has to tell about the best life.

Particularly in one section of the Politics the practical and contemplativ
life are juxtaposed in a way that discloses their problem. The section in
question is Pol.VII, 3 (1325a15-25b32). Aristotle raises the question if the
bios politikos is the best life or the tou eleutherou bios (25a19-20) as something different from the life of the statesman. He accepts and denies both
possibilities, i.e. he tries as usual to solve this aporia by means of qualifications. But the formulation of the solution rather stresses the discrepancy.
The qualifications do not lead out of the difficulties this time, but more
deeply into them. Aristotle attempts to save the argument by means of a
rhetorical point, using the ambiguity of the expression praktikos bios
(25b16). Suddenly, he employs the word praxis synonymously with energeia
in a sense which includes both political and theoretical activity. Facing the
same problem in EN, Aristotle carefully distinguishes between theōria on
the one hand and poiēsis and praxis on the other (cf. §28). Pol.VII, 3 makes
the confusion complete. After raising the question mentioned above,
Aristotle makes an evasive trip discussing another matter, namely the relation between power and virtue, before he returns to an apparent repetition
of the doctrine of EN X, 6-8.

The only real solution of this problem hinted at in the Corpus is the
solution connected with the idea of philautia (cf. §24): that the theōrōn is
politician by representing the pattern of human freedom and perfection for
the lawgiver. This solution is not incompatible with the answer given here,
even if it is not expressly stated. Pol.VII, 3 concludes with the contention

that thinking is the supreme praxis. Practical life need not concern others,
i.e. theoria is a praxis of privacy. A state may also be a state without
foreign policy, Aristotle says. Correspondingly, a man may also be a man
without external actions (exoterikai praxeis, 25b29). This is indicated by the
life of the theos and the kosmos "who have no external actions over and
above their own energies". Thus they are patterns of virtuous perfection
(Pol.1325b23-32). Here Aristotle repeats something which was said some
passages above:

> Let us acknowledge, then, that each one has just so much of happiness
> as he has of virtue and wisdom, and of virtuous and wise action. God
> is a witness to us of this truth, for he is happy and blessed, not by
> reason of any external good, but in himself and by reason of his own
> nature (Pol.1323b22ff.; cf. Xen. Mem.3.9.14-15).

Rolfes reads into those passages the idea of philautia recorded in § 24.
He says in his commentary (Leipzig 1912) ad 1325b29:

> Gott braucht keine anderen Götter, um selig zu sein, die Welt keine
> anderen Welten, um vollkommen zu sein.

And further:

> Es kann aber hier in der Politik um so weniger die Meinung des
> Aristoteles sein, die Einwirkung Gottes auf die Welt in Abrede zu
> stellen, da er ja gerade damit beschäftigt ist, zu zeigen, wie das
> beschauliche und abgeschiedene Leben des Weisen für die Umwelt
> fruchtbar sein kann. Auch hierfür, scheint's, soll Gott als Beispiel
> dienen.[5]

If this interpretation can be accepted, the doctrine is identical with the
doctrine of EN. This implies: the inclusion of theoria in praxis cannot
change the problematic structure pointed out in the commentary on EN X,
6-8. Newman reaches the same conclusion but notes a certain distance
between the two treatises:

> Aristotle's object in the passage of the Politics before us (i.e. 1324a27ff.,
> 1325a19ff.) seems to be to represent the political and the contemplative
> life as akin, both rich in kalai praxeis, whereas in EN he had sharply
> distinguished hai kata tas aretas praxeis from hē tou nou energeia or
> theōrētikē (1177b18ff.). In both discussions, however, the contemplative
> life is viewed as autotelēs in comparison with the political.[6]

This minor difference may be due to the different perspectives. The account of the bios theōrētikos as autotelēs and the analogy to the life of God obviously revive the dilemma of EN X, 7 unaltered.

EN is written for the lawgiver and the supreme happiness of theōria appears within its horizon merely as the aim of the lawgivers. It does not approach men who seek the supreme happiness for themselves, but men who are supposed to secure its conditions (EN 1102a23ff.). This is perhaps the reason why the ideal in EN X, 6-8 seems so highly strung: the readers or listeners are supposed to stick to their last, but at the same time they have to be converted to loyal devotion to philosophy. In this sense we have spoken of quasi-protreptics. At any rate, the relation between the philosopher and the lawgiver reflects the thoughts of Aristotle on how the philosopher is supposed to determine political life. Firstly we will take a look at the Protrepticus and then examine the corresponding doctrine of the Politics.

In Plato, politics should be based on theoretical knowledge. This is his reason for making the philosopher king, or the other way round. The philosopher and the lawgiver are clearly identical in his Republic because he knows no practical or political thought besides the theoretical knowledge of the Good in itself. Aristotle, however, underlines the practical character of political knowledge, and we should expect, then, that he wou distinguish sharply between the philosopher and the lawgiver. The outcome however, is rather complex.

In the Protrepticus it is not said that the philosopher and the lawgiver are identical in principle, but it is apparently regarded as desirable that they are one in person. Hentschke, in her great book on the political thought of Plato and Aristotle, rightly sees the importance of the philosopher for the constitution of the state. But she is wrong in maintaining that the phronimos in the Protrepticus (who corresponds to the sophos of EN) is plainly identica with the nomothetēs.[7]

In the Protrepticus theoretical knowledge is of supreme value even if useless for other purposes. But it is useful, Aristotle contends, for the medical practitioner, for the teacher of gymnastics, and particularly for the lawgiver. For all of them must know nature well (B44-46). The knowledge of the philosopher is theoretical, but all the same it may determine our actions.[8] Like the faculty of seeing (cf. EN 1144b12; Protr.B24) it does not produce anything, but it makes clear the different possibilities of choice and action. It is a knowledge which leads us to everything that is good (B51). The crucial advantage of the philosopher is that he contemplates things as they really are, and not their representations (B48). Nobody can be a spoudaios or a good nomothetēs who merely imitates another, Aristotle says. The philosopher does not procure representations, but patterns. Therefore his laws are permanent and his actions right and noble (B49).

Philosophy is, then, a necessary condition for right political and practical decisions. We must be philosophers to put the affairs of the state in order (B8). But philosophy is much more than an aid to right political action. It would also be desirable if it were useless for political work. In fact, it is regarded as a sort of praxis itself. As a mere accident it may also be useful for external actions (B52).

The philosopher is thus no more identical with the lawgiver than with the medical practitioner or the teacher of gymnastics. Here the bios theōrētikos does not exclude the realisation of the bios politikos in the same person as it did in EN. Speaking to Themison, Aristotle probably regards a combination desirable, but the supreme value is attached to philosophy and not to the business of the lawgiver. The ideals differ even if they may be realised in the same person.

Moreover, the 'seeing' of the phronimos in the Protrepticus is more obviously directed to good and bad actions than the more sublime ideal of EN. The phronēsis of the Protrepticus apparently falls apart in two faculties on the way to EN (cf. §4, n.6), the nous praktikos and the nous theōrētikos (cf. §28, n.1). On the first one, EN gives some scanty comments. The second one takes over the position of phronēsis as the best part of man, the activity of which will give the best life. Accordingly, it dominates the scene in EN X, 6-8.

It must be repeated, because it is ignored even by the best commentators (cf. §23, n.3), that Plato's philosopher-king falls apart in Aristotle owing to his concept of political science. Burnet says: "Plato had referred the science of the king or statesman to the cognitive class (Polit.259c); Aristotle, on the contrary, never tires of insisting on its practical character. This is a fundamental distinction".[9] The relation between the sophos and the nomothetēs in EN and the Politics is accordingly marked by a certain distance. Themistius says: Aristotle recommends that the ruler should listen to the philosopher, but he should not himself become one (cf. §21, n.5).

Firstly, the job of the nomothetēs is not theoretical; it is the supreme sort of phronēsis (EN 1141b25, 32). The lawgiver should study the voluntary and the involuntary (EN 1109b34), plan the education in the state (EN 1179b34, Pol.1266b27), know which political measures save and which destroy a democracy (Pol.1309b35), and he should be concerned entirely with the state (Pol.1274b37). He is the source of both written and unwritten laws (Pol. 1319b38), and his aim is zōe agathē (Pol.1256b32, 1325a7ff.; EN 1180b23ff. The practical character of his job is underlined by the frequent mention of him in the company of the politikos (Pol.1274b36, 1326a4, 1288b27, 1309b35)

Secondly, the relation between the figure of the philosopher and the law-giver is such that his work gets its essential aim from the support of the life of the sophos, whereas the sophos contributes to lawgiving per accidens.

Thirdly, the distinction between the two lives is mediated by the concept of scholē. The legislator and politician who are concerned entirely with the state (Pol.1274b37) cannot enjoy leisure from the affairs of the polis themselves, but this is a necessary condition for the business of the philosopher. Newman says: "Leisure is the true end; but then the virtues necessary for a right use of leisure are not only those which find exercise in leisure, but also those which find exercise in active work".[10]

Accordingly, the life of action is accepted as a condition of the best life and so far it can be said to be virtuous and happy. But in the world as it is, it has other necessary purposes as well: "Even if the life of action (bios politikos) is not admitted to be the best, either for individuals or states, still a city should be formidable to enemies, whether invading or retreating" (Pol.1265a25). But the acts that first and foremost justify the business of the politikos are the acts which secure the supreme freedom and perfection of the bios theōrētikos. Newman says rightly: "The legislator must legislate with a view to call forth the activities of all parts of the soul, but especially those which have most of the nature of ends".[11] This happens when he provides the conditions for scholē, a position which other men enjoy: "But leisure of itself gives pleasure and happiness and enjoyment of life (to zēn makariōs), which are experienced, not by the busy men (ou tois ascholousin), but by those who have leisure" (Pol.1338a1ff.).

The difficulty with this account of the doctrine of the Politics is that the bios theōretikos is hardly discussed at all in the treatise although it is of crucial importance for the systematic exposition of the ideas in it. Like EN, the Politics represents the theme of the best life as extremely important and rather superfluous at the same time. In EN the sophos was the most virtuous man, without being virtuous in the usual sense. His essential virtue was different in kind from that of the phronimos. In the Politics, the sophos is the real politician without sharing the acts of the practical ruler and lawgiver. In both treatises the philosopher is set in a position where he can move everything without moving himself. Bröcker says:

> Da aber das Höchste, wir wir aus der Ethik wissen, die theōria ist, so besteht der höchste Zweck des Staates im Dasein dieser. Nicht darauf kommt es an, dass alle philosophicren, sondern dass Philosophen da sind.[12]

Theōria constitutes the order of the individual preferences and the state hōs erōmenon (cf. Meta. 1072b3). For "in men rational principle (logos) and mind (nous) are the end towards which nature strives ..." (Pol. 1334b13).

Both EN and the Politics are primarily concerned with the pros to telos pherousai praxeis (cf. Pol. 1331b28) even more than with the telos itself. One would think, then, that men being different have different ends. But the supreme end for man absorbs the relative value of the other kinds of living. The argument ends up in an apparent circle. Political actions and practical virtues are there for the sake of the supreme human perfection, and this perfection is justified through its directive effect on common men's life and work. The bios praktikos is absorbed in this state of mutual dependence, but the bios theōretikos is represented as partly independent of external goods and the work of others. The conclusion is that the state and the acting man need the philosopher more than he needs them.

If the argument is dubious, its purpose is obvious enough. The bios theōretikos has to be saved from the suspicion that it is superfluous and a mere oddity. Aristotle tries to include philosophy as an important element in the course of events, to nullify its isolation and give it the position he thinks that it deserves. It may be said that he did not succeed in this attempt. The reason was probably that his aspirations on behalf of the business of the philosopher were too high. His concept of the philosopher is as curious as his concepts of nous in the psychology and of God in the Metaphysics, concepts that are constructed to support the first one.

§36. THE FACULTIES OF THE HUMAN SOUL

Different aspects of Aristotle's psychology have already been treated in §§13, 15, 24, 26. It remains, however, to give a summary of the evidence that the account of the faculties of the human soul is determined in its structure by the ideal of the bios theōrētikos no less than EN and the Politics. The structural correspondence between the treatises is easily seen. Dirlmeier says:

> Nun ist unter den der Menschennatur gegebenen inneren Vorzügen der wertvollste die theoretische Vernunft. Und so erreicht Aristoteles, ähnlich wie im dritten Buch von De Anima eine letzte Steigerung, indem er am Schluss der EN im 10. Buch das theoretische Leben, das Glück des Denkens, des Weisen schildert.[1]

This correspondence raises the question if the two summits, which both represents doctrinal peculiarities, have a common origin.

Düring is wrong in calling De Anima "eine naturwissenschaftliche Untersuchung der psychophysischen Prozesse".[2] Its main thought is as metaphysical as anything in the Corpus. It is equally wrong to look for the scientific anthopology of Aristotle in De Anima and to regard it as pre-supposed in EN. The ethics of Aristotle is not constructed on conclusions from the dispassionate work of the natural scientist. The rhetorics noted in EN X, 6-8 is also present in the treatise on psychology. Moreover, EN X, 7 apparently reveals the background for the fundamental distinctions of the other treatise. The doctrine of De Anima on nous is, in our opinion, formulated to serve the justification of philosophy of which EN X, 6-8 is the most striking instance.

In EN, nous is presented as the malista anthrōpos (cf. §24). It is the opinion of Aristotle that the philosopher is the man who realises the malista anthrōpos, and because he, his virtue, and his happiness are something apart, nous is similarly depicted as a thing apart. The crucial point here is the concept of freedom: <u>autarkeia</u>. The freedom of independence belongs to the philosopher most of all. It is not unexpected, then, that the basic faculty of his work is regarded as independent of the other faculties of the soul.

"The Aristotelian idea of the soul is, indeed, a new and original conception: for in Plato the soul is not generally distinguished from intelligence", Caird says.[3] The new thing is that Aristotle thinks of the soul as an actuality of a given body, its sort of life. The soul is not a thing for itself, like Plato's concept of the soul in the <u>Phaedo</u> (cf. §4), but a 'quality of the body', <u>sōmatos de ti</u> (De An. 414a21). Both in plants, animals, and men the soul is the <u>eidos</u> of the body. Man as a natural species has no exceptional position. In this <u>scala</u> from plants to human beings there is not only an addition of faculties: "In the transition to a higher stage of development, the elements of the lower stage are preserved, but they are, in the language of Aristotle, reduced to potentiality; they are absorbed and taken up into a new form of being", Caird says.[4]

But the Platonic concept of the soul as a thing different from the body is apparently (but only apparently) preserved in the case of <u>nous</u>. <u>Nous</u> is not <u>sōmatos de ti</u>; it is not the form of the body. Thus Aristotle ends up with a divided soul instead of the old Platonic division between soul and body. He says:

> It indubitably follows that the soul is inseparable from its body, or at any rate that certain parts of it are (if it has parts) – for the actuality of some of them is nothing but the actualities of their bodily parts. Yet some may be separable because they are not the actualities of any body at all (<u>De An.</u> 414a19ff.).

Aristotle as a rule hesitates before speaking of 'parts of the soul'. Only things can have parts, and the Aristotelian soul is not a thing, but the proper function of a concrete body. Nevertheless, Aristotle distinguishes clearly enough between the parts of the soul that are functions of bodily organs and the part of the soul that has nothing to do with the body. One may ask, then, if <u>nous</u> can be a part of the soul. For the soul cannot exist without the body, whereas <u>nous</u> can (<u>De An.</u> 429a24). We will take a closer look at this division inside the human soul.

The soul, in so far as it belongs to the body, is even subject to another science than the <u>nous</u>, which is <u>kechōrismenos</u>. The first subject is examined by the physikos (403b5-12), the second subject by the protos philosophos (403b15-16). Still another division is found. In De An. 415a5ff. nous and theōria are distinguished from the treatment of the logismos, dianoia, and phantasia.[5] The examination of the theoretical nous belongs to another logos, Aristotle says (415a11-12). Nous is so different from the rest of the soul that whereas the soul is named sōmatos de ti, "it is better for nous not to be embodied, for the union must be undesirable for it" (De An. 407a35-7b5).

Aristotle realises himself that his concept of the soul falls into different parts:

> We have no evidence as yet about mind or the power to think (peri tou nou kai tēs theōrētikēs dynameōs); it seems to be a widely different kind of soul, differing as what is eternal from what is perishable; it alone is capable of existence in isolation from all other psychic powers (De An. 413b24ff.).

As we shall see later, his concept of nous also falls apart. This business of dividing represents exceptionally bad thinking in Aristotle. It seems that some primary decisions have already been taken, and Aristotle tries to arrange the account around these decisions.[6]

If the remaining parts of the soul have the structure of the bodily organs between them, nous has no structure of its own. It is not a thing, but a function which is non-existent before it is set in operation. In the act of knowing, it adopts the structure of the reality known. Thus it recognises truth without any element of disturbance or distortion. Nous becomes the things which it knows (De An. 430a19, 431a1, 431b17), and it sees the unity of all things (430b6). The soul is like the hand as organon organōn, and nous is similarly the eidos eidōn (432a1), i.e. without nous the impressions of reality are as meaningless as a heap of instruments which nobody can make use of.

But the concept of nous is generally overloaded. Too many threads have to be tied together in the concept of the telos, therefore it is often or mostly depicted with a certain vagueness. So nous is the circular movement of revolution (407a19ff.), the eye of the soul (EN 1096b29); it is man at his most (EN 1178a7), and the form of forms (432a2). Here, two things should be noted: a) this general overloading of the telos must not be mixed up with the phenomenon that we have called the 'dilemma' of Aristotle. To this dilemma belong only the observations which reflect the clash between ideology and reality in the evaluation of the bios theōrētikos; b) the attempt to find a system is not only futile, but veils the character of this thought, which rests on metaphors and analogies.

A system of thought may, of course, also rest on analogies. But in Aristotle the analogies overlap each other and replace each other in slightly different contexts. Their purpose is to solve problems, not to reflect the architecture of reality. At any rate, this is the work of the metaphorical analogies. The case of the conceptual analogies may be somewhat different.[7]

The metaphorical analogy describes a relation by means of a reference to the world of things, e.g.:

nous : soul = eye : body

The conceptual analogy describes a relation by means of a reference to metaphysical concepts, e.g.:

nous : soul = energeia : dynamis

In the second case, Aristotle may have thought of describing the architecture of reality, but even this description is guided by preferences which have to be explained. Already his careless use of terms tells us that he thinks with his mind directed towards concrete problems, which must be solved.

In De An. 412a1ff., Aristotle develops a concept of theōria similar to the one observed in EN X, 6-8: the soul is the eidos of the body and this eidos has two forms, as hexis and energeia. To make this last division clear, Aristotle refers to the relation between sleeping and being awake (412a25). But theoria cannot be the energeia of the soul complete. It is merely the energeia of its epistēmē - whatever Aristotle means by that. In De An. 429a27ff. the analogy is repeated in a slightly different form:

body : soul = dynamis : energeia = soul : theōria

Not all bodily organs contribute to the life of the soul, and similarly not all parts of the soul contribute to the life of theōria.

There seems to be a sort of displacement at work here. Theōria is both given a particular position and bound to the soul through this continuous ana-

logy. The soul in question is two things at the same time. The soul that is
the eidos of the body is clearly the soul with its vegetative and animalistic
component. But the soul that gives rise to theōria must be the particular
human component. This displacement in the analogy must mean either that
one step in the argument is presupposed, i.e.:

complete soul : human part = dynamis : energeia = human part : theōria

Or, we may regard it as an instance of the now well known transmission of
power to the end, the urge of the end to dominate the whole and be identified
with it, in Aristotelian thought. It is undoubtedly an instance of "Systemzwang"
as Düring says,[8] but even the compulsion of the system has a purpose which
should be investigated.

The relation of nous to the soul is, then, described by a number of
different metaphorical analogies besides the references to concepts like
energeia and entelecheia. Nous is (1) the ruling element in the soul, like
the father in the household (EN 1177a14-15). Then it is (2) the theion in the
soul like God in the kosmos (EE 1248a26). It directs the soul (3) as the eye
directs the body (EN 1096b29), and (4) orders the eidē as the hand orders
the instruments (De An. 432a1). A number of related analogies support this
doctrine, e.g. the analogy of sleeping/being awake to dynamis/ergon (cf.
§13), the latter being a metaphorical analogy clearly different from the
conceptual analogy of dynamis/energeia.

Aristotle reads a similar dualism into all relations. He firmly maintains
that the happiness of seeing and thinking is the supreme reality, the supreme
end. Accordingly, all relations are placed in a hierarchic structure with
theoretical thought on the summit. And this outcome is partly due to the
arguments from analogy. In his concept of God, who is pure energeia and
the supreme entelecheia, this conviction is stated metaphorically. Everything is estimated as to its contribution or likeness to this activity. And,
of course, this applies especially to the faculties of the human soul. A short
note on the puzzle of De An. III, 5 will illustrate this problem and probably be helpful for the solution of our question.

Jaeger, Nuyens, and Bröcker, and others, regard De An. III, 5 as a
remainder of Aristotle's youthful Platonism.[9] It is, however, easy to see
that this is a guess which hardly explains the problems raised by this passage

As regards the contents of III, 5, the questions are not solved by this hypothesis, but somehow they need elucidation. The doctrine of poiētikos and pathētikos nous is an answer to the problem stated in 429b22-29: How can nous know the real things if it is haploun, apathes, and mētheni mēthen echei koinon? "How can it come to think at all? For interaction between two factors is held to require a precedent community of nature between them" (429b23ff.). As often elsewhere Aristotle solves the problem of the relation of nous to the real world of things with a distinction or rather by extending a well-known analogy. If nous can be set in a continuous connection with the body, then its connection with the material things is saved. The principle of the ratios is dynamis/energeia:

body: soul = soul : nous = nous path. :nous poiēt.

Needless to say, this is an excellent instance of the "Gesetz der super-ponierten Formen" (cf. §13, n. 8). A whole is cut up in analogous relations to explain the diversity of its functions and to disclose its intrinsic order. But this cutting up is more than an analytical procedure; it is apt to destroy the whole as a whole.

Nous, as we have seen, is clearly cut off from the rest of the soul, and its relation to corporeal realities is in fact mysterious. Now Aristotle gives two arguments for its supreme position and power: 1) nous is potentially whatever is thinkable (pathētikos), and 2) it makes all other realities think-able itself (poiētikos). So the doctrine of nous poiētikos saves the self-sufficiency of nous and at the same time gives it some urgently needed connection with reality. It should be noted that the distinction is not a piece of a system, but presents two aspects of nous as arguments for its essential importance.

The alternatives set forth in 429b27ff. are examined immediately: the nous pathētikos in 429b29-30a9, and nous poiētikos in 430a10-25. Reason is both the eye (pathētikos) and the light (poiētikos). Pathētikos resembles hylē because it can become anything. Poiētikos resembles causa efficiens because it brings about everything. The distinction is meant, then, to defend the supreme position of nous, as an answer to the objection that hits the doctrine of Anaxagoras on nous. The solution gets its form, however, from the compulsion of analogical inference.

Ross does not see more than a systematic order which may be recon-structed.[11] But in the Aristotelian Corpus there lies hidden a real structure as well, reflected in the formal arrangement of his 'system'. This arrangement may be interpreted as reflecting certain preferences of interest. Plainly stated, at some places Aristotle makes divisions and distinctions from conviction, whereas at other places he is merely occupied with saving those principal decisions from their own dubious consequences. In our opinion, De An. III, 5 makes distinctions meant to justify the principal decision that nous is the 'best thing in us', the key to freedom, from the adjacent consequence of this doctrine as it was formulated by Anaxagoras: that it cannot think of reality as it is. In other words, the doctrine of nous poiētikos and pathētikos is an argument for the possibility and importance of the bios theōrētikos as the best life. Bröcker says:

> Man darf wohl vermuten, dass die aristotelische Psychologie hier durch die Theologie bestimmt wird. Ohne den göttlichen unkörperlichen nous bricht die aristotelische Theologie zusammen, aber damit auch seine Physik, denn die Theologie ist ja, wie wir uns klar gemacht haben, zu-gleich die allgemeine Philosophie. Die göttliche Vernunft muss es geben damit nicht die Physik in einem regressus in infinitum strandet. Und nur wenn es so etwas wie den göttlichen nous auch im Menschen gibt, ist die Annahme des göttlichen nous mehr als eine Phantasie.[12]

This is correct as regards the connection between the different pragmateiai, but in our opinion the protreptics concerning the best life is the source of this theology and not the weight attached to physics, as is generally assumed.

The establishment of nous as something for itself is a part of the establishment of the bios theōrētikos as something particular and unassail-able, beyond practical claims and considerations of usefulness. Nous is both a part of the soul and something else. It is like the ugly duckling which turns out to be the pride of the pool. This reflects Aristotle's dilemma: the useless business of the philosopher has to be defended without putting him completely beyond the life as lived by most men.

In EN we found two concepts of virtue. The one was the opposite of vice, but the supreme virtue of theōria was the opposite of inactivity. In the Politics we found two concepts of praxis. The one was the practical work of the politician and citizen, but the supreme praxis was theōria,

which represented the good that the other praxeis pointed at. Thus theōria
was present in all practical actions as their remote end. In De An. we have
seen a division in the concept of the soul. The one part was the actuality of
the body, but the supreme part, the basic faculty of theōria, was not.

We read this as one single opposition. Man is sometimes identified
with all his faculties and all his actions, but at other times he is identified
with his supreme aspect only. This ambiguity in the Aristotelian anthropology is not only reflected in his doctrine of virtue, praxis, and the faculties
of the human soul. This ambiguity is also transferred to his metaphysics.
For the living being is a mikros kosmos (Phys. 252b26). This has always
been understood as if the nature and structure of the universe were stamped
into the single living being. But it can also be understood the other way
round. Nature is constructed as the well-ordered human being, and as such
its architecture must make room for a reality corresponding to the life
which is considered the best for man. And in fact, we find an ambiguity in
the Metaphysics similar to that in the pragmateiai treated above. It presents two different concepts of reality. The one is the complete thing, the
ousia, but the supreme reality is a thing apart: the circular movement of
the superlunary region.

That there is a connection here is obvious (cf. §§14, 15, 16, 28; for the
relation between Lambda and the psychology, see De An. 407a19ff.). It is,
however, hard to determine the nature of this correspondence. Man is not
only constructed after the pattern of the universe or the ideal state. Nor is
the universe as it is presented in the Metaphysics a mere construction from
the Aristotelian anthropology. The primary pattern is given by neither
politics, natural science, or psychology. These, have a common structure
impressed on them from the source of the tradition which is conserved and
renewed in Aristotle's thought (cf. §§3, 31). But his main concern in this
summing up of Greek philosophy is, as far as we can see, the commitment on
behalf of thought and its life, the bios theōretikos.

§37. METAPHYSICS AND THEOLOGY

As to EN, the Politics, and De Anima, they all concern ta anthrōpina directly and comply more or less easily with our thesis that they reflect the interest of Aristotle in defending philosophy in spite of the difficulties connected with its position. The case of the Metaphysics is different. Apparently, its distinctions are used, e.g. in the conceptual analogie, as a source for the understanding of things human. In most commentators the realm of abstract matrices is given a sort of independence, whereas ta anthrōpina is regarded as a particular case which may be examined by means of these matrices. But the relationship between the Metaphysics and EN is more complex.

The ethics is not only thrown upon metaphysical concepts (in the solution of the aporiai of the tradition). In the Metaphysics these concepts are developed to explain why and how human thought is possible. It is, then, perhaps not unreasonable to suppose that there is a relation of dependence the other way round too: that the structure of the Metaphysics reflects the preferences of Aristotle as to the best life. But we are well aware that this is no complete explanation of the structural ambiguities of the treatises known to us as the Metaphysics. It should, however, be asked how far this hypothesis applies to it. That this is the case to some extent, we have already presupposed in the commentary above (cf. §§15,16,18,28).

The reduction of structural ambiguities to conflicting interests does not imply that the internal problems of Aristotle's thought are not taken seriously On the contrary, only this kind of investigation can show why the problems were so important to him. Our reading is not an attempt to reduce it all to a matter of conflicting interests. Our hypothesis is not meant to explain why Aristotle is writing in general, but is intended as a contribution to the understanding of some structural anomalies in his thought.

As in the case of EN, the Politics, and De Anima, the Janus-face of the Metaphysics has been noted for a long time. The most recent study on this theme is also one of the best.[1] Routila examines the relation between the theology and ontology in the Metaphysics and refers to the main points of the discussion till now. Jaeger, of course, treated the discrepancy between the ontology and the theology as an argument for his pisture of the development of Aristotle.[2] His hypothesis underlined the correspondence between the sections of EN, the Politics, De Anima, and the Metaphysics, which are found incompatible with the rest of their respective pragmateiai. Jaeger contended that the religious and speculative characters of these sections were due to the immaturity of the author, who was not yet an 'empiricist'. No thesis can replace the contention of Jaeger, which does not show consideration for the correspondence between the irregular passages of the different treatises. We have found that this agreement does not consist in their assumed speculative character, which should be foreign to the ripe 'empiricist'. The cracks in the structure of the treatises result from their common theme: they all turn on philosophy and its conditions. Routila considers particularly the theses of Natorp, Jaeger, and Aubenque. Of these, Jaeger is the only one who attempts to explain the structural difficulties of the Metaphysics with reference to similar phenomena in the other pragmateiai. Routila himself makes the contradiction as insignificant as possible and aims at a synthesis not far from the conclusions of Owens and Bröcker.[3]

There is no contradiction here, Routila says, but we disagree with him. Not so much, however, in his analysis as in his concept of contradiction. For Routila, a contradiction is something indisputable, inherent in the subject-matter, so that it can be seen by all who really want to. In the case of simple expressions, it may be possible to reach such an agreement, but in the case of a comprehensive work the question of contradiction or non-contradiction is a more complex matter. It is often so that the point of view can set off or hide an assumed contradiction. The serious problem is not, then, if there is a contradiction between certain lines of argument, but which points of view will make the contradictions obvious and which will make them disappear. It is a simple, but meaningless task to take sides in the question of contradiction or non-contradiction in the Metaphysics as if it could be answered by the subject-matter alone. In this work, certain contradictions appear from certain points of view. So it is with the two elements of the paramount science, ontology and theology. As in the case of EN, most of the structural difficulties disappear for the understanding which starts from the summit. EN, the Politics, De Anima, and the Metaphysics each represents a sort of unity if read in the light of the question urgent to Aristotle: the justification of the bios theōrētikos in the plurality of possibilities. We think that the structural anomalies which occupy the commentators are less conspicuous from this point of view, even though they will not disappear completely.

The main structural problem of the Metaphysics is recognised by Aristotle himself. It is an aporia, he says, "whether first philosophy is universal or concerned with a single kind of being" (Meta.1026a23f.). This aporia is solved by showing that the 'single kind of being' which is the subject-matter of metaphysics has the particular character of totality. Accordingly, he must not make a decision. The paramount theoretical science of being and the study of the Prime Unmoved Mover are one. But he distinguishes theology from the other theoretical sciences in such a way that the unity is threatened and seems indefinitely established. The main place is Meta.1026a15ff.:

> The first science deals with things which both exist separately and are immovable. Now all causes must be eternal, but especially these; for they are the causes that operate on so much of the divine as appears to us. There must, then, be three theoretical philosophies, mathematics, physics, and what we may call theology, since it is obvious that if the divine is present anywhere, it is present in things of this sort. And the highest science must deal with the highest genus. Thus, while the theoretical sciences are more to be desired than the other sciences, this is more to be desired than the theoretical sciences.

Here, Aristotle clearly favours the assumption that the supreme science is 'theology'. Thus he repeats the opinion expressed in Alpha:

> And the science which knows to what end each thing must be done is the most authoritative of the sciences (archikōtatē de tōn epistēmōn), and more authoritative than any ancillary science; and this end is the good of that thing and in general the supreme good in the whole nature (to ariston en tē physei pasē) (Meta.982b3-7).

The connection between the study of the different archai, the considerations of the metaphysical concepts, and this paramount science is basically clear. We have already seen how the theōria of God is the contemplation of the principle of the principles. If God is the supreme archē, the examination of the archai must start from an understanding of his role and effects. Bröcker says: "Die ersten Gründe aber betreffen in der Tat alles Seiende, und so ist die Einsicht in sie Einsicht in alles, weil sie Wissenschaft des Allgemeinen ist".[4]

The physikē epistēmē is clearly different from this paramount science both as theology and as the abstract consideration of the principles of being. Physics is called 'second philosophy' (Meta. 1004a7ff., 1005b1, 1037a13ff.), because its subject-matter is different from that of 'first philosophy'. Physics is concerned with achōrista (Meta. 1025b26-28), whereas first philosophy is concerned with 'separable and immovable' ousiai (Meta. 1069a30-34).[5] The question arises, however, if there is an analogical differentiation within the first philosophy. Aristotle shows some reserve in the reference to celestial things, here as in EN and De anima. God is depicted as fairly superfluous and extremely important at the same time. He embraces all things being their cause and the ultimate source of their movements.[6] Therefore the concept of God represents the possible unity of all knowledge. The remaining part of the prime philosophy, however, seems to be more closely connected with physics than with the concept of God.

This is the problem: the doctrine of the general principles of being (with the exception of the celestial ousiai) appears as reflection on physics and not as deduced from the concept of God. Thus the concept seems somewhat superfluous, whereas Aristotle insists upon its great importance. By means of this concept he ties the doctrine of principles to the celestial sphere in spite of the impression on the reader that this doctrine could be distilled from his Physics. Bröcker, Oehler, and Routila attempt to show the idea behind this arrangement, and there is, in fact, something to be said for the unity of the prime philosophy. Undoubtedly, the intention of Aristotle can be worked out, but the artificial arrangement justifies the question for its purpose.

Bröcker comments on the Aristotelian idea of God:

Wenn es solches Seiendes gibt ... dann ist seine Erkenntnis, als die Erkenntnis des im eigentlichsten Sinne Seienden, zugleich die Erkenntnis des Seienden als Seienden überhaupt, da von ihm aus alle Abwandlungen des Seienden verstanden werden müssen.[7]

This is perhaps just what Aristotle wanted to show, but it is not a correct account of what he did. The analysis of the principles of being shows a considerably intact outline even without the theology. Lambda looks more like an appendix in spite of the admonitions on the way through the preceding books and the indubitable attempt at integration there. Oehler admits: "Die Gotteslehre ist nirgendwo in der 'Metaphysik' identisch mit der Ersten Philosophie, sondern ist nur ihr höchster Punkt. Was zu diesem höchsten Punkt hinführt, ist aber auch schon Erste Philosophie!".[8]

As may be seen, the problem of the unity of the Metaphysics correspond[s] remarkably to the problem of the relation between the bios theōrētikos and the other virtues in EN. There, the bios theōrētikos represents the point where all aspirations to happiness converge. Here, the life of God marks the convergence of all sciences and the unity of being. This is not a mere analogical structure, because the life of God is the pattern of the best life for man. Thus the supreme knowledge has an ethical aspect. The contempla-tion of the last archē unites the different impulses of acting man in the same way as it gives rest to him who seeks a completion of his knowledge of the world. Bröcker says ad Meta. 982b4-7: "Auch das 'Gute' und das Worumwille[n] haben den Character des Grundes. Daher ist die Einsicht in die ersten und letzten Gründe auch die Einsicht in das worauf es erstlich und letztlich an-kommt, also die Herrschende Einsicht".[9] The connection between the Metaphysics and EN justifies the question if there are practical preferences at work in this construction of reality. But firstly we have to consider the concept of God, which discloses an ambiguity similar to that of the concept of the 'first philosophy'.

In general, we have treated the Aristotelian notion of God above (cf. §28). But the fragmentary character of the accounts on this point leave many prob-lems unsolved. Oehler says: "In dieser stark verkürzten Zusammenfassung der Ersten Philosophie in Lambda vermisst man in der zweiten Hälfte manches, wovon man sich nicht vorstellen kann, dass darüber Aristoteles keine Meinung gehabt hat".[10] But a more complete account is nowhere pre-sented. The considerations on the bios theōrētikos in EN X, 7 clearly presuppose a close correspondence between the best life of man and the life of God. In fact, God is the ideal of human freedom and the philosopher imitates him. Thus, the philosopher in his turn is the ideal of human per-fection for other men. The role played by God in the universe is played by the philosopher in the state (cf. §35). Like the life of God, the bios theōre-tikos (a) is the life of nous, (b) has the best objects, (c) is most synechēs,

(d) enjoys the supreme pleasure, and (e) represents a pattern of self-sufficiency (cf. §§13-18). One may ask, then, if either God or the philosopher is not superfluous. Why are there two nearly identical patterns of perfection?

Firstly, Aristotle thinks that the bios theōrētikos needs justification, whereas the life of God does not. The latter is the core of the life of nature, which is necessarily so. Human life, however, may be otherwise. Its form and contents depend on the choice and decisions of the person in question. The analogy to the life of God supports and sets off one possibility of human choice as the best one. Secondly, the divine pattern of perfection needs mediation to affect human choice. It must represent itself as a possibility for human beings, and this possibility to adopt the shape of nature resting in itself is represented by the bios theōrētikos.

God mediates his perfection to human society through the philosopher. But how does he mediate necessity to nature? God is the model of perfection and the last archē, which as such prevents the scientist from a regressus ad infinitum. But, as Verdenius says, "the final cause sometimes develops an efficient aspect", and he refers to Meta.1075a11:

> We must consider also in which of two ways the nature of the universe possesses the good and the highest good, whether as something separate and by itself, or as the order of the parts. Probably in both ways, as an army does; for its good is found both in its order and in its leader, and more in the latter; for he does not depend on the order, but it depends on him.

Verdenius comments:

> The image of the leader shows that the principle of order not only transcends the world as a model of perfection, but also pervades the world as a force exercised by the supreme power. Consequently, the Aristotelian god, who is the ultimate source of the good, brings about the order of the world, primarily as the object of the world's desire, but secondarily as a regulative force (cf. Phys. 267b8; Gen.Corr. 322b21; Meta. 1074b1ff.).[11]

Firstly, the references of Verdenius are scanty. Secondly, we should remember that the telos is considered by Aristotle effective enough as such. But there is an ambiguity here which should not be ignored. The model of perfection is perhaps too immovable even for Aristotle and he develops his

doctrine of the plurality of movers to explain the plurality of celestial movements through which God or the gods operate in this world. Verdenius is probably right in stressing the problem of mediation, and he is equally right in
using Aristotle's treatment of traditional religion as an argument for the
effective aspect of God. He says further:

> There is an interesting passage in which he praises the ancients for
> regarding the primary substances which act as the unmoved movers of
> the planets, as gods, and only criticizes the fact that they imagined
> these gods in the form of men (Meta. 1074a38). This seems to show that
> Aristotle took the traditional gods to be imperfect representations of the
> unmoved movers of the planets.[12]

Aristotle often criticises traditional religious representations (cf.
Meta.1000a9ff.), but he never hesitates to use them if they fit in his picture
(cf. Mot.An.699b35ff.; 699a27). Here the old gods are models for the crowd
of immovable movers. Thus the solitariness of the sublime pattern of perfection is broken, and his necessity is mediated to nature. It must be admitted that it is said on one occasion that the unmoved movers also have the
best and most self-sufficient life (De Cael.279a20), but as a rule they represent the efficient aspect of the divinity, whereas God Himself is the model of
unity and perfection. Needless to say, this problem of mediation corresponds
to the attempts of breaking the isolation of the bios theōrētikos in EN and
the Politics and the isolation of nous (through the distinction. poiētikos/
pathētikos) in De Anima. More important, this mostly ignored problem of
mediation determines the ambiguity of the 'first philosophy' in the Metaphysics. By now we may recognise the interest behind the constructions of
this work.

In EN and the Politics, the bios theōrētikos had to be distinguished
from the striving for money and pleasure and from the business of the citizen
occupied with civic duties. In De Anima, nous had to be distinguished from
the unfree faculties tied to the body and its needs. Here, philosophy has to
be distinguished from the special sciences:

> We answer that if there is no substance other than those which are
> formed by nature, natural science will be the first science; but if
> there is an immovable substance, the science of this must be prior and

must be first philosophy, and universal in this way, because it is first.
And it will belong to this to consider being qua being - both what it is
and the attributes which belong to it qua being (Meta.1026a27-32).

The union of the study of the principles of being with theology was
necessary to avoid the absolute mastery of natural science. Oehler has
seen clearly that Aristotle thus conjures the end of philosophy:

> Denn die Analyse der natürlichen Substanzen in Zeta, Eta, Theta steht
> ganz im Dienst jenes umfassenden Begriff einer Ersten Philosophie,
> den der Leser der'Metaphysik'-Bücher schon aus den sogenannten ein-
> führenden Erörterungen in Alpha bis Epsilon kennt ... das fundamentale
> Faktum der Rückbindung der Seinsanalyse an die Lehre von einem
> übersinnlichen, tranzendenten Sein eines höchsten Eidos. Diese feste
> Klammer seines eidologischen Systems hat Aristoteles nie preisge-
> geben, denn dann wäre für ihn der Grund der Möglichkeit einer Ersten
> Philosophie überhaupt entschwunden.[13]

There must be somebody who is above even the natural philosopher
(Meta.1005a33-b1), otherwise the unity of knowledge is broken and the
philosopher would be out of work. The contention: pros hen hapanta
syntetaktai (Meta.1075a18) is the unique opportunity of the philosopher.

In the Presocratics the study of nature and theology was one thing.
There, the metaphysics was not yet working with entities beyond the realm
of sensible things. The change comes with Plato. Metaphysics as dialectics
was developed as a special branch of science, which nevertheless advanced
the claim of superiority. Through the thought of Plato, the contrast between
metaphysics and natural science was established. Plato manages to keep his
universe together by means of an ethical point of reference (the Idea of Good)
because he was more occupied with ethics and politics than with nature.
Aristotle, however, was a natural scientist and considered it a supreme task
to reestablish the unity of the Presocratic view of the universe. This he
could only do through an adoptive transformation of the Platonic unity in the
justification of philosophy as the supreme and comprehensive science.
Aristotle would not let the special sciences run off and scatter. What Plato
accomplished through his dialectics, Aristotle tries to do with his construction
of the best life as the imitation of the life of God.

The incitement to preserve the unity of science was ethical. As long as
this unity was preserved, the bios theoretikos in the traditional sense could

be retained in spite of the rise of natural sciences. For ethics, psychology and physics could, then, converge in the concept of God, who is no more than the guarantor and pattern of the best human life. But in Aristotle's life-time the unity of science was threatened and dissolving. This is one of the reasons for his polemics against the mathematicians (cf. Meta. 991b13, 995a6, 1078b10, 1084b24ff.). The supreme freedom was only to be found in the science which dealt with subjects both chōrista and akinēta which could be a paragon of imperturbability. A triangle would not do, because it has no energeia in which we can share.[14]

To avoid misunderstanding it must be repeated: we do not defend the opinion that practical thought is the source of theoretical thought in general. Nor is it the other way round. A philosophy is completed when the internal development of speculation in some way or other meets the interest of thinking man. This meeting is hardly ever complete, but it often betrays tensions, as in the case of Aristotle. From these tensions, however, we may collect information on the respective contributions of the internal necessity of the argument and the external necessity of justification and persuasion.

§38. ARISTOTLE'S DILEMMA

A certain ambiguity in Aristotle's thought was noted by Zeller (cf. §1, n. 3). Jaeger attempted to determine more exactly the nature of this ambiguity and offered his developmental hypothesis as a solution. Most commentators have noted a similar dilemma without offering any solution at all. There were, of course, many points which Zeller found problematic which could not be explained through the reading of Jaeger. And other formulations of the ambiguity of Aristotelian thought centre more or less around the problem without hitting it convincingly. Zeller and Jaeger took their point of departure in the impression that not only were single passages or treatises problematic, but they pursued conflicting motives in Aristotle's thought in general. The same conviction we find in modern interpreters, e.g. Verdenius:

> It has often been suggested that the contradictions in Aristotle's system ultimately derive from the conflict between two forces in his mind,

Platonism and empiricism. But his respect for nature is something more than empiricism: it is not only a belief in the observation of nature, but also, and in the first place, a belief in Nature itself. This belief in Nature was an inheritance from Plato, and the main conflict was not between Platonism and something else, but between the different aspects of Platonism as they were developed by Aristotle.[1]

With this we fully agree, but the expressions are too vague to be helpful in the textual interpretation. The same is the case with Düring: "In Aristotle's writings, we can always expect to meet side by side the two dominant trends: Platonic abstraction and biological empiricism".[2] Or, at another place: "Aristotle was struggling to become a Platonist and to reconcile his empirical and common sense approach to nature with Plato's idealism".[3]

Readers who have worked primarily with one of the pragmateiai have tried to formulate the nature of the ambiguities there, disregarding the similar character of the other treatises. Thus, Rodier says about EN: "Mis en demeure d'opter entre l'utilitarisme et l'intellectualisme, il se serait, sans doute, prononcé pour ce dernier, mais non sans quelque regret".[4] This general charge of 'intellectualism' is also laid by Caird and Wundt (cf. §34, n. 6). But the dichotomy of EN is not found only in the ethics. Léonard also isolates the phenomenon of "une scission dans la doctrine" and says: "Eudémonisme et moralisme, deux points de vue; vie théorique et vie pratique, deux genres de vie; sophia (sagesse théorique) et phronēsis (sagesse pratique), deux perfections".[5] Aubenque similarly isolates the ambiguity of the Metaphysics and regards it as a consciously elaborated aporia.

In Frank, on the other hand, the frame of reference is too wide. He regards the antagonism between rational argumentation and need for redemption as something characteristically Greek, and tries thus to explain Aristotle's doctrine of happiness.[6] Even Hardie misses the point when he regards the ambiguity of EN as a mere slip of Aristotle's reasoning due to his old-fashioned ideas of theology.[7]

We have tried to argue that there is some connection between EN, the Politics, De Anima, and the Metaphysics referring to the fact that it is the same subject that creates the difficulties in all of them, namely the theme of philosophy. Our hypothesis is not designed to explain all the problems noted by Zeller, Jaeger, Rodier, Léonard, Frank, and others, but it can be used to explain the dilemma in the way we have reformulated it, and this does not seem irrelevant to the questions asked by the other commentators.

In the strict sense, a dilemma is the position of having two possibilities of choice, which are both bad. The dilemmatic situation par excellence is the choice between Scylla and Charybdis. This is not the position of Aristotle On the contrary, he wants two things that cannot easily be had at the same time. When we use the word 'dilemma' here, it is, then, in the wide sense denoting a difficult position in general.

Aristotle is a pioneer of natural science, but cannot give it a separate justification (cf. Part.An. 644b22-45a36). He tries with all his might to keep its traditional connection with theology and philosophy in the grand manner. Thus Aristotle attempts to keep science and knowledge within the frame of ethical relevance. The unity of knowledge is as important to him as the possible unity of man's aspirations.[8] The telos that unites both of them is the theological concept of theōria. As we have noted: the natural scientist and the theologian never cooperate quite convincingly. But Aristotle would not have been content to do the one or the other thing. In his justification of the bios theōretikos, he defends not only the unity of knowledge, but also the connection between science and ethics. Thus Aristotle protects his variety of the Platonic conjunction of truth and goodness. But he works with more disparate elements than Plato did in the Republic, and the return to Preplatonic thought is not possible any more.

The association between ethics, natural science, and theology dissolves, and we can trace the process in Aristotle's doctrine of man and his condition. This is already done, and there is no need to repeat the outcome here. The concepts of the divided virtue, the divided soul, and the divided reality correspond, however, to a recently rediscovered dichotomy in Aristotle's concept of the telos.

In §5 we noted that the telos of something should comprehend its whole nature, but that this was hardly the case with nous. However, Aristotle often warns the reader: dichōs to hou heneka. K. Gaiser has examined the passages where this expression occurs (Meta. 1072b1-3; EE 1249b15; De An. 415b2-3; 415b20-21; Phys. 194a35-46), but it is not easy to grasp the meaning of the ambiguity that Aristotle notes in his concept of telos.[9] The difference between the telos tini and the telos tinos is never unmistakably stated by Aristotle in spite of its importance. Gaiser quotes Bernays, who said: "Die Kategorie des Zweckes ist gleichsam das Zentralorgan der aristotelischen Philosophie, dessen kleinste Modifikationen nicht ohne die durchgreifendsten Wirkungen für den gesamten Organismus erfolgen können."[10]

The conclusions of Gaiser seem to have some impact on our own problem: if the telos of man is to be identified with the perfect cooperation of his different faculties, or with his 'best part' only. Moreover, they procure an argument for the universality of Aristotle's dilemma. For the distinction in the concept of telos is not only a difference in the relation of the telos to its subject, Gaiser contends: "Der Charakter des Telos selbst wird durch die Unterscheidung modifiziert".[11]

With some hesitation, Gaiser compares the division in the concept of telos with the distinction agathon haplos/agathon tini (cf. EE 1228b18-30, 1235b30-36a15; EN 1129b3, 1152b26-33). Further, it probably corresponds to the account of the two technai in Phys. 194b2 ff.: one that "uses the product" and another that "directs the production of it". The telos tinos should, then, mean: "übergeordnetes Ziel, das durch seine Vollkommenheit wirkt, ohne für sich selbst etwas nötig zu haben". And the telos tini: "ein Subjekt, das ein eigenes Interesse hat und anderes für sich braucht".[12]

Accordingly, God and the energeia theoretike are tele in the first sense, whereas the phronimos and the man with moral virtues, who need external means and fellow men for their perfection, work on their tele in the second sense. If not perfectly, the distinction corresponds to the difference between end (tinos) and completion (tini) in English. The ultimate perfection and the specific perfection are not different things as regards most natural objects. But man has a particular position among them. He is called upon to realise more than his specific perfection. For a short time, at any rate, he can reach the ultimate perfection which in principle is reserved for God. The condition of man is marked by the tension between the completion of his natural faculties and the supreme end which depends on his nous coming in from outside (cf. §§ 13, 23, 26, 36).

The reading of Aristotle is not sure on this point, and Gaiser concludes with a careful question mark:

Wollte Aristoteles also in dem verlorenen Werk (i.e. On Philosophy) damit begrifflich feststellen, dass sich die teleologische Ordnung einerseits in dem universalen Streben nach dem Göttlichen manifestiert, anderseits aber auch auf mehrfach abgestufte Weise in der je besonderen Vollkommenheit und Zweckmässigkeit der einzelnen Lebewesen?[13]

The assumption of Gaiser is probably right, but in our context, it is important to recall the unique position of man in this picture of reality.

The circle is teleios, and the natural telē are in Aristotle's representation of the universe figured as sort of circular movements resting in themselves. Gaiser refers to the concluding chapters of Gen.Corr. where the circular movement of the heavens, of the seasons, of the generation and corruption of natural species, and of the elements in transformation, are all figured as imitating the supreme perfection of God within their own circles (Gen.Corr.336b27ff., 337a17ff.; Gen.An.731b18–32a1). But the telos tinos is not reserved for God. Man shares in the circular movement of the natural species in birth and death, probably also in health and renewal, but man particularly shares in a circular movement similar to that of the divine life:

> We must identify the circle referred to with mind (nous); for it is mind whose movement is thinking, and it is the circle whose movement is revolution, so that if thinking is a movement of revolution, the circle which has this characteristic movement, must be mind (De An.407a19ff.)

Thus man is a universe of his own as well as a part of the natural world. The imitative structure of the different possibilities of man is obvious: the morally acting man must look at the phronimos for a paragon of right action. The phronimos must look at the sophos for a paragon of human freedom. And the sophos must contemplate the life of God to share in the supreme perfection. To the scala naturae there corresponds, then, a scala humana.

The problem consists in the fact that this scala is not continuous. In the natural universe there is a rift between the things sub luna and the things super lunam. In the human world, there is a rift between the specific completion and the supreme end of man. Theōria is the end of human life, but not the completion of man as a natural species. In fact, theōria is also figured as a completion, not of man's natural faculties, however, but of the different 'lives': it is both the most pleasant, most virtuous, and most free life (cf. §7, n.5).

Against this background, we understand better the arguments from analogy in §§13 and 36. As was said in the Introduction (cf. §3), Aristotelian science is not a science of discovery, but a science of understanding. The inferences from analogy do not disclose new facts. Oehler says:

> Gerade die analogische Bestimmung immer abstrakterer Relations-
> begriffe musste schliesslich an einem höchsten und letzten Beziehungs-
> pol gleichsam hängen bleiben - an jenem Prinzip, von dem Aristoteles
> sagt, an ihm hänge der Himmel und die Natur (Meta. 1072b13).[14]

But this is hardly right if Oehler is trying to explain why Aristotle needs a concept of God, nor is it correct to regard this concept as a product of mere 'Systemzwang'. The concept of God was given as the ideal unity of knowledge and being. The arguments from analogy do not establish the ultimate telos, but are used to secure the connection between the ultimate telos tinos, and the many different instances of telē tini. In this, it corresponds to the syllogism which never tries to establish the conclusion as a fact, but as a necessary fact. Oehler rightly sees the importance of the inference from analogy for all parts of the Metaphysics. But asked what its real import is, he knows no answer.[15]

In §4, n.6 we contrasted the readings of Jaeger and Wehrli as to the relation between ethics and theoretical knowledge in Plato and Aristotle. There we could not yet take sides in the dispute, but here we find it settled. Wehrli says:

> Erst Aristoteles schuf eine an der Fülle empirischer Erfahrung ausge-
> richtete Lehre vom menschlichen Verhalten die aller kosmischen und
> metaphysischen Spekulationen gegenüber autonom war. Damit wurde
> aber auch die platonische Verbindung zwischen den beiden Lebensformen
> des Schauens und Handelns endgültig zerschnitten; im aristotelischen
> Werke traten die aussermenschliche Welt als Gegenstand zweckfreien
> Forschens einerseits und die in den ethischen und politischen Traktaten
> behandelten Probleme als faktisch getrennte Komplexe nebeneinander.[16]

As regards the outcome and final impression of Aristotle's literary work, this is right. But it is not a fair interpretation of his intentions. Aristotle set himself against this 'Zerschnittung' and tried with all his might to bridge the gap between empirical science and metaphysics. Jaeger, on the other hand, renders the intentions of Aristotle without neglecting the difficulties connected with the accomplishment of his project:

> Though Aristotle separates ethics from metaphysics and makes it a special discipline, at the decisive point he connects the two together as Plato did: he holds fast to the significance of intellectual cultivation and knowledge for the moral culture of the personality. He assigns the theoretic life the highest rank both in the state and in the orders of the moral world; and the individual human being's happiness, the aim of human striving, is achieved on his view not in moral perfection or at any rate not in that alone, but only in the full development of the intellectual powers of human nature. In the end, indeed, exactly like Plato, he makes specifically moral insight dependent on the knowledge of the ultimate source of reality. The primacy of the theoretical over the practical reason is his enduring Platonic conviction.[17]

Thus the struggle between Jaeger and Wehrli through the present work has a genuine Aristotelian solution: even though each apparently rejects the thesis of the other, they are both right in the way that Jaeger describes Aristotle's intentions, whereas Wehrli depicts the actual outcome.

The concept of God guarantees the unique position of the philosopher and gives him ideological protection in the fight with other forms of life and with the special sciences. The tragedy of this god and his philosopher is that their freedom is won through isolation (cf. §18). Thus the last word of Aristotle is the first word of Hellenism. On the border between two ages his interests were divided in the same way as the soul of man in <u>De Anima</u>. And this can be seen from the contrast between his closest adherents: Theophrastus, the natural scientist, and Epicurus, the wise gentleman.

SUMMARY

In the Presocratic <u>kosmos</u>-poetry, theology and physics were one and the same thing. <u>Physis</u> was more or less abstractly perceived as an aggregation of divine powers. Nature was, accordingly, both the ruler and the ruled, both <u>natura naturans</u> and <u>natura naturata</u>. Aristotle commented on this situation by saying that they had not yet separated the different causes. A century ago, in Zeller, this phenomenon was called 'hylozoism', i.e. the matter was perceived as a living thing.

The course of philosophy from Thales to Plato was extremely curious. Matter was perceived as ever more "material" in our sense, i.e. as ever more dead; whereas the principles which fashion and rule its movements were pulled ever farther away from the sensible and material world. In Plato, the dialectics, though comprising everything, develop into a special science dealing with specific subjects. The rift between the sensible and the intelligible, which was propounded by Parmenides, was completed in a debasement of matter and the sensible and a corresponding concentration on those things which were subjects of thought only. In this sense we can say that Plato established a division between metaphysics and physics that put an end to speculation on the unity of nature in the Presocratics.

Admittedly, a sort of unity is preserved, but it is supplanted into the world of thought. As the supreme point of reference, the Good in itself keeps the theological and political universe of Plato together. Plato's works were always surrounded by an air of morality, so he could himself afford to ignore the world of actual things. But to Aristotle this concentration on the intelligible was unbearable, for the simple reason that he took trouble to perceive nature not as the unchangeable constitution of the universe, but as the things that live, grow, and decay.

Accordingly, Aristotle tried to reintegrate the natural world, to reha-
bilitate the Presocratic unity. This doctrine of unity could not be repeated
in the form that Thales propounded it. It had to be worked out as a doctrine
of the connection between the four causes: form, matter, movement and
completion. Firstly, matter and form was understood as essentially dependent on each other, at any rate sub luna. Aristotle preserved the unity
of the thing (ousia) as both a subject of the senses and a subject of thought.
In this way he reconstituted the unity of Presocratic speculation through his
criticism of Plato. The one and only target of this criticism is the tmēsis
or chorismos that Plato put between the thing as subject of thought and as
subject of the senses, i.e. between form and matter.

Aristotle's solution to this problem of unity is not complete. He was
so occupied by the simple things, or by the different species of things, that
the connection between the manifold areas of study was strained. Aristotle
must, we think, repay the unity of the simple thing with the unity of kosmos
and the sciences. The reason for his splitting the universe of knowledge
into different compartments is that to every special sort of subjects it
should correspond a special pragmateia, with its proper method.

We have tried to show in this book that Aristotle must accede to a
Platonic redoubling of the makrokosmos to save the unity of the mikro-
kosmos. He comes out of this dilemma with a separation in the concept of
the soul, two different concepts of the real, two different concepts of
virtue, and two concepts of the politician. This structural ambiguity runs
through all his authorship. A short course in his anthropology will make
the point clear.

If we reconsider the course of philosophy from Thales to Plato as
regards the development of the picture of man, we discover the same thing
as in the development of physics. In the Presocratics man was both body
and soul, both thought and passions. This is clearly stated in Empedocles
who perceived both man and the universe as a field of battle between love
and hate. Through his rationalistic prepossessions Parmenides separated
body and soul in stating the absolute difference between the sensible and the
intelligible. In Plato's Phaedo we can study a completely developed dualistic anthropology. There the doctrine of man becomes a doctrine of the

soul. Because, in the Phaedo, the soul is man. Accordingly, the man who has the greatest soul is the greatest man. Of course, in the end, this anthropology confines itself to a doctrine and a glorification of the philosopher.

We are used to saying that Aristotle puts the parts of man together again. He overcomes the duality between matter and form by considering the simple thing (ousia) as the primary existant, and he overcomes the duality between soul and body by considering man as a natural being with certain functions depending on both his body and his soul. In Aristotle's anthropology the soul is not a guest in a strange body, but the principle of its organization, the range of its functions. Aristotle perceives man as being at home in nature where he belongs to a place, a topos; whereas man in the Phaedo is not only identified with a soul in a strange body, but is regarded as a being who is a stranger in the world.

In a certain sense, however, one might say that anthropology and psychology are one and the same thing also in Aristotle because he lets the soul comprehend all the functions of the living being. But psychology is more extensive than anthropology. Man is not the only being with a soul – animals and plants also have souls. We would not, then, expect to find a sharp division between philosophers and other people in Aristotle. Undeservedly, we ascribe to him too much common sense. Aristotle overcame the dualism of Plato's doctrine, but he paid·for it with a new duality. This was the subject of our treatise: to interpret and show how this new duality is expressed.

nous	God	theōria
|	|	|
eternal	super lunam	supreme happiness
perishable	sub luna	secondary happiness
|	|	|
soul ⎫ body ⎬ man	form ⎫ matter ⎬ thing	logos ⎫ orexis ⎬ phronēsis

Aristotle reunited body and soul in his new concept of man. But, in addition, he had to postulate the existence of an eternal reason (nous). He reunited form and matter in his new concept of the simple thing (ousia). But, in addition, he had to postulate the existence of an eternal God behind the moon. He reunited thought and passion in his new concept of prudence (phronēsis). But, in addition, he had to set the philosophic contemplation (theōria) as the supreme activity and happiness. Many commentators have remarked on these structures individually. Only one, however, has tried to interpret them together as an expression of one single ambiguity. Jaeger propounded the thesis that the dilemma between "empiricism" and "theology" in Aristotle resulted from his development. At first Aristotle was - in his opinion - a pupil of Plato concerned with metaphysical entities. In the end he developed his own "empirical" interpretation of reality. Jaeger believed that the doctrines of nous, God and theōria were reminiscences from Aristotle's Platonic youth. In his ripe years, however, Aristotle repudiated thi religious metaphysics in favour of "empirical" science, he thinks.

Jaeger's theory of development has the advantage in that it interprets these structures as an expression of one single problem. We think it opportune to supplant this thesis with a single explanation which can connect and throw light on these analogical structures. For the theory of development is not sufficient. The rift in these structures should be understood rather as a difficulty connected with the philosophical problems that occupied Aristotle all his life, problems that resulted from his historical situation and the place of philosophy in this.

Yet another structure must be mentioned: Aristotle reunited the ruler and the ruled in his new concept of the politikos. But, in addition, he had to postulate a special form of life, namely scholē, the time of philosophic leisure with its self-sufficient occupations.

scholē

|

for its own sake

---

for the sake of something else

|

ruler)
ruled)   politikos

Aristotle tried with this concept of <u>politikos</u> to overcome the opposition between the ruler and the ruled in Plato's <u>Politeia</u>. This he said himself in so many words. But he had to pay for this unity with the reservation of a special category for the philosopher – superior to political life in one sense, at the centre of political life in another. This, we think, is the key to the understanding of the rift in the structures mentioned above: Aristotle took trouble to rescue the <u>bios theōrētikos</u> not only as a particular form, but as the supreme form of life. For only the concept of the philosopher can connect the particular supremes in these structures:

- <u>Scholē</u> is the social condition of philosophy, the framework of the <u>bios theōrētikos</u>.

- <u>Nous</u> is the psychological condition of philosophy, its base in the faculties of man.

- <u>Theōria</u> is the activity of the philosopher, that which makes him deserve the name.

- God is the pattern of the freedom of the philosopher, and the supreme subject of his theory. Besides, God is the source of the necessity and the coherence of the universe. The philosopher unveils this necessity and brings about the pattern of freedom in the world of humans.

The philosopher communicates the cosmic order into the realm of moral possibilities. He is no more king or lawgiver in the <u>polis,</u> as he was in Plato's <u>Politeia.</u> Now, the philosopher imitates the <u>energeia akinesias</u> of God, his imperturbable activity, and thus he becomes the pattern of human completion and happiness. As the <u>telos</u> of the state is to realise the ultimate completion of man, the philosopher is both more and less of a politician than he who chooses it as his profession.

This representation of the <u>bios theōrētikos</u> is a plea made by a thinker who could not give up the unity of science or philosophy in the grand Presocratic manner, despite the historical situation which questioned this unity and the resulting comprehensive construction.

Jaeger's thesis may be given a new twist. His interpretation of the supreme point of these structures as being due to Aristotle's dependence on Plato, may be true in an unexpected sense. The essence of Plato's political and theological project is to save the norms and standards in a world which seems to ignore them. This he accomplishes by saving them from this world of confusions. Justice, goodness, and beauty are elevated into the beyond so that they should not be maimed by the actual injustice, cruelty and ugliness of this world. Here we find the reason for the primacy of the intelligible in Plato: he had to point at justice even if it was not present in the actual world of things. He had to point at beauty and goodness even if the actual world knew none or but a few actual instances.

Aristotle did just the same thing with the concept of philosophy. He elevated it and its conditions from this world, where its actual existence was threatened, into the beyond.

He undoubtedly regarded himself as the last Greek philosopher, and that he was, at least in one reasonable sense. He summed up the tradition as if he was indeed the last thinker ever. EN X, 6-8 was his effort to retain the supreme position of theōria and thus to keep the sciences together in one single kosmos of knowledge. But this great construction of the universe of human activities and knowledge was in his own lifetime desintegrated into a lot of "professions" with no ethical relevance. Thus EN X, 6-8 is the last defence of Greek philosophy in the grand manner. The successors of Aristotle failed in the attempt to justify science from the point of view of ethics. So science and philosophy drifted apart.

In the notes, the references are often abbreviated. For the full title, the number of the edition, etc. see the Bibliography.

§1. PRELIMINARY REMARKS

1. W. Jaeger. _Aristoteles._ Berlin 1923. Transl. by R. Robinson, Oxford 1934. A short account of the development of Aristotelian studies is given in F. Wehrli. _Theoria und Humanitas._ Zürich/ München 1972, 229-33. The discussions immediately following Jaeger's book are recorded by A.-H. Chroust in _Classica et Mediaevalia_ 24(1963), 27-57. In _Wiener Studien_ 76(1963), 54-67, F. Dirlmeier presents the most urgent problems now in connection with the latest research on Plato. The typical sorts of understanding are denoted by W. Wieland. _Die aristotelische Physik._ Göttingen 1962, 19-34.

2. J.H. Randall Jr. _Aristotle._ New York 1960, 21. The criticism of the genetic method started with two articles of H.-G. Gadamer (in _Logos_ 17(1928), 132ff. and _Hermes_ 63(1928), 138-64). It was formulated as a programme by Dirlmeier in _Jahrbuch für das Bistum Mainz_ 5(1950), 161ff., and it has got further arguments from K. Oehler (_Zeitschrift für philosophische Forschung_ 17(1963), 604-13). For the complications attached to the developmental point of view when it is maintained in spite of the unlimited plurality of possible constructions, see Gauthier/Jolif. _L'Éthique à Nicomaque._ Tome I.

Introduction. Louvain/Paris 1970, 10-62. We may note that Jaeger's thesis in its time was a real simplification. To maintain it now, however, seems to be at variance with the principle of economy: it creates more problems than it solves.

3. Cf. E. Zeller. Die Philosophie der Griechen II, 2. 3. ed. Leipzig 1879, 304-51. The same dichotomy determines the still readable account in A. Hägerström. Aristoteles etiska grundtankar och deras förutsättningar. Upsala 1893.

4. W. F. R. Hardie. Aristotle's Ethical Theory. Oxford 1968, 347.

5. It may be comforting to see that readers of Aristotle in the antiquity were also puzzled by apparent inconsistencies. Cicero says about the Aristotelian concept of God: "For now he ascribes all divinity to mind, now he says that the world itself is a god, now he sets another god over the world and ascribes to him the role of ruling and preserving the movement of the world by a sort of backward rotation. Then he says that the heat of the heavens is a god, not realizing that the heavens are part of the world, which he has himself elsewhere called a god" (Translation by W. D. Ross. Select Fragments. The Works of Aristotle transl. into English. Vol. XII. Oxford 1952, 97). The perplexity will, however, be greater than it needs to be if we do not share the knowledge of Randall: "The Aristotelian Corpus can be said to present a totality, not of results, but of problems. It is the problems that are for him primary, the systematic interest secondary" (op. cit. 31).

6. Cf. G. Schneeweiss. Der Protreptikos des Aristoteles. Diss. München, Bamberg 1966, 220ff., 228.

7. Cf. W. Jaeger. Aristotle. 2nd ed. Oxford 1967, 54-101; I. Düring. Aristotle's Protrepticus. Gothenburg 1961. For the work of Schneeweiss see note 6. One may profitably note the scepticism of G. Rabinowitz. Aristotle's Protrepticus and the Sources of its Reconstruction. Berkeley 1957. Nevertheless, the reading surprises the sceptic. As G. Müller says: "Wenn wir den Aristoteles des Protreptikos suchen, wie wir es seit Bernays und Bywater mit Recht tun, so finden wir dogmatisch genau dasselbe, was in den esoterischen Schriften steht. Wo es anders scheint

begegnet uns nicht ein sich entwickelnder Aristoteles sondern ein kontaminierender Jamblich" (Ethik und Politik des Aristoteles ed. by F.-P. Hager. Darmstadt 1972, 394). We must remember, however, that the Protrepticus is a sort of tract and not a treatise on ethics.

8. Cf. Dirlmeier. Aristoteles. Magna Moralia. 2nd ed. Berlin 1966, 93-147.

9. Jaeger says about MM: "Problems have become facts, and the whole has shrunk to a textbook for students" (Scripta Minora II, Rome 1961, 507). Its most thorough commentator judges thus: "Von der Aktualität des aristotelischen Geistes ist nichts zu verspüren", and "aus den intensiven methodischen Erwägungen des Aristoteles ist feste Schultradition geworden" (R. Walzer. Magna Moralia und aristotelische Ethik. Berlin 1929, pp.1 and 266).

10. J. Burnet. The Ethics of Aristotle. London 1900, xiii.

11. Burnet. op.cit. xiv.

12. For fuller information, cf. the Bibliography. Indispensable for the study of EN are, moreover, the commentary of W.L. Newman. The Politics of Aristotle. 4 vols. Oxford 1887-1902, and the commentary of H.-G. Gadamer on Plato's Philebus, now in Platos dialektische Ethik und andere Studien zur platonischen Philosophie. Hamburg 1968, 81-178. G. Widmann presents a short survey of the latest research on the three ethics ascribed to Aristotle in Autarkie und Philia in den aristotelischen Ethiken. Stuttgart 1967, 7-23.

13. Jaeger. Aristotle. 2nd ed. Oxford 1967, 434.

14. A. Grant. The Ethics of Aristotle. 2 vols. 3rd ed. London 1874, I, 178.

§2. PLATO AND THE PROBLEM OF CONTEMPLATIVE LIFE

1. One of the most instructive books on Plato's thought regards it as his main theme: A.-J. Festugière. Contemplation et vie contemplative selon Platon. 3rd ed. Paris 1967.

2. I. Düring. Aristoteles. Heidelberg 1966, 470.

3. The first small account was given by F. Boll. Vita Contemplativa. Heidelberg 1920. The discussion was renewed after an article by Jaeger, cf. n.6, thoroughly discussed by R. Joly, cf. n.10. The work of Festugière in Acta Congressus Madvigiani 2 (1958), 131-74, considers the history of the notion both before and after Aristotle, and the concept of contemplation in Plato and the Presocratics is examined by G. Picht in Wahrheit, Vernunft, Verantwortung. Stuttg. 1969, 108-35.

4. Cf. F. Boll. op.cit. 4: "Es ist im innersten Wesen des Griechentums begründet, über das nur Individuelle hinaus, dem es eine nie ermattende, freudige wie gehässige Aufmerksamkeit geschenkt hat, zu Typen fortzuschreiten, das heisst unter Verzicht auf die zufällig gegebenen Besonderheiten das Gemeinsame und allgemein Gültige zu erfassen". This is the theme of the famous I. Bruns. Das literarische Porträt der Griechen im 5. und 4. Jahrhundert vor Chr. Geb. Berlin 1896.

5. Diog. Laertius IX, 35-6.

6. W. Jaeger. 'On the Origin and Cycle of the Philosophic Ideal of Life'. Written and published in 1928. Now in Aristotle. 2nd ed. Oxford 1967, 426-61. The texts are collected and translated by B. Snell. Leben und Meinungen der Sieben Weisen. 4th ed. München 1971. On the fame of Anaxagoras, cf. §31.

7. W. Jaeger. op.cit. 429. The conclusion of Jaeger is adopted in Dirlmeier's commentaries on EN and EE.

8. For the suspicion of ordinary men concerning the philosophers, cf. the extraordinarily useful work of L. Schmidt. Die Ethik der alten Griechen. 2 vols. Berlin 1882. Reprinted Stuttgart/Bad-Cannstatt 1964, II, 433f. F. Boll gives references to the mocking of the comedy in op.cit. 33f. The most famous instance is, of course, Aristophanes' picture of Socrates in Nubes. Cf. Plato's Republic 488e.

9. W. Jaeger. op.cit. 427.

10. A.-J. Festugière. Contemplation et vie contemplative selon Platon. 3.ed. Paris 1967, 13-44. The account of R. Joly. Le thème philosophique des genres de vie dans l'antiquité classique. Bruxelles 1956, is on crucial points too confiding, cf. the criticism of W. Spoerri in Gnomon 30 (1958), 186-92. A lot of new perspectives on the ancestry of the philosopher are pointed out in F. Wehrli. Hauptrichtungen des griechischen Denkens. Zürich/Stuttg. 1964, 31-44. For the work of G. Picht, see note 3.

11. Diels/Kranz. Fragmente der Vorsokratiker (DK). 6.ed. Dublin/Zürich 1971, 21B 2. Cf. the argument from the concept of God, §28.

12. G. Picht. op.cit. 114.

13. Concerning the Pythagoreans, it is not yet clear if they used the term 'philosophy' in the later, Platonic sense. W.K.C. Guthrie supports the assumption of the ancestry of the term in his History of Greek Philosophy. Cambr.1971, I, 204f.

14. W. Jaeger. op.cit. 433. Cf. F.M. Cornford in Classical Quarterly 6 (1912), 246-64.

15. Correctly in R.-A. Gauthier. La Morale d'Aristote. Paris 1953, 52. Cf. §§3 and 31.

16. This does not, of course, imply a rejection of the basic unity of Plato's thought. F. Wehrli may be right: "Weder Theaitetos noch Phaidon widersprechen der Forderung des Staatswerkes, dass der Philosoph, statt in der Seligkeit der Kontemplation zu verharren, seinen Herrscherpflichten zu genügen hat" (op.cit.158). The question is only what Wehrli means by the term 'contradict'. There is a difference between the late and the earlier dialogues of Plato on this point, but it is perhaps more profitably interpreted as a difference of the relative importance of permanent themes than as a question of contradiction or non-contradiction.

17. Festugière gives the reason for calling it a paradox. He says about the claim of the philosopher to rule the city: "Aux yeux du peuple, ce vaeu est plus choquant que d'imposer aux femmes le service militaire ou

d'etablir le partage des épouses et des enfants" (op.cit. 39). - Still the best short account of the philosopher in the state: W. Jaeger. Paideia II. 3rd ed. Berlin 1959, 338-60. On the supposed origin of Plato's philosopher/statesman, cf. J.S. Morrison in Classical Quarterly 52 (1958), 198-218. Instructive is, moreover, H.G. Wolz. 'The Protagoras Myth and the Philosopher-Kings'. Review of Metaphysics 17(1963/64), 214-34. See also R.K. Elliott. 'Socrates and Plato's Cave'. Kant-Studien 58(1967), 137-57.

18. W. Jaeger. op.cit. 430f.

19. A.-J. Festugière. op.cit. 17.

20. Leges should be used carefully in developmental constructions because neither the author nor its time is sufficiently established. Hentschke in her Politik und Philosophie bei Plato und Aristoteles. Frankf. am Main 1971, neglects the importance of the Theaetetus and the Timaeus for the problem of the bios theōrētikos in Plato and constructs a greater difference between him and A. than the sources allow (p.344f.). We adhere to the opinion that the crack in the relation between theōria and praxis takes place in the work of Plato, and not in the transition from Plato to Aristotle.

21. This topic has been thoroughly examined by Festugière in the book mentioned above in n.10 and also in his Le Dieu Cosmique. Paris 1949, 132ff. The concept of divinity and the divine in the later Plato is brilliantly treated by F. Solmsen in Plato's Theology. New York 1942. The notion of kosmos in Plato's thought is recorded by W. Kranz, Kosmos. Archiv für Begriffsgeschichte 2. Bonn 1955, 27-58. On the origin of its philosophical use, cf. H. Ryffel. 'Eukosmia'. Museum Helveticum 4(1947), 23-38. The difference between Plato and Aristotle is often hard to establish. G. Schneeweiss puts it thus: "Nach Aristoteles jedoch gibt nicht die Natur des Universums, sondern die Geistesnatur des Menschen als Entelechie die Norm für das sittlich Gute" (op.cit. 315). Verdenius also neglects the role of mimēsis in the thought of Aristotle, cf. Phronesis 5(1960), 63f. But we will see later that the motives of energeia and mimēsis balance evenly in Aristotle's ethics.

22. This is, of course, not the appropriate place to discuss the problem of
    Socrates. Except for the well-known extremes of Burnet and Gigon,
    there is no disagreement among scholars as to the ethical and political
    impact of Socratic thought. The account in W.C.K. Guthrie: Socrates
    (Cambridge 1971), gives references to the discussion and argues for a
    reasonable conclusion not far from the position of W. Jaeger. Paideia
    II, 3rd ed. Berlin 1959, 63-73.

23. W. Jaeger. Aristotle, 434.

§3. THE METHOD OF ARISTOTLE'S ETHICS

1. On the polemics against Plato in EN, see now H. Flashar. 'Die Kritik
   der platonischen Ideenlehre in der Ethik des Aristoteles'. Synusia
   (Festgabe für W. Schadewaldt). Pfullingen 1965, 223-46. A comparison
   between their notions of dialectics is found in F. Solmsen. 'Dialectics
   without the Forms'. Aristotle on Dialectic (ed. by G.E.L. Owen).
   Oxford 1968, 49-68; cf. P. Wilpert. Kant-Studien 48(1956/57), 247-57.
   For the notion of dialectics in Plato, see H.-G. Gadamer. Platos dialektische Ethik. Hamburg 1968, 1-80.

2. J. Burnet. The Ethics of Aristotle. London 1900, p.v.

3. L.H.G. Greenwood. Aristotle. Nicomachean Ethics. Book Six.
   Cambridge 1909, 127-44. Cf. the rather pointless polemics of W.F.R.
   Hardie in op.cit. 28-45.

4. A. Grant. op.cit. I, 72f. Cf. R. McKeon. 'Aristotle's conception of
   Moral and Political Philosophy'. Ethics 51(1941), 253-90. Now also the
   discussion of S. Cashdollar. 'Aristotle's Politics of Morals'. Journ. of
   the Hist. of Philosophy 11(1973), 145-60.

5. J.H. Randall Jr. Aristotle. New York 1960, 40. The most comprehensive and profound account of the method and character of Aristotelian
   science is still. J.M. LeBlond. Logique et Méthode chez Aristote. Paris
   1939. Although ethics is not their primary concern, valuable remarks on
   the problem of method are found in R. McKeon. Journ. of the Hist. of
   Ideas 8(1947), 3-44, and W. Kullmann. 'Zur wissenschaftliche Methode

des Aristoteles'. Synusia (Festgabe für W. Schadewaldt). Pfullingen 1965, 247-74.

6. In this resignation we may also see polemics against the Academy, against the students that had made mathematics out of philosophy (Meta. 992a32). On the opposition between mathematics and rhetorics, see Theaet.162e. The inexactitude of ethics may be due to its complexity, because simplicity means exactness (Meta.1079a9). The notes on akribeia in the Politics are hardly relevant here (1337b8-15). The problems connected with this discussion of exactness are propounded by E. Kapp in Mnemosyne (1938), 179-94.

7. E. Caird. The Evolution of Theology in the Greek Philosophers. 2 vols. Glasgow 1904, I, 303. This account of Platonic and Aristotelian philosophy is marked by Hegelian thought, but extremely well written and, until the works of Festugière, far the best on the subject.

8. For this particular thought, see L.-M. Régis. L'opinion selon Aristote. Paris/Ottawa 1935; J.M. LeBlond. Eulogos et l'argument de covenance chez Aristote. Thèse compl. Paris 1938. Now also K. Oehler in Antike und Abendland 10(1961), 103-29. Cf. §31.

9. In his commentary to the Politics. Newman formulates it thus: "Politica Science is not called upon, as a deus ex machina, to bring passive matte to intermingle with the Ideas: on the contrary, it finds a natural process already in action, and its business is to study this process, to assist it and amend it" (op.cit. I, 56).

10. Cf. I. Düring. Aristotle's Protrepticus, 33-35; and the well considered work of E. Mikkola. Isokrates. Helsinki 1954, 193-212.

11. J. Burnet. op.cit. xvii.

12. This is, obviously, the weakest part of Burnet's thesis. Whenever he comes to a passage which is difficult to understand, he can say: this is merely a part of Aristotle's dialectical exposition, i.e. he does not really mean it. What we have called Aristotle's dialectical method in the ethics, does not imply this lack of seriousness. L.H.G. Greenwood has shown both in principle and in detail that Burnet is wrong on this point (cf. Greenwood. op.cit. 137ff.).

13. J. Burnet. op.cit. xiv.

14. Well presented by A. Stigen in The Structure of Aristotle's Thought.
    Oslo/New York 1966, 53-76. Cf. moreover McKeon in Ethics 51(1940/
    41), 66-101. For the connection between dialectics and the regular
    scientific procedure, see J.M. LeBlond. Logique et Méthode etc. pp.
    1-56, and E. Kapp. Der Ursprung der Logik bei den Griechen. Göttingen
    1965, 7-26.

15. For the transition from judgements which are "true, but not clear" to
    judgements which are "true and clear", cf. Plato's Pol.275a, 281c.

16. Cf. J.D. Monan's article in Aristote et les problèmes de méthode (ed.
    by S. Mansion). Louvain/Paris 1961, 252ff. There are also essential
    remarks on this topic in W. Wieland. Die aristotelische Physik. Göttingen
    1962, 141ff. Cf. §11.

17. Some themes are well, but summarily stated by G.E.R. Lloyd. Polarity
    and Analogy. Cambridge 1966, 360ff., 403ff.; cf. also M. Hesse in
    The Philosophical Quarterly 15(1965), 328-40. For Aristotle as for
    Plato the inference from analogy seems to be the solution when the subject-
    matter is especially difficult to handle: "It is hard to exhibit except by
    analogies, any of the things that are most important: for each of us
    seems to know everything as in a dream, and, again, in waking reality
    to know nothing at all" (Plato's Politicus 277d). Cf. R. Bambrough's
    article in Philosophy, Politics and Society (ed. by P. Laslett). Oxford
    1970, 98-115.

18. W. Jaeger. 'Aristotle's use of medicine as model of method in his
    ethics'. Scripta Minora II, Rome 1960, 491-509. The problem is also
    well treated by F. Wehrli in Theoria und Humanitas. Zürich/München
    1972, 177-206; 206-14. For the historical complexity of the problem,
    see H. Diller. 'Hippokratische Medizin und attische Philosophie'.
    Hermes 80(1952), 385-409. Now also J. Longrigg. 'Philosophy and
    Medicine'. Harvard Studies in Classical Philology 69(1963), 147-75.

19. W. Jaeger. op.cit. 499.

20. Jaeger treated this theme in Paideia II, 3rd ed. Berlin 1959, 11-58. For the impact of medical thought on the philosophy and the concept of philosophy in Plato, see R.E. Cushman. Therapeia. Plato's Conception of Philosophy. Chapel Hill 1958.

21. J. Burnet. op.cit. §26, n.7. For the similar idea in Plato, see the references in Gauthier/Jolif ad EN 1104a9-10.

22. Cf. the famous speech of Creon in Sophocles' Antigone 163ff. and 189. The theme is also found in Alcaeus and Aeschylus. References in Jebb's big commentary ad loc. Cf. Plato's Republic 488a and Politicus 299c.

23. W. Jaeger. op.cit. 507. Cf. EN 1096b32ff.

24. G.E.R. Lloyd in Phronesis (1968), 76ff.

§4. ETHICS AND THE DOCTRINE OF MAN

1. Pointfully represented by B. Groethuysen. Philosophische Anthropologie Darmstadt 1969, 8-47.

2. Plato never stops by man as he is. The species of man is in Plato not even justified by an eidos. G. Picht says sharply, but justly: "Aber man versteht von der Philosophie Platons nichts, wenn man nicht weiss, dass der Schöpfer der Ideenlehre eine Idee des Menschen nicht kennt ... Wenn man überhaupt von einer Idee Menschen sprechen wollte, so wäre diese Idee die Wahrheit als solche" (op.cit. 122). For the problem of Parm. 130c, cf. B. Snell. The Discovery of Mind. Oxford 1953, 246f.

3. A.W.H. Adkins. Merit and Responsibility. Oxford 1960, 344. Cf. the dictum of Festugière: "On peut dire que les neufs premiers livres de l'Éthique à Nicomaque sont consacrés à l'étude de la vertu du politikos. À l'opposé, si l'homme est, avant tout, l'être pourvu d'un intellect spéculatif dont l'office est de contempler les choses divines, l'activité morale humaine consiste à pratiquer d'abord la theoria. Le dixieme livre de EN est consacré à l'étude de la vertu du theoretikos. Il en résulte, tout au long de l'Éthique, une sorte de malaise et de gêne" (Contemplation et vie contemplative. p.41).

4. L.H.G. Greenwood. op.cit. 47.

5. Ibid. 48.

6. These remarks are only valid for EN. For the meaning of phronēsis in
   all the ethical writings attributed to Aristotle, see G. Schneeweiss. op.
   cit. 263ff.; 301-313. P. Aubenque argues strongly for the originality
   of the Aristotelian concept of phronēsis in his full monograph on the
   theme: La prudence chez Aristote. Paris 1963. Nothing has been debated
   more intensively than the systematic import of the concept of phronēsis
   and its relation to theōria. Here we will only recall that (a) the interest
   of modern interpreters in 'the origin of moral principles' in Aristotle is
   due to the importance of the theory of knowledge in modern philosophy,
   and the interest of the interpreters surpasses Aristotle's own interest in
   this question by far. He takes no explicit or clear stand in the question
   of dependency or independency as regards the relation between the acts
   of phronēsis and theōria. Accordingly, (b) there is no place for sweeping
   statements. Jaeger's judgement: "In the end, indeed, exactly like Plato,
   he (i.e. Aristotle) makes specifically moral insight dependent on the
   knowledge of the ultimate source of reality" (Aristotle, 435) is as diffuse
   and inconclusive as Wehrli's contradiction: "Die Ablösung des sittlichen
   Handelns von der kontemplativen Einsicht ist in der EE genau so Tatsache
   wie in der EN" (Theoria und Humanitas, 180, n. 11).

7. L.H.G. Greenwood. op.cit. 59.

8. See §1, n.6; §5, n.2. M. Verbeke also argues for a different origin of
   EN X, 7 in Revue philos. de Louvain 46(1948), 342-45. But the reference
   to the Protrepticus is a vain attempt at solution because a similar problem
   appears there: (a) it shows a maximum of indecision as to the final determination of happiness (cf. B94-96), and (b) the relation between moral
   and theoretical knowledge is just as problematic as in EN. See Düring's
   commentary ad B21. We treat this problem of the Protr. in §35.

9. That Aristotle tries to justify his work against attacks, is obvious from
   many passages, cf. especially Part.An. 644b22-45a36. The problems of
   justification turns up in the introduction to the different pragmateiai.

10. J. Burnet. op.cit. 345. This possibility is seriously considered in §24 and §35.

11. More exactly: the praxis thoroughly described in EN as the interplay between the rational and the irrational part of human soul, is peculiar to man. There is, however, also another use of the term in Aristotle. Praxis in the widest sense may replace bios or energeia or kinēsis. It is not only used about the activity of animals and men, but also about the movement of the stars (Hist.An.487a11ff.; Part.An.646b15; Pol. 1254a7; EE 1220b27; De Cael. 292b1ff.).

12. It is essential for the understanding of Aristotle's ethics not to ascribe to him a concept of duty more or less like the modern post-Kantian one. On this point we take sides with V. Brochard. Études de philosophie ancienne et de philosophie moderne. Paris 1912, 492ff. and A.W.H. Adkins. Merit and Responsibility. Oxford 1960, 253, - against R.-A. Gauthier. La morale d'Aristote. Paris 1963, 86-96 and W.F.R. Hardie Aristotle's Ethical Theory. Oxford 1968, 124-28. Nobody will deny the Greeks the experience of moral obligation. Leonidas knew exactly what he had to do to preserve his honour. When we speak of 'duty', however, we think more or less consciously of the ethical theory of Kant, and Leonidas' fear of dishonour was certainly very far from Kant's categorical imperative. The difference between the ancient Greek and the modern concept of moral obligation is lucidly described in the book of Adkins mentioned above. See moreover W. Bröcker. Aristoteles. 3.ed. Frankf. am Main 1964, 289-300. What remains is the translator's problem: how to translate a Greek text into a modern language without mixing modern concepts into the ancient discussion? Here, the work of R.-A. Gauthier fails on a decisive point.

13. J. Burnet. op.cit. xxxiv.

14. The theological aspect of the Aristotelian concept of eudaimonia may be seen from the indiscriminate use of makarios and eudaimōn (EN 1101a1, 1176a27, 1178b9; Pol.1323b24, 1331b25). Thus Aristotle expresses the kinship between the state of the gods and the state of the happy men, cf. §28. On Aristotle's forerunners in this genre, see B. Gladigow. 'Zum Makarismos des Weisen'. Hermes 95 (1967), 404-33.

§5. HAPPINESS IS NOT A DISPOSITION

1. J.A. Stewart. Notes on the Nicomachean Ethics of Aristotle. 2 vols.
   Oxford 1892, ad loc.

2. Cf. H. Margueritte in Revue d'hist. de la philosophie 4(1930), 176–88;
   249–73. The close relationship between Books I and X was already noted
   by G. Riva. Il concetto di Aristotele sulla felicità terrestre. Prato 1883.

3. W. Theiler. Zur Geschichte der teleologischen Naturbetrachtung bis auf
   Aristoteles. 1925/reprinted 1965. Cf. K. Gaiser. 'Das zweifache Telos
   bei Aristoteles' in Naturphilosophie bei Aristoteles und Theophrast (ed.
   by I. Düring). Heidelberg 1969. This article is discussed in §38.

4. A. Grant. op.cit. I, 229.

5. A. Grant. op.cit. I, 223.

6. R.-A. Gauthier. La morale d'Aristote. Paris 1963, 46.

7. On this problem, cf. §4,n.12. See moreover: H. Reiner. 'Das Kantische
   Sittengesetz im sittlichen Bewusstsein der Antike'. Kant-Studien 39(1934),
   1–26; and S. Krohn. 'Aristoteles som grundläggare av den normativa
   etiken'. Ajatus 28(1966), 89–101.

8. On Aristotle's use of hexis, Jaeger says: "These (i.e. strength, health,
   etc.) are called a permanent disposition of the body (hexis) in medical
   terminology, and Aristotle does not hesitate to apply the same word to the
   ethical phenomenon of virtue, especially since Plato had been the first to
   see this similarity and to use medical terms like hexis or diathesis in
   an ethical sense" (Scripta Minora II, Rome 1960, 502). Cf. the following
   citation from Plato's Philebus.

9. On the origin of this problem and its treatment in the Academy, see now
   R. Nickel. Das Begriffspaar Besitzen und Gebrauchen. Ein Beitrag zur
   Vorgeschichte der Potenz-Akt-Beziehung in der aristotelischen Ethik.
   Diss. Berlin 1970. In the Topics, Aristotle once mentions the name of
   the counterpart: Xenocrates said that the happy man (eudaimōn) has a
   good soul. For the soul is the daimōn of the person (112a36).

10. Cf. Diels/Kranz. op.cit. 22B 1, 21, 26, 73, 88, 89.

11. See the Protrepticus B90: "For such reasons we assign life to the man who is awake rather than to him who is asleep, to him who thinks rather than to him who is thoughtless, and we say that the pleasure of living is the pleasure we get from the exercise of the soul; for that is true life". Cf. B80, 83, 101. The notation and translation follow Düring's edition: Aristotle's Protrepticus. An Attempt at Reconstruction. Gothenburg 1961.

12. This is clearly formulated in De Anima: "Now the word actuality (entelecheia) has two senses corresponding respectively to the possession of knowledge (epistēmē) and the actual exercise of knowledge (theōria). It is obvious that the soul is actuality in the first sense, viz. that of knowledge as possessed, for both sleeping and waking presuppose the existence of the soul, and of these waking corresponds to actual knowing (theōrein), sleeping to knowledge possessed, but not employed, and, in the history of the individual, knowledge comes before its employment or exercise. That is why the soul (psychē) is the first grade of actuality (entelecheia) of a natural body having life (zōē) potentially in it" (412a22-28).

13. Therefore the judgement of F. Dirlmeier is an obvious overstatement: "Zwischen dem Peripatos und der Aussenwelt ist eine Mauer, auch wenn über sie die Tiere und die Pflanzen hereinkommen" (Aristoteles. Nikomachische Ethik. Darmstadt 1969, 249f.). Cf. however, §§20-21.

§6. AN ACTIVITY DESIRABLE IN ITSELF

1. The same thing is said in the Protrepticus: "A thing pursued as an end in itself is always superior to one pursued as a means to something else, so too that which is free to that which is not" (B25). The concept of happiness as that which is always and merely wished for its own sake, is also found in Rhet.I, 5-6. An adjacent criticism of this concept is given by Gauthier/Jolif. op.cit. ad 1176b2-6: "Nous retrouvons la position typiquement aristotélicienne du probleme du bonheur. Le bonheur ne peut être qu'une activité qu'on choisit pour elle-même sans que rien nous y contraigne. Est dès lors exclue du bonheur toute la vie

de travail, à laquelle nous contraint la nécessité de gagner notre vie, et entre seule en ligne de compte la vie de loisir. Tout le problème du bonheur consiste à se demander comment peupler ses loisirs: par le plaisir, par la politique ou par l'étude". Cf. the cognate criticism of G. Redlow. Theoria. Berlin 1966, 104-120.

2. W.F.R. Hardie. op.cit. 356.

3. I. Düring. Aristoteles. 46.

4. The graduation and the idea of different forms of happiness are seldom explicitly confirmed in Aristotle. It may, however, be inferred from sayings like e.g. EN 1099b18ff. Aristotle there contends that the end of human activity (i.e. happiness) "would be widely spread through the community; for it may be attained, through some study and practice, by anyone who is not maimed in respect of arete".

5. A. Grant. op.cit. I, 141.

6. For the place and role of this concept in Aristotle's thought, cf. G. Widmann. Autarkie und Philia in den aristotelischen Ethiken. Diss. Tübingen 1967.

7. On the relation between the concepts of praxis and poiesis, see EN 1094a5, 1105a28, 1105b12, 1139b1, 1140a5, 1140b3ff.; Pol.1254a5ff.; Meta.1048b22, 1050a21-b2; cf. Plato's Charm. 163b-3. The meaning of this distinction is brilliantly disclosed by H.-G. Gadamer. Wahrheit und Methode. 3.ed. Tübingen 1972, 295-307.

8. Autarkes means both the negative: 'not to require anything else', and the positive: 'to have what is needed' (cf. Pol.1253a28, 1256b31f., 1261b11f.; Gen.An.776b8f.). See, M. Pohlenz. Griechische Freiheit. Heidelberg 1955, and F. Tomberg. Polis und Nationalstaat. Darmstadt/ Neuwied 1973. For further interpretations, see notes to §18.

9. Cf. P. Merlan. 'Aristoteles' und Epikurs müssige Götter'. Zeitschrift für philosophische Forschung 21(1967), 485-98, and K. Kleve. Gnosis Theon. Oslo 1963. The last work discusses Cicero's presentation of Epicurean theology, an important theme for the student of Aristotle's theology. But the author disregards the relation between Aristotle and

Epicurus. The standard work on this relation, E. Bignone. L'Aristotele perduto e la formazione filosofica di Epicura. 2 vols. Firenze 1936, should be read with criticism.

10. The account of energeia in Aristotle's thought given by A. Grant is still instructive (op. cit. I, 230-51). The citation is from op. cit. I, 243.

§7. VIRTUOUS ACTIONS AND AMUSEMENTS

1. This, of course, does not contradict the contentions concerning the structure of EN X, 6-8 given at the end of §4.

2. The references to Rodier and Gauthier ad loc. apply to their commentaries, see the Bibliography. For the understanding of spoudaios as well as other key terms of Greek ethical thought, one may profitably consult L. Schmidt. Die Ethik der Griechen. 2 vols. Berlin 1882, 289-376. For the different meanings of the main words, the indexes in Newman's commentary to the Politics are also indispensable.

3. J. Léonard says about the account of hēdonē given in Book VII: "L'impression générale, laissée par ces chapitres, est qu'Aristote se trouve amené, par la force des raisonnements, à un hédonisme qui l'etonne un peu lui-meme" (Le bonheur chez Aristote. Bruxelles 1948, 70). The examination of pleasure in the Aristotelian ethics is fully and conscientously treated by Festugière. Le plaisir. Paris 1936, and recently by G. Lieberg. Die Lehre von der Lust in den Ethiken des Aristoteles. München 1958.

4. F. Dirlmeier. Aristoteles. Nikomachische Ethik. Darmstadt 1969, 229.4.

5. Düring says rightly: "Die einen sehen in der philosophischen Einsicht das grösste Gut, die anderen in der ethischen Tugend, wieder andere in der Lust. Der Kernsatz der aristotelischen Ethik ist, dass diese drei Werte zusammen das Lebensglück stiften" (Aristoteles, 434). And for the support of his thesis, Düring refers to EN 1098b23-26; EE 1214a31, 1218b34; Protr. B41, 94; Pol. 1323b1-3; MM 1184b5-6. The dialectics leading up to the conclusion of Aristotle is, however, far from simple and must be considered in detail.

§8. THE TYRANTS SPEND THEIR LEISURE IN AMUSEMENTS

1. G. Rodier. Introduction et notes au livre X de l'Éth. à Nic. Paris 1897, 47. Cf. J. Derbolav. 'Freiheit und Naturordnung im Rahmen der Aristotelischen Ethik'. Kant-Studien 57(1966), 32-60.

2. See the account of F. Wehrli. Hauptrichtungen des griechischen Denkens. Zürich/Stuttg. 1964, 69-79, and the article of O. Regenbogen in Das humanistische Gymnasium 41(1930), 1-20.

3. Diels/Kranz. op.cit. 22B 4.

4. This objection is, of course, also given by Aristotle: "not to have one's life organized in view of some end, is a mark of much folly" (EE 1214b10).

5. On amusements and the estimation of them in Greek thought, see F. Wehrli. op.cit. 22-31. We repeat: Aristotle rejects the life of pleasure, but not the pleasure of life: "If certain pleasures are bad, that does not prevent the chief good from being some pleasure" (EN 1153b7). Cf. §7.

6. For Aristotle's doctrine of friendship, see E. Hoffmann in Ethik und Politik des Aristoteles (ed. by F.-P. Hager). Darmstadt 1972, 149-83, and R. Ritter. Die aristotelische Freundschaftsphilosophie nach der Nikomachischen Ethik. Diss. München 1963. Critical reflections on Aristotle's concept of friendship from the point of view of personalism, are given by M.S. Shellens. Das sittliche Verhalten zum Mitmenschen im Anschluss an Aristoteles. Hamburg 1958.

7. Reason, nous, is used in so many different ways in the Aristotelian Corpus that Aristotle can hardly be said to have a single concept of nous. In the present context he may remind us of a passage in De Anima: where there is a sense of time, nous can oppose the appetites, "for nous bids us resist because of the future (dia to mellon), while appetite has regard for only the immediate present" (433b5ff.). - For the complexity of nous, see now H. Seidl. Der Begriff des Intellekts (nous) bei Aristoteles. Meisenheim am Glan 1971. Cf §13.

8. For the personification of the possibilities of moral decision, see W. Schultz. 'Herakles am Scheidewege'. Philologus 1909, 489-99. Cf. Pol.V, 10 on the tyrant.

9. Diels/Kranz. op.cit. 68B 53.

10. In the Categories. The point of this doctrine is clearly stated in A. Stige 'Aristoteles kategorilære'. Ajatus 29(1967), 103-27.

§9. THE DISPOSITION DECIDES WHAT IS PLEASANT

1. Cf. the Protrepticus: "Now since all men choose by preference what accords with their own characters (the just man choosing to live justly, the brave man to live bravely, the temperate man to live temperately), similarly it is clear that the wise man will choose, above all things, to think wisely, that being the exercise of his faculty" (B40). For this problem of Greek thought, see C.W. Müller. Gleiches zu Gleichem. Ein Prinzip frühgriechischen Denkens. Wiesbaden 1965; as regards Aristotl notably 187-90.

2. The really pleasant is that which is pleasant to sensation unspoiled. "So with the soul; what is pleasant to children or brutes, but to the adult, is really pleasant" (EE 1235b37, 1235a10, 1237a28, 1238a34).

3. For the medical analogy, see §3 and the end of §8.

4. What is firstly chosen for the sake of pleasure may, however, develop into a more serious thing. In EE the author indicates a possible develop- ment from friendship for the sake of pleasure to a friendship for the sake of virtue (1236a37). It is even suggested that this way is the only possible one: "the road is through pleasure" (1237a6).

§10. HAPPINESS DOES NOT LIE IN AMUSEMENTS

1. Cf. the important remarks on Damon, Plato and the concept of education, plattein, in G. Picht. op.cit. 118ff. See, moreover, W.D. Anderson. Ethos and Education in Greek Music. Cambridge, Mass. 1966; A. Busse in Rhein. Museum 77(1928), 34-50, and E. Koller in Museum Helveticur 13(1956), 1-37; 94-124.

2. Aristotle thus takes an intermediate stand between Eudoxus, who held pleasure to be the supreme value, and Speusippus, who said that pleasure is never a good thing. See I. Düring. _Aristoteles._ 147ff.

3. The idea that amusements and toil must replace each other in alternating succession is, of course, not new. It is found in the story about Amasis in Herodotus (II, 173) and also in the famous funeral oration of Pericles in Thucydides (II, 38).

4. Düring says: "Stewart und Dirlmeier halten mit Recht daran fest, dass Aristoteles eine Hierarchie konstruiert; die Höchstform schliesst in sich die anderen Formen ein" (op.cit. 471). The word 'Hierarchie' is not well chosen because the doctrine is more implicitly assumed than explicitly stated. The same point is well put by G. Müller: "Es war nicht des Aristoteles Meinung, dass ein ungerechter oder böser Mensch zur göttlichen Eudaimonie aufsteigen könnte, noch eher er sich gewandelt und in den Besitz der menschlichen Eudaimonie gesetzt hätte. Das Niedere ist um des Höheren willen da, nach aristotelischer Stufenlehre; aber das Höhere verwirklicht sich nicht, ohne dass das Niedere vorher verwirklicht war" (Ethik und Politik des Aristoteles ed. by F.-P. Hager). Darmstadt 1972, 381. - It should be remarked, however, that the relation between the bios politikos and the $\overline{\text{bios theoretikos}}$ is more complex than that. Firstly, the distinction of Müller between divine and human happiness cannot be justified. Both politics and contemplation are human forms of activity. Otherwise their examination would not belong to the ethics (EN 1102a13: "But clearly the virtue we must study is human virtue; for the good we were seeking was human good and the happiness human happiness"). That the happiness is often also called 'divine', is another matter. It is never done to mark that it lies beyond human possibilities, but rather to mark that it is the limit of human experience. Secondly, the prosperity of the state is also called 'god-like', theioteron (EN 1094b9). Thirdly, there is no transition from the complete $\overline{\text{bios}}$ politikos to the $\overline{\text{bios theoretikos}}$. The philosopher need not be politician first. But the philosopher does need the politician to defend and secure his form of life. In other words: the 'Hierarchie' is not a picture of the way of the individual to supreme happiness. Cf. the considerations in §§4 and 35.

5. For the interpretation of philosophy in Alpha 1-2 as malista eidenai, see W. Bröcker. Aristoteles. Frankf.am Main 1964, 9-23. Differently: K. Ulmer. Wahrheit, Kunst und Natur bei Aristoteles. Tübingen 1953, 61ff., and H.-G. Gadamer. Platos dialektische Ethik. Hamburg 1968, 15ff. We are not likely to understand rightly the different sorts of hierarchical exposition in Aristotle if we try to make them too analogous. There is a likeness between the account of the stages of knowledge, the faculties of the human soul and the different forms of life, but this likeness does not justify the reconstruction of a 'system'.

§11. THE MORE SERIOUS ACTIONS ARE THE BETTER

1. J.D. Monan. 'Two Methodological Aspects of Moral Knowledge in EN'. Aristote et les problèmes de méthode (ed. by S. Mansion). Louvain/ Paris 1961, 253.

2. W. Wieland. Die aristotelische Physik. Göttingen 1962, 148.

3. W. Wieland. op.cit. 145. It is hard to avoid the impression that this account is a simplification. The distinctions between word and thing, between statements and matters of fact are not as foreign to Aristotle's thought as Wieland will have us believe. Cf. the introductory remarks in A. Stigen. 'Aristoteles' kategorilære'. Ajatus 29(1967), 103-27. As to certain discussions they hit the point better who find "ein heilloses Durcheinander" (Wieland. op.cit. 146). See now the thorough criticism of Wieland in K. Oehler. Antike Philosophie und Byzantinisches Mittelalter. München 1969, 95ff.; and the remarks in W. Bröcker. Aristotel Franf. am Main 1964, 244-50.

4. See the references in J.D. Monan. op.cit. 252-61; Wieland op.cit. 141-61; and J.M. LeBlond. Logique et Méthode chez Aristote. Paris 1939, 308-26.

§12. HAPPINESS IS NOT FOR ANY CHANCE PERSON

1. Andrapodos (77a7) means a slave (cf. the mistake of O. Gigon. Entretiens sur l'antiquité classique. Tome XI. p.281), but Aristotle's dictum does not only concern them. It also refers to the man he calls tychon, 'any chance person' (Ross) or 'the man in the street' (cf. W.K. C. Guthrie. Socrates. Cambridge 1971, 92). These two are contrasted with ho aristos (77a8), 'the best man' (Ross). The difference is due to the supposition that the last one may freely set an aim before him and actually has decided for the highest aim, whereas the first ones either cannot or will not do the same. For this use of tychon, cf. Xenophon Mem. 3.9.10.

2. Ad EN I,5 Grant's commentary supports this view: "Bios is the external form, opposed to zoē, the internal principle of life. Thus bios is 'line of life', 'profession', 'career'".

3. I. Düring. Aristoteles. Heidelberg 1966, 12. Cf. e.g. Pol. 1329a19: "Besides, the ruling class should be the owners of property, for they are citizens, and the rulers of a state should be in good circumstances; whereas mechanics, or any other class which is not a producer of aretē, have no share in the state".

4. W.F.R. Hardie. Aristotle's Ethical Theory. Oxford 1968, 340.

5. Cf. O. Gigon. 'Die Sklaverei bei Aristoteles'. Entretiens sur l'antiquité classique. Tome XI. Vandoeuvres/Geneve 1964, 247-76.

6. For the interpretation of EN as a programme for paideia, see E. Fink. Metaphysik und Erziehung im Weltverständnis von Plato und Aristoteles. Frankf. am Main 1970.

§13. REASON IS THE BEST THING

1. See, K. von Fritz in Class.Phil. 40(1945), 223-42; 41(1946), 12-34; Archiv für Begriffsgeschichte 9(1964), 87-102. G. Jaeger. Nus in Platons Dialogen. Hypomn. 17. Göttingen 1967. H. Seidl. Der Begriff des Intellekts (nous) bei Aristoteles. Meisenheim am Glan 1971. The last one is merely a sketch of the book that should be written on this theme.

2. W.F.R. Hardie op.cit. 336.

3. See, F. Dirlmeier's commentary ad loc., and Greenwood op.cit. 75-78.

4. See, Gauthier ad loc. and the article of G. Verbeke in Fontes Ambrosiani 25, Milan 1951, I, 79-95.

5. E. Frank. Wissen, Wollen, Glauben. Zürich/Stuttgart 1955, 64-66.

6. K. Oehler. Die Lehre vom noetischen and dianoetischen Denken bei Platon und Aristoteles. Zetemata 29. München 1962.

7. Greenwood op.cit. 75-78.

8. Quoted in E.A. Wyller. Der späte Platon. Hamburg 1970, 25 ff.

9. See, E. Frank. op.cit. 115-19.

10. J. Léonard. Le Bonheur chez Aristote. Bruxelles 1948, 146.

11. Cf. I. Düring. Aristoteles. 451-54.

12. See V. Rose. Aristoteles. Fragmenta. Lipsiae 1886, frg. 49.

13. Düring op.cit. 27 and 32.

14. Cf. E. Frank op.cit. 26-50.

15. H.H. Joachim. Aristotle. The Nicomachean Ethics. Oxford 1951, 289.

16. See, G. Jaeger op.cit. 52 and 67.

17. Beare op.cit. 56-96. Particularly p. 89.

18. J.H. Randall Jr. Plato. The Dramatist of the Life of Reason. New York, London 1970, 49. See also, G. Rudberg in Class. et Mediaevalia 5(1942) 159-86.

19. E. Caird op.cit. I, 94.

20. E. Caird op.cit. I, 333.

21. J. Léonard op.cit. 29. Cf. §4.

22. Newman. The Politics of Aristotle. I, 65.

23. P. Defourny in Ethik und Politik des Aristoteles (ed. by F.-P. Hager). Darmstadt 1972, 222.

§14. CONTEMPLATION IS THE BEST ACTIVITY

1. Cf. §4, n.6. Phronēsis is used also in EE to denote the core of the
   bios theōrētikos: 1214a32, 1215a34, 1215b1, 1216a19, 29, 38 etc.

2. Cf. S. Mansion in Aristotle in the Mid-Fourth Century (ed. by I. Düring
   and G.E.L. Owen). Gothenburg 1960: "A. devotes all his intellectual
   power to vindicating, as his master had done, the supremacy of the
   philosophical life" (p. 75).

3. J. Léonard op.cit. 148.

4. Ibid. 151.

5. Cf. F. Boll op.cit. 26ff.; H. Koller in Glotta 36(1958), 273-86; and
   J. Ritter in Metaphysik und Politik. Frankf. am Main 1969, 9-32.

6. J. Burnet op.cit. 258.

7. I. Düring. Aristoteles. 472.

8. Ibid. 28.

9. J. Stenzel. Metaphysik des Altertums. Darmstadt 1971, 176.

10. Cf. Festugière. Le Dieu Cosmique. Paris 1949, 132-52.

11. W.D. Ross. Select Fragments. The Works of Aristotle etc. Vol.XII.
    Oxford 1952, frg.8 (p.81f.). Cf. I. Düring. Aristoteles, 110.

12. R.-A. Gauthier. La Morale d'Aristote. Paris 1963, 99.

13. J. Burnet op.cit. 265f.

14. Cf. S.H. Rosen in Phronesis 6(1961), 127-37.

15. W.F.R.Hardie op.cit. 339: "But to the extent that Aristotle's case for
    the supremacy of 'theory' rests on the kinship between a divine spark in
    Man and the objects of theological and cosmological speculation, the
    exclusion of physics is inevitable, and of mathematics also if, as
    Aristotle inclines to think, mathematical propositions are about sensible
    substances in respect of certain of their properties".

16. On the idea of ergon anthrōpou, cf. G.E.R. Lloyd in Phronesis 1968,
    68-83, and S. Clark in Ethics 82(1972), 269-83. See moreover, H.J.
    Krämer. Arete bei Platon und Aristoteles. Amsterdam 1967, 118ff.

17. R.-A. Gauthier op.cit. 13. Cf. the judgement of W. Jaeger on the conclusion of EE: "Against such an ethics of pure devotion to God the famous picture of the contemplative life in book ten of the Nicomachean Ethics fades, and becomes little more than an objective if idealized description of the life of the scholar devoted to research, rising at the end to the intuition of the ultimate force that guides the spheres. Some of the old notes sound again in this picture, but not quite with their old power" (op.cit. 243).

18. I. Düring. Aristoteles. 445. He says further: "Daher steht in den drei Ethiken das tugendhafte Leben im Zentrum, nicht die theoria, die eine Ausnahmeform für wenige Auserwählte ist (spanion ist das Schlüssel- wort sowohl bei Platon als Aristoteles)" (p.470). In Plato, Düring can refer to the Phaedo 90a and the Republic 476b, but in Aristotle the only reference that may have some bearing on this point is that to EN 1145a27 Differently, W.J. Verdenius in Untersuchungen zur eudemischen Ethik (ed. by P. Moraux and D. Harlfinger). Berlin 1971, 285-97.

19. A.-J. Festugière. La contemplation et vie contemplative etc. p.5.

20. See P. Defourny op.cit. and W.J. Verdenius' commentary on the last section of EE (1249b3 and out) referred to in note 18 above.

21. F. Boll op.cit. pp.5 and 6.

22. F. Solmsen. Kleine Schriften. Vol.II. Hildesheim 1968, 1-28. His judgement is supported by the account of M.P:n Nilsson on the spirit of the last half of the fourth century, cf. Grekisk Religiositet (2.ed.). Stockholm 1960, 65-89.

23. F. Dirlmeier in Jahrbuch für das Bistum Mainz 5(1950), 170f.

24. I. Düring. Aristoteles. 472.

§15. THE OBJECTS OF REASON ARE THE BEST

1. "Es ist ganz unrichtig, in Aristoteles einen Gegner der Erkenntnis des Gleichen durch Gleiches sehen zu wollen" (C.W. Müller. Gleiches zu Gleichem. Wiesbaden 1965, 189). Important remarks on Aristotle in C.W. Müller pp.187-90.

2. A. Grant ad end of EN I, 2. Cf. H.-G. Gadamer. 'Über das Göttliche im frühen Denken der Griechen'. Das Altertum und jedes neue Gute (Festschrift für W. Schadewaldt). Stuttgart/Berlin 1970, 397-414; and R. Mugnier. Le sens du mot THEIOS chez Platon. Paris 1930.

3. Aristotle's metaphysics of movement and its relation to his theology is excellently considered in M.J. Buckley. Motion and Motion's God. Princeton 1971, 15-86. The concept of motion is the main key of inter- pretation in the work of W. Bröcker. Aristoteles. Franf. am Main (3rd ed.) 1964.

4. Cf. H. Happ. 'Kosmologie und Metaphysik bei Aristoteles' in Parusia. (Festschrift für J. Hirschenberger) 1965, 155-87.

5. W.L. Newman op.cit. I, 23.

6. For its prehistory, see B. Gladigow. Sophia und Kosmos. Hildesheim 1965.

§16. CONTEMPLATION AND CONTINUITY

1. Cf. J. Christensen in Class.et Mediaevalia 19(1958), 7-40, and the presentation of Aristotle's theology between that of Plato and that of Plotinus in F.-P. Hager. Der Geist und das Eine. Bern/Stuttgart 1970.

2. This expression is used on the universe in On Philosophy, see W. Theiler. Zur Geschichte der teleologischen Naturbetrachtung. Berlin 1965, p. 83ff.

3. E. Frank op.cit. 56.

4. H. Bonitz. Index Aristotelicus. Darmstadt 1955, p.728.

5. See S. Sambursky. 'The World of the Continuum' in his Physical World of the Greeks. London 1960, 132-57. F. Solmsen. Aristotle's System of the Physical World. New York 1960, 199ff. E. Frank sums up the importance of this concept thus: "While the Pythagoreans and Plato did not recognize the continuum (syneches) as a mathematically exact concept and therefore did not accept it among their definitions (Meta.1036b9), Aristotle tried to reduce the mathematical concepts, especially that of the

infinite, to the concept of the continuum which, as a mathematical concept, is still unknown to Plato and which Aristotle himself may have been first to introduce into mathematical discussion" (op.cit. 101f.).

6.   Cf. J. Burnet ad 1098a18.

§17. PLEASURE AND CONTEMPLATION

1.   L.H.G. Greenwood op.cit. 76f.

2.   A. Grant ad 77a26.

3.   See W.D. Ròss' big commentary on the Metaphysics. 2 vols. Oxford 1924, ad loc. (Meta. 1072b14).

4.   The doctrines of pleasure and the theology are, then, as closely related in Aristotle as in Epicurus, cf. P. Merlan. Studies in Epicurus and Aristotle. Wiesbaden 1960.

§18. CONTEMPLATION IS SELF-SUFFICIENT

1.   For the idea of autarkeia, see O. Gigon in Ajatus 28(1966), 39-50, and the recent study of F. Tomberg. Polis und Nationalstaat. Darmstadt/ Neuwied 1973.

2.   M. Pohlenz. Griechische Freiheit. Heidelberg 1955.

3.   O. Gigon op.cit. 40.

4.   In his doctrine of 'la vie mixte', R.-A. Gauthier makes nearly the same mistake: "Il ne s'agit pas pour Aristote de distinguer deux types de bonheur séparables qui seraient les bonheurs de deux hommes différents, l'un le bonheur parfait du philosophe et l'autre le bonheur secondaire du politique, mais de hierarchiser les deux types de vie que mene conjointement le même homme, à la fois philosophe et homme politique" (op.cit. 108).

5.   G. Rodier op.cit. 47.

6.   I. Düring. Aristoteles. p.16.

237

7. On the canon of virtues in Plato and Aristotle, see F.E. Sparshott in The Monist 54(1970), 40-65.

8. See G. Widmann. Autarkie und Philia in den aristotelischen Ethiken. Stuttgart 1967, treats the problem of autarkeia well, but does not expound sufficiently clearily the paradox that theōria is at the same time a transgression of friendship and the fulfilment of it. Cf. §24.

§19. LOVED FOR ITS OWN SAKE

1. L.H.G. Greenwood op.cit. 145-66.

2. Newman op.cit. I, 59.

3. Cf. A. Mansion in Revue philos. de Louvain 48(1950), 465-77.

§20. WE ARE BUSY THAT WE MAY HAVE LEISURE

1. E. Mikkola in Arctos (1958), 68-87.

2. Cf. I. Düring. Aristoteles (p.142f.) and Protrepticus (pp.33ff.). See, moreover, E. Koller in Museum Helveticum 13(1956), 1-37; 94-124.

3. F. Solmsen. Kleine Schriften II. Hildesheim 1968, 1-28. Cf. the works of Curtius, Mikkola, Stocks and Welskopf in the Bibliography.

4. F. Solmsen op.cit. p.4,n.19.

5. Ibid. p.9.

6. The definitions of E. Mikkola are not satisfactory. Ascholia: "die vom Zwang diktierte alltägliche Arbeit". Scholē: "die eigene Zeit eines jeden" (op.cit. 75). Curiously, I. Düring adopts the conclusions of Mikkola in his big book on Aristotle. Solmsen's work is probably unknown to him.

7. F. Solmsen op.cit. 12.

8. Ibid. p.19. "Exalted by the philosopher", so also Mikkola: "Wir können feststellen, wie der prosaische Aristoteles sich zu poetischem Schwung

erhebt, wenn er beschreibt, was der Begriff schole̅ umfasst" (Mikkola op. cit. 76, with reference to Pol. 1334a28–34).

9. F. Solmsen op. cit. 13f.

10. Ibid. p. 15.

11. Ibid. p. 25. Cf. Pol. 1337a27.

12. Ibid. p. 28.

§21. CONTEMPLATION IS BETTER THAN POLITICS

1. H. Bonitz. Index Aristotelicus. Darmstadt 1955, p. 613.

2. F. Dirlmeier. Aristoteles. Nikomachische Ethik. 1969.

3. J. Burnet op. cit. xxix. Cf. the examination of Newman in his commentary I, 234ff., and E. Braun. Aristoteles über Bürger- und Menschentugend. Wien 1961.

4. L. H. G. Greenwood op. cit. 78.

5. See W. D. Ross. Select Fragments. frg. 2 from 'On Kingship', p. 66.; in V. Rose. Aristoteles Fragmenta. p. 409.

6. L. H. G. Greenwood op. cit. 83.

7. E. Caird op. cit. I, 358.

8. cf. E. Zeller op. cit. II, 2, 616.

§22. HAPPINESS AND THE NATURE OF MAN

1. J. Burnet op. cit. 122. Cf. Gauthier/Jolif ad EN 1126a30.

2. H. Seidl says in op. cit.: "Nach Aristoteles ist also der Mensch offenbar von solcher Natur, dass er aus sich selbst heraustreten und über 'nur menschliches' Verhalten hinauszugehen vermag" (p. 161). Whereas S. Clark puts it thus: "Beasts grow up, whether they will or not, and so do we at some levels, but it is up to us to grow up fully. If Aristotle is correct, we have very far to grow" (Ethics 82(1972), 283).

3. Against the opinion of F. Nuyens as quoted in Gauthier/Jolif ad 77b33.

§23. MAKE YOURSELF IMMORTAL

1. F. Dirlmeier in Jahrbuch für das Bistum Mainz 5(1950), 171. Now also in Aristoteles in der neueren Forschung (ed. by P. Moraux). Darmstadt 1968, 144-57. On hybris and the ideal of measure, see F. Wehrli. Hauptrichtungen des griechischen Denkens. Zürich/Stuttgart 1964, 69-79, and E. Milobenski. Der Neid in der griechischen Philosophie. Wiesbaden 1964.

2. See B. Gladigow (§4, n.14) and G. Müller in Ethik und Politik des Aristoteles (ed. by F.-P. Hager). Darmstadt 1972, 368-402. E. Frank presents valuable comments on the language of the Mysteries (op.cit. 62-63). He says about Plato and Aristotle: "An Stelle des Mysterientempels tritt das ganze Universum, die ganze Natur, und das höchste Mysterium, das sich in ihr abspielt, ist das menschliche Leben ..." (p.68).

3. F. Dirlmeier op.cit. 170f.

4. G. Müller op.cit. 372.

5. Cf. Festugière. Le Dieu Cosmique. Paris 1949, 206-209, and M. P:n Nilsson. Grekisk Religiositet (2.ed.). Stockholm 1960, 135-147.

6. Cf. A. Mansion in Revue philos. de Louvain 48(1950), 465-77.

7. J.H. Randall Jr. Plato. The Dramatist of the Life of Reason. New York/London 1970, 218.

8. J. Léonard op.cit. 171. Cf. the statement of De Anima: "The discursive reason and the feelings of love and hate are not modes of affections of reason, but of the subject in which it is realised, though they are due to that realisation. Hence, when this subject is destroyed, reason ceases to remember and to love; for such states belong not to it, but to the being in whom soul and body are combined (tou koinou), and this, of course, perishes. But the reason in itself is something more divine and cannot be the subject of any such modes as these" (408b25ff.).

9. J. Léonard op.cit. 155.

10. A still readable consideration of Plato's erotics is found in W.H. Thompson's edition of the Phaedrus. London 1868.

11. L.H.G. Greenwood op.cit. 82.

§24. MAN MUST CHOOSE THE LIFE OF HIS SELF

1. A.W.H. Adkins. From the Many to the One. London 1970, 204. The historical background for the idea of philautia in Aristotle is given in L. Schmidt. Die Ethik der alten Griechen. 2 vols. Berlin 1882, II, 394–454.

2. W. Bröcker. Aristoteles. Frankf. am Main 3.ed. 1964, 28.

3. R.-A. Gauthier. La Morale d'Aristote. Paris 1963, 86–96.

4. E. Arleth. 'Die Bedeutung von ongkos bei Aristoteles'. Wiener-Studien 22(1900), 11–17.

5. Stob. 3,3,45, quoted by B. Snell in Leben und Meinungen der Sieben Weisen. München 1971, 112. Cf. on the contrary, the story of Thales in Pol.1259a6ff. and Newman's note ad oligon, op.cit. II, 205.

6. Due to the ethereal character of the objects in question. Aristotle does not describe or analyse matters of fact, but creates useful fiction as background for the propounding of ideals.

7. See E. Frank. 'Begriff und Bedeutung des Dämonischen in der girechischen Philosophie'. op.cit. 51–69. He says: "Und so ist auch das theoretische Selbstbewusstsein nur ein Derivat des christlichen Gewissen das heisst den Griechen noch unbekannt" (p.56). H. Seidl maintains on the contrary: "Der Gedankengang in I, 9 zeigt, dass mit der Tätigkeit des nous ein reflexives Moment gegeben ist, durch das der Intellekt sich seiner Tätigkeit bewusst ist und sie als sittlich gut erfährt" (op.cit. 159), and he refers to De An. 429b9, 26–29; 430a5–9. However, it is not nous that implies a reflexive element, but energeia. Cf. the quotation from A. Grant at the end of §8.

8. C.W. Müller op.cit. 189f.

9. I. Düring. Aristoteles. pp.400 and 469ff.

§25. THE VIRTUES OF ACTION ARE SECONDARY

1. I. Düring. Aristoteles, 471.

2. For the idea of 'la vie mixte', see also R.-A. Gauthier. La Morale d'Aristote. Paris 1968 (cf. §18, n.4).

3. Cf. §23, n.3. Dirlmeier later gave up this opinion, cf. §33, n.4.

4. Cf. §7, n.5. Düring does not himself note the full relevance of this observation for the understanding of the 'Hierarchie'.

5. H. Seidl op.cit. 169.

6. For the role of the idea of initiation in the philosophy of Parmenides, see A.P.D. Mourelatos. The Route of Parmenides. New Haven 1970.

7. L.H.G. Greenwood op.cit. 84.

8. J. Léonard says: "Qu'on les regards dans leurs objects la sagesse et la prudence paraîtront tout à fait distinctes, comme le nécessaire se distingue du contingent; qu'on les envisage dans leur sujet, elles paraîtront radicalement une, fonction double d'un seul nous; qu'on les envisage dans leur but, elles se hierarchisent parfaitement, car vue dans son but, la prudence échappe elle aussi à la contingence, pour servir avec amour l'immuable sagesse" (op.cit. 127).

§26. THE EXCELLENCE OF REASON IS A THING APART

1. This syntheton as cooperation is lucidly described by A. Stigen. Aristoteles etikk. Oslo 1973 (the introduction). But he tends to ignore the exceptional position of nous and treats it as a mere appendix. Syntheton or hē synthetos ousia is translated thus by H. Bonitz: "id quod compositum est ex materia et forma vel ex substantia et accidente", and with regards to EN 1177b28, he remarks: "opp to theion". Nous is neither the form nor the substance of man as a whole, therefore to syntheton cannot comprise nous in any way.

2. I. Düring. Aristoteles. 471.

3. For Aristotle's criticism of Plato, see E. Frank op.cit. 86-119, and H. Flashar. 'Die Kritik der platonischen Ideenlehre in der Ethik des Ari stoteles'. Synusia (Festgabe für W. Schadewaldt). Pfullingen 1965, 223-46.

4. On nature as having phronēsis: Part.An. 786a10f., 694a20f., 661b28f.; Gen.An. 766a5.

5. On nous poiētikos, see §36 for literature and a short treatment.

6. W.F.R. Hardie. Aristotle's Ethical Theory. Oxford 1968, 354f.

7. See Gauthier/Jolif ad loc. and W. Jaeger. Aristotle. 332ff.

8. M. De Corte. La doctrine de l'intelligence chez Aristote. Paris 1934, p.34.

9. E. Caird op.cit. I, 278.

10. Ibid. I, 284.

11. Ibid. I, 272.

§27. CONTEMPLATION AND EXTERNAL EQUIPMENT

1. J. Léonard op.cit. 52. For the general attitude of the Greeks to property see L. Schmidt op.cit. II, 369ff.

2. This contradiction is underlined in the work of O. Gigon on slavery, see §12, n.5.

3. In Rhet. 1360b18-28, Aristotle gives a list of external goods, cf. Plato's Rep. 491c and Meno 87e.

4. Criticism from a communist point of view in G. Redlow and E.C. Welsko From a liberal point of view in E. Barker and W.L. Newman. For a thorough criticism of ideology, see F. Tomberg (further information in the Bibliography).

5. The best study of prohairesis is presented by E. Kullmann. Beiträge zum aristotelischen Begriff der Prohairesis. Basel 1943, cf. also H. Kuhn in Das Sein und das Gute. München 1962, 275-95.

6. 'Pour vivre en homme' (Gauthier).

7. G. Rodier asks: "N'est-ce pourtant pas l'intellect qu'Aristote a appelé un peu plus haut, <u>malista anthrōpos</u>?" There is no answer to this question. Aristotle mixes the terms, but this problem we have already treated in §§4 and 24.

§28. THE GODS ARE HAPPY IN THEIR CONTEMPLATION

1. We do not comment here on the so-called 'practical' <u>nous</u>. It belongs to another line of argument. See the note of J. Burnet in <u>op.cit.</u> xxi, n.5.

2. "For heaven's sake, shall we let ourselves easily be persuaded that motion and life and soul and mind are really not present to absolute being, that it neither lives nor thinks, but awful and holy, devoid of mind, is fixed and immovable?" (Plato's <u>Soph.</u> 248e-49a).

3. Cf. I. Düring. <u>Aristoteles,</u> 214, 219. For literature, see F. Solmsen. <u>Plato's Theology.</u> New York 1942, 74, n.19.

4. Especially naive is the account in O. Gilbert. <u>Griechische Religions-philosophie.</u> Leipzig 1911.

5. H.H. Joachim <u>op.cit.</u> 294-95.

6. I. Düring. <u>Aristoteles,</u> p.27.

7. In the case of man, whose <u>telos</u> is an activity, the position of having attained the <u>telos</u> (<u>entelecheia</u>) is of course an <u>energeia.</u> But in general the terms are not synonymous (cf. <u>Meta.</u> 1048b5-35).

8. See W. Jaeger. <u>The Theology of the Early Greek Philosophers.</u> Oxford 1947, and the works of Solmsen, Caird, and Gilbert just noted.

9. I. Düring <u>op.cit.</u> 117, 186. Cf. the exceptionally instructive article of W.J. Verdenius in <u>Phronesis</u> 5(1960), 56-70.

10. For interpretation and references, see the introductory chapter of F. Solmsen <u>op.cit.</u>, and W.K.C. Guthrie. <u>A History of Greek Philosophy</u>. Vol. III. Cambridge 1969, 226-47.

§29. MEN AND ANIMALS

1. For general instruction on the philosophical language of Plato and Aristotle, see K. von Fritz. Philosophie und sprachlicher Ausdruck bei Demokrit, Plato und Aristoteles. New York 1938. Still readable is R. Eucken. Geschichte der philosophischen Terminologie. Leipzig 1879. Reprinted 1964.

2. Cf. H. Meinhardt. Teilhabe bei Platon. Freiburg/München 1968.

3. J. Léonard op.cit. 131.

4. Cf. §26, n.3.

5. See Gauthier/Jolif ad 1097a11-13.

6. Cf. §5, n.2.

§31. THE WISE MEN AGREE WITH US

1. Cf. §3, W.K. C. Guthrie in Journ. of Hellenic Studies 77(1957), 35-41, and O. Gigon in Arch. di Filosofia 1954, 129-50.

2. K. von Fritz in Histoire et historiens dans l'antiquité. Vandoeuvres/ Geneve 1958, 92.

3. J.W. Verdenius in Phronesis 5(1960), 58.

4. J. Ritter. Metaphysik und Politik. Frankf. am Main 1969, 122f.

5. J.M. LeBlond. Logique et méthode chez Aristote. Paris 1939, p.252.

6. Dirlmeier says ad loc.: "Wie in der Komposition des platon. Staates zwischen I und X Symmetrie hergestellt wird durch das Motiv der Unter-weltsmythen (I 330d8: X 614b2), so in der NE durch das Solon-Motiv (I 11, 1100a11): an die Stelle des Mythos ist die Weisheit griechischer Tradition getreten".

7. H. Margueritte in Revue d'hist. de la philosophie 4(1930); 186, 263. As to Anaxagoras, he is not the unquestionable pattern for Aristotle, not an instance of the best life exactly as Aristotle wishes to have it. Anaxa-goras represented, as he was, the bios xenikos described and critisised

in <u>Pol.</u>1324a15-30. Aristotle treats the figure of Anaxagoras like an old opinion that should be interpreted to disclose its element of truth.

§32. THE THEORY DEFENDED BY 'THE FACTS OF LIFE'

1. See J. Burnet ad 1098b11.

2. It is a severe flaw of Gauthier's interpretation not to see the great difference between the viewpoint of ethics and that of psychology. This is probably the reason behind his uncritical use of the work of F. Nuyens. Cf. the Bibiliography.

§33. THE GOODS DO CARE FOR HUMAN AFFAIRS

1. In 1935, see §34, n.1.

2. J.W. Verdenius <u>op.cit.</u> 59.

3. See J.W. Verdenius in <u>Untersuchungen zur eudemischen Ethik</u> (ed. P. Moraux and D. Harlfinger). Berlin 1971, 286, 294.

4. Dirlmeier says <u>ad loc.</u>: "Sein 'Freund der Gottheit' wird nicht als Normgeber in Verbindung gebracht mit dem 'Leben gemäss der Tugend'. Er ist ein Sonderfall. Er ist der Philosoph des platon. Staates, aber ohne dessen bildnerische, nomothetische Aufgabe. Der arist. Nomothet muss erst gefunden werden." Note the plain contradiction to §23, n.3. (It is, of course not that bad to contradict oneself if only the last statement is the right one. And so it is here).

5. Cf. Dirlmeier <u>ad loc.</u>

§34. THE PHILOSOPHER IS DEAREST TO THE GODS

1. F. Dirlmeier. 'Theophilia - Philotheia'. <u>Philologus</u> 90(1935), 57-77 and 176-193. Moreover his notes in the commentary <u>ad loc.</u>

2. Cf. §§11 and 3.

3. G. Widmann. <u>Autarkie und Philia in den aristotelischen Ethiken.</u> Stuttgart 1967, 81ff.

4. J.W. Verdenius in Phronesis 5(1960), 60.

5. A. Grant op.cit. I, 215.

6. E. Caird op.cit. I, 318f. This corresponds exactly to the charge in M. Wundt. Der Intellektualismus in der griechischen Ethik. Leipzig 1907.

§35. THE PHILOSOPHER AND THE LAWGIVER

1. W. Jaeger. Aristotle. p. 264.

2. Newman op.cit. I, 297. The quotation presupposes his own order of the books of the Politics.

3. Newman op.cit. I, 347.

4. Ibid. I, 303.

5. E. Rolfes. Aristoteles. Politik. Leipzig 1912, p. 305.

6. Newman op.cit. I, 303.

7. A.B. Hentschke. Politik und Philosophie bei Platon und Aristoteles. Frankf. am Main 1971, 341ff.

8. See S. Mansion. 'Contemplation and Action in Aristotle's Protrepticus'. Aristotle and Plato in the Mid-Fourth Century (ed. by I. Düring and G.E.L. Owen). Gothenburg 1960, 56-75.

9. Burnet op.cit. p. xxii.

10. Newman op.cit. I, 346.

11. Ibid. I, 345.

12. W. Bröcker. Aristoteles. p. 307.

§36. THE FACULTIES OF THE HUMAN SOUL

1. F. Dirlmeier. Jahrbuch für das Bistum Mainz 1950, 170.

2. I. Düring. Aristoteles. p. 572.

3. E. Caird op.cit. I, 275.

4. _Ibid._ I, 288.

5. On the difference between discursive and noetic thought, see W. Bröcker op.cit. 284ff. and the full treatment in K. Oehler. _Die Lehre vom noetischen und dianoetischen Denken bei Platon und Aristoteles._ München 1962.

6. A readable account of the exceptional position of _nous_ in W. Bröcker. _Aristoteles._ p.280.

7. The distinction is new and does not correspond to any of the distinctions in the notion of analogy mentioned in G. Patzig. _Kant-Studien_ 52(1960/61), 185-205.

8. I. Düring. _Aristoteles._ p.583, n.135.

9. W. Jaeger. _Aristotle._ p.332ff.; W. Bröcker. _Aristoteles._ p.288. F. Nuyens follows Jaeger in his method and in his main constructions.

10. Cf. F. Brentano. _Die Psychologie des Aristoteles._ Darmstadt 1967, with the criticism of T. Ando. _Aristotle's Theory of Practical Cognition_ (3.ed.). The Hague 1971, and H. Cassirer. _Aristoteles' Schrift 'Von der Seele'._ Darmstadt 1968, 140ff.

11. W.D. Ross. _Aristotle_ (5.ed.). London 1966, 129ff.

12. W. Bröcker. _Aristoteles._ p.284.

§37. METAPHYSICS AND THEOLOGY

1. Cf. L. Routila. _Die aristotelische Idee der Ersten Philosophie._ Amsterdam 1969.

2. L. Routila op.cit. 27ff.

3. Cf. W. Bröcker op.cit. 229-38; J. Owens. _The Doctrine of Being in the Aristotelian Metaphysics_ (2. ed.). Toronto 1963.

4. W. Bröcker op.cit. 16.

5. See K. Oehler. _Antike Philosophie und Byzantinisches Mittelalter._ München 1969, 192f.

6. K. Oehler says: "Der Terminus prōtē ousia als Bezeichnung der Transzendenz hat aber noch eine zweite Bedeutung. Er bezeichnet daneben in singularischer Weise Gott, den Ersten Beweger, und zwar als den Inbegriff der Transzendenz - und im begründend umfassenden Sinne als den Inbegriff alles Seidenden überhaupt" (op.cit. 195).

7. W. Bröcker. Aristoteles. p.48.

8. K. Oehler op.cit. p.208.

9. W. Bröcker op.cit. p.17.

10. K. Oehler op.cit. 215.

11. W.J. Verdenius in Phronesis 5(1960), 61.

12. W.J. Verdenius op.cit. 62.

13. K. Oehler op.cit. 204.

14. Cf. Meta. 996a36: "The mathematical sciences take no account of goods and evils". Cf. the exposition in A. Stigen. The Structure of Aristotle's Thought. Oslo/New York 1964, 89-99.

§38. ARISTOTLE'S DILEMMA

1. W.J. Verdenius op.cit. 63.

2. Arctos 1(1954), 76.

3. Eranos 54(1956), 112.

4. G. Rodier op.cit. 55.

5. J. Léonard op.cit. 117f.

6. See L. Routila op.cit. 33ff.

7. Cf. E. Frank op.cit. 65f.; W.F.R.Hardie op.cit. 356.

8. See E. Berti. L'Unità del Sapere in Aristotele. Padua 1965.

9. K. Gaiser. 'Das zweifache Telos bei Aristoteles'. Naturphilosophie bei Aristoteles und Theophrast. (ed. by I. Düring). Heidelberg 1969, 97-113.

10. J. Bernays. Die Dialoge des Aristoteles in ihrem Verhältnis zu seinen übrigen Werken. Berlin 1863, 108.

11. K. Gaiser op.cit. 98.

12. Ibid. p. 100.

13. Ibid. p. 111.

14. K. Oehler op.cit. 211.

15. Ibid. p. 209ff.

16. F. Wehrli. Hauptrichtungen des griechischen Denkens. Zürich/ Stuttgart 1964, 160.

17. W. Jaeger. Aristotle. 435. This suggestion is brilliantly worked out by A. Brémond in Le Dilemme aristotélicien. Paris 1933. But the structural difficulties of Aristotle's thought cannot be explained altogether by the reference to his dependence on the matrices of Platonic philosophy. Brémond forgets that A. defends a particular case of his own as well, and the creative moment is an unhistorical point of departure. History becomes inescapable only for the later consideration.

BIBLIOGRAPHY

A valuable bibliography is presented in Gauthier's commentary Vol.I, 315-334
and Vol.II, 917-940. A more comprehensive catalogue is now under preparation, directed by Paul Moraux, in the 'Aristoteles-Archiv' in Berlin.

The list below contains books and articles that are referred to in the notes
or otherwise regarded as useful.

The sources for the present work have been the Oxford editions of Burnet
(Plato), Bywater (EN), Jaeger (Meta.), Ross (De An., Pol., Rhet., Phys.),
and the Loeb editions of Guthric (De Cael.) and Rackham (EE). For other
texts and recommendations in the choice of texts, see the 'Bibliographie' in
Düring's standard work on Aristotle (623ff.).

For Plato, we have freely used the classical translation of Jowett, and
for Aristotle: The Works of Aristotle. Translated into English under the
editorship of J.A. Smith and W.D. Ross. Oxford 1908-13. 12 vols.

Adkins, A.W.H. Merit and Responsibility. A Study in Greek Values. Oxford
      1960.
-      From the Many to the One. A Study of Personality and the View of
      Human Nature, etc. London 1970.
Anderson, W.D. Ethos and Education in Greek Music. Cambridge, Mass.
      1966.
Ando, T. Aristotle's Theory of Practical Cognition (3.ed.). The Hague 1971.
Arleth, E. 'Die Bedeutung von ongkos bei Aristoteles'. Wiener-Studien
      22(1900), 11-17.
Aubenque, P. La prudence chez Aristote. Paris 1962.
-      Le problème de l'être chez Aristote. Essai sur la problématique
      aristotélicienne. Paris 1962.

Bambrough, R. 'Plato's Political Analogies'. Philosophy, Politics and Society (ed. by P. Laslett). Oxford 1970, 98-115.

Barker, E. The Political Thought of Plato and Aristotle. New York 1959.

Beare, J.I. Greek Theories of Elementary Cognition. Oxford 1906.

Berti, E. L'Unità del Sapere in Aristotele. Padua 1965.

Bignone, E. L'Aristotele perduto e la formazione filosofica di Epicuro. 2 vols. Florence 1936.

Boesch, P. Theoros. Untersuchung zur Epangelie griechischer Feste. Berlin 1908.

Boll, F. Vita contemplativa (Festrede). Heidelberg 1922.

Bonitz, H. Index Aristotelicus. Darmstadt 1955.

Braun, E. Aristoteles über Bürger- und Menschentugend. Wien 1961.

Brémond, A. Le Dilemme aristotélicien. Archives de Philosophie. T.10, ch.2. Paris 1933.

Brentano, F. Von der mannigfachen Bedeutung des Seienden nach Aristoteles Freiburg im Br. 1862.

-      Die Psychologie des Aristoteles. Insbesondere seine Lehre vom nous poiētikos. Mainz am Rhein 1867.

-      Aristoteles und seine Weltanschauung. Leipzig 1911.

Brochard, V. Études de philosophie ancienne et de philosophie moderne. Paris 1912.

Bröcker, W. Aristoteles (3.ed.). Frankf. am Main 1964.

Bruns, I. Das literarische Porträt der Griechen im 5. und 4. Jahrhundert v.Chr. Geb. Berlin 1896.

Buckley, M.J. Motion and Motion's God. Thematic Variations in Aristotle, Cicero, Newton and Hegel. Princeton 1971.

Burnet, J. The Ethics of Aristotle. Edited with an introduction and notes. London 1900.

-      Aristotle on Education. Extracts from the Ethics and Politics, translated and edited. Cambridge 1967.

Busse, A. 'Zur Musikästhetik des Aristoteles'. Rheinisches Museum 77(1928), 34-50.

Caird, E. The Evolution of Theology in the Greek Philosophers. 2 vols. Glasgow 1904.

253

Cashdollar, S. 'Aristotle's Politics of Morals'. Journal of the History of
Philosophy 11(1973), 145-60.

Cassirer, H. Aristoteles' Schrift 'Von der Seele'. Tübingen 1932.

Cherniss, H. The Riddle of the Early Academy. Berkeley/Los Angeles 1945.

Christensen, J. 'Actus Purus'. Classica et Mediaevalia 19(1958), 7-40.

Chroust, A.-H. 'The first thirty years of modern Aristotelian scholarship'.
Classica et Mediaevalia 24(1963), 27-57.

- 'Aristotle's religious convictions'. Divus Thomas 69(1966), 91-97.

Clark, S. 'The Use of 'Man's Function' in Aristotle'. Ethics 82(1972), 269-
83.

Cook, A.B. Zeus. A Study of Ancient Religion. Vol.I. Cambridge 1914.

Cornford, F.M. 'Psychology and Social Structure in the Republic of Plato'.
Classical Quarterly 6(1912), 246-64.

Curtius, E. Arbeit und Musse (Festrede). Berlin 1875.

Cushman, R.E. Therapeia. Plato's Conception of Philosophy. Chapel Hill
1958.

DeCorte, M. La doctrine de l'intelligence chez Aristote. Paris 1934.

Defourny, P. 'Die Kontemplation in den aristotelischen Ethiken'. Ethik und
Politik des Aristoteles (ed. by F.-P. Hager). Darmstadt 1972, 219-34.

Derbolav, J. 'Freiheit und Naturordnung im Rahmen der Aristotelischen
Ethik'. Kant-Studien 57(1966), 32-60.

DeVogel, C.J. 'Aristotele e l'ideale della vita contemplativa'. Giornale di
Metafisica 16(1961), 450-66.

Diemer, A. 'Gott und Zeit bei Aristoteles'. Kant-Studien 50(1958/59), 273-
86.

Diller, H. 'Die philosophiegeschichtliche Stellung des Diogenes von Apollonia'.
Hermes 76(1941), 359-81.

- 'Hippokratische Medizin und attische Philosophie'. Hermes 80(1952),
385-409.

Dirlmeier, F. 'Aristoteles'. Jahrbuch für das Bistum Mainz 5 (1950), 161-
71.

- 'Beobachtungen zur Nikomachischen Ethik'. Wiener-Studien 69(1956),
171ff.

- Aristoteles. Magna Moralia. Berlin 1966.

254

Dirlmeier, F. Aristoteles. Eudemische Ethik. Darmstadt 1969.

-    Aristoteles. Nikomachische Ethik. Darmstadt 1969.

Düring, I. 'Aristotle, the Scholar'. Arctos 1(1954), 61-77.

-    'Aristotle and Plato in the Mid-Fourth Century'. Eranos 54(1956),
     109-20.

-    Aristotle's Protrepticus. An Attempt at Reconstruction. Göteborg
     1961.

-    Aristoteles. Darstellung und Interpretation seines Denkens.
     Heidelberg 1966.

-    'Personlighetsetik och samhällsetik hos Platon och Aristoteles'.
     Ajatus 28(1966), 63-88.

Elliott, R.K. 'Socrates and Plato's Cave'. Kant-Studien 58(1967), 137-57.

Festugière, A.-J. Le Plaisir. Éthique à Nicomaque H. et K. Introduction,
     traduction et notes. Paris 1936.

-    'Autarcie et communauté dans la Grèce antique'. Liberté et
     civilisation chez les Grecs. Paris 1947, 109-26.

-    Hippocrate. L'ancienne médicine. Paris 1948.

-    La révelation d'Herme Trismegiste II. Le Dieu Cosmique. Paris 1949

-    Personal Religion among the Greeks. Berkeley/Los Angeles 1954.

-    'Les trois vies'. Acta congressus Madvigiani. Vol.II. Copenhagen
     1958, 131-78.

-    Contemplation et vie contemplative selon Platon. Paris 1967.

Flashar, H. 'Die Kritik der platonischen Ideenlehre in der Ethik des
     Aristoteles'. Synusia (Festgabe für W. Schadewaldt). Pfullingen
     1965, 223-46.

Fortenbaugh, W.W. 'Aristotle's Rhetoric on Emotions'. Archiv für Geschichte
     der Philosophie 52(1970), 40-70.

-    'Ta pros to telos and Syllogistic Vocabulary in Aristotle's Ethics'.
     Phronesis 10(1965), 191-201.

Frank, E. Wissen, Wollen, Glauben. Zürich/Stuttgart 1955.

Fritz, K. von. Philosophie und sprachlicher Ausdruck bei Demokrit, Plato
     und Aristoteles. New York 1938.

Fritz, K. von. 'Nous, noein and their derivatives in pre-Socratic philosophy, excluding Anaxagoras'. Classical Philology 40(1945), 223-42; 41 (1946), 12-34.

- 'Der nous des Anaxagoras'. Archiv für Begriffsgeschichte 9(1964), 87-102.

Gadamer, H.-G. 'Der aristotelische Protreptikos und die entwicklungs-geschichtliche Betrachtung der aristotelischen Ethik'. Hermes 63 (1928), 138-64.

- Recension of W. Jaeger's Aristotle in Logos 17(1928), 132ff.

- Platos dialektische Ethik und andere Studien zur platonischen Philosophie. Hamburg 1968.

- 'Über das Göttliche im frühen Denken der Griechen'. Das Altertum und jedes neue Gute (Festschrift für W. Schadewaldt). Stuttgart 1970, 397-414.

- Wahrheit und Methode. Grundzüge einer philosophischen Hermeneutik (3. ed.). Tübingen 1972.

Gaiser, K. 'Das zweifache Telos bei Aristoteles'. Naturphilosophie bei Aristoteles und Theophrast (ed. by I. Düring). Heidelberg 1969, 97-113.

Gauthier, R.-A. La Morale d'Aristote. Paris 1963.

- (with J.Y. Jolif) L'Éthique à Nicomaque. Introduction, traduction et commentaire. 2 vols. Louvain/Paris 1970.

Gigon, O. Sokrates. Sein Bild in Dichtung und Geschichte. Bern 1947.

- 'Die Geschichtlichkeit der Philosophie bei Aristoteles'. Arch. di Filosofia 1954, 129-50.

- . Grundprobleme der antiken Philosophie. Bern/München 1959.

- 'Die Sklaverei bei Aristoteles'. Entretiens sur l'antiquité classique. Tome XI. Vandoeuvres/Genève 1964, 247-76.

- 'Autarkiebegreppet i den klassiska grekiska filosofin'. Ajatus 28(1966), 39-50.

Gilbert, O. Griechische Religionsphilosophie. Leipzig 1911.

Gillies, J. Aristotle's Ethics and Politics comprising his Practical Philosophy transl. from the Greek. 2 vols. London 1797.

Gladigow, B. Sophia und Kosmos. Untersuchungen zur Frühgeschichte von sophos und sophie. Hildesheim 1965.

- 'Zum Makarismos des Weisen'. Hermes 95(1967), 404-33.

Gould, J. The Development of Plato's Ethics. Cambridge 1955.

Gould, T. 'The Metaphysical Foundations for Aristotle's Ethics'. Essays in Ancient Greek Philosophy (ed. by J.P. Auton). New York 1971, 451-61.

Grant, A. The Ethics of Aristotle. Illustrated with essays and notes. 2 vols. 4.ed. London 1885.

Greenwood, L.H.G. Aristotle. Nicomachean Ethics Book VI. With essays, notes and translation. Cambridge 1909.

Grilli, A. Il problema della vita contemplativa nel mondo greco-romano. Milan/Rome 1953.

Groethuysen, B. Philosophische Anthropologie. Darmstadt 1969.

Guthrie, W.K.C. 'The Development of Aristotle's Theology'. Classical Quarterly 27(1933), 162-71; 28(1934), 90-98.

- 'Aristotle as a Historian of Philosophy'. Journal of Hellenic Studies 77(1957), 35-41.

- A History of Greek Philosophy. 4 vols. Cambridge 1962-75.

Hägerström, A. Aristoteles' etiska grundtankar och deras forutsättningar. Upsala 1893.

Hager, F.-P. Der Geist und das Eine. Untersuchungen zum Problem der Wesensbestimmung des höchsten Prinzips als Geist oder als Eines in der griechischen Philosophie. Bern/Stuttgart 1970.

Hardie, W.F.R. Aristotle's Ethical Theory. Oxford 1968.

Hentschke, A.B. Politik und Philosophie bei Platon und Aristoteles. Frankf. am Main 1971.

Hesse, M. 'Aristotle's Logic of Analogy'. The Philosophical Quarterly 15(1965), 328-40.

Hoffmann, E. 'Aristoteles' Philosophie der Freundschaft'. Ethik und Politik des Aristoteles (ed. by F.-P. Hager). Darmstadt 1972, 149-83.

Hüffmeister, F. 'Phronesis in den Schriften des Corpus Hippocraticum'. Hermes 89(1961), 51-84.

Jaeger, G. Nus in Platons Dialogen. Hypom. 17. Göttingen 1967.

Jaeger, W. Paideia. Die Formung des griechischen Menschen. 3 vols.
Berlin 1959.

– The Theology of the Early Greek Philosophers. Oxford 1947.

– 'Aristotle's Use of Medicine as Model of Method in his Ethics'.
Scripta Minora. Vol. II. Rome 1960, 491-509.

– Aristotle. Fundamentals of the History of his Development. 2. ed.
Oxford 1967.

Janóska, G. 'Zum Begriff der Metaphysik: Aristoteles und das Meta-
physische'. Kant-Studien 57(1966), 61-71.

Joachim, H.H. Aristotle. The Nicomachean Ethics. Oxford 1951.

Joly, R. Le thème philosophique des genres de vie dans l'antiquité
classique. Bruxelles 1956.

Kapp, E. 'Theorie und Praxis bei Aristoteles und Platon'. Mnemosyne
1938, 178-91.

Kearny, J.K. 'Happiness and the Unity of Nicomachean Ethics Reconsidered'.
Proceedings of the American Catholic Philosophical Association
40(1966), 135-43.

Kleve, K. Gnosis Theon. Die Lehre von der natürlichen Gotteserkenntnis
in der epikureischen Theologie. Oslo 1963.

Koller, E. 'Musse und musische Paideia'. Museum Helveticum 13(1956),
1-37; 94-124.

Koller, H. 'Theoros und Theoria'. Glotta 36(1958), 273-86.

Krämer, H.J. Der Ursprung der Geistmetaphysik. Amsterdam 1964.

– Arete bei Platon und Aristoteles. Zum Wesen und zur Geschichte der
platonischen Ontologie. Amsterdam 1967.

– 'Das Verhältnis von Platon und Aristoteles in neuer Sicht'. Zeitschrift
für philosophische Forschung 26(1972), 329-53.

Kranz, W. Kosmos. Archiv für Begriffsgeschichte. Bonn 1955.

Kretschmar, M. Otium et studia litterarum. Philosophie und bios theōrētikos
im Leben und Denken Ciceros. Würzburg/Aumühle 1938.

Krohn, S. 'Aristoteles som grundläggare av den normativa etiken'. Ajatus
28(1966), 89-101.

Kuhn, H. 'Der Mensch in der Entscheidung: Prohairesis in der Nikomachisc Ethik'. Das Sein und das Gute. München 1962, 275-95.

- 'Wissenschaft der Praxis und praktische Wissenschaft'. Werden und Handeln (Festschrift für Gebsattel) 1963, 157ff.

Kullmann, E. Beiträge zum aristotelischen Begriff der Prohairesis. Basel 1943.

Kullmann, W. 'Zur wissenschaftlichen Methode der Aristoteles'. Synusia (Festgabe für W. Schadewaldt). Pfullingen 1965, 247-74.

LaFontaine, A. Le Plaisir d'apres Platon et Aristote. Paris 1902.

LeBlond, J.M. Eulogos et l'argument de covenence chez Aristote. Thèse compl. Paris 1939.

- Logique et méthode chez Aristote. Étude sur la recherce des principes dans la physique aristotélicienne. Paris 1939.

Leisegang, H. Der Heilige Geist. Das Wesen und Werden der mystisch-intuitiven Erkenntnis in der Philosophie und Religion der Griechen. Leipzig/Berlin 1919.

Léonard, J. Le Bonheur chez Aristote. Bruxelles 1948.

Lieberg, G. Die Lehre von der Lust in den Ethiken des Aristoteles. Zetemata 19. München 1958.

Lloyd, G.E.R. Polarity and Analogy. Cambridge 1966.

- 'The role of medical and biological analogies in Aristotle's ethics'. Phronesis 1968, 68-83.

Lobkowicz, N. Theory and Practice: History of a Concept from Aristotle to Marx. Notre Dame/London 1967.

Loening R. Die Zurechnungslehre des Aristoteles. Jena 1903.

Longrigg, J. 'Philosophy and Medicine'. Harvard Studies in Classical Philology 69(1963), 147-75.

McKeon, R. 'Plato and Aristotle as Historians: A Study of Method in the History of Ideas'. Ethics 51(1940/41), 66-101.

- 'Aristotle's Conception of Moral and Political Philosophy'. Ethics 51(1941), 253-90.

- 'Aristotle's Conception of the Development and the Nature of Scientific Method'. Journal of the History of Ideas 8(1947), 3-44.

Mansion, A. 'L'existence d'un fin dernière de l'homme et la morale'.
Revue philos. de Louvain 48(1950), 465-77.

– 'L'immortalité de l'âme et de l'intellect d'apres Aristote'.
Revue philos. de Louvain 51(1953), 444-72.

Mansion, S. 'Contemplation and Action in Aristotle's Protrepticus'.
Aristotle and Plato in the Mid-Fourth Century (ed. by I. Düring
and G.E.L. Owen). Göteborg 1960, 56-75.

Margueritte, H. 'Une lacune dans le 1er livre de l'Éthique à Nicomaque'.
Revue d'hist. de la philosophie 4(1930), 176-88.

– 'La composition du livre A de l'Éthique à Nicomaque'. Revue
d'hist. de la philosophie 4(1930), 250-73.

Meinhardt, H. Teilhabe bei Platon. Ein Beitrag zum Verständnis
platonischen Prinzipiendenkens unter besonderer Berücksichtigung
des "Sophistes". Freiburg/München 1968.

Merlan, P. Studies in Epicurus and Aristotle. Wiesbaden 1960.

– 'Zum Problem der drei Lebensarten'. Philosophisches Jahrbuch
74(1966/67), 217-19.

– 'Aristoteles' und Epikurs müssige Götter'. Zeitschrift für philosophische Forschung 21(1967), 485-98.

Mikkola, E. Isokrates. Seine Anschauungen im Lichte seiner Schriften.
Helsinki 1954.

– 'Scholē bei Aristoteles. Arctos (1958), 68-87.

Milobenski, E. Der Neid in der griechischen Philosophie. Wiesbaden 1964.

Monan, J.-D. 'La connaissance morale dans le "Protreptique" d'Aristote'.
Revue philos. de Louvain 58(1960), 185-219.

– 'Two methodological aspects of moral knowledge in the Nicomachean
Ethics. Aristote et les problèmes de méthode. Louvain/Paris 1961,
247-71.

– Moral Knowledge and its Methodology in Aristotle. Oxford 1968.

Morrison, J.S. 'The Origin of Plato's Philosopher-Statesman'. Classical
Quarterly 52(1958), 198-218.

Müller, C.W. Gleiches zu Gleichem. Ein Prinzip frühgriechischen Denkens.
Wiesbaden 1965.

Müller, G. 'Probleme der aristotelischen Eudaimonielehre'. Ethik und
Politik des Aristoteles (ed. by F.-P. Hager). Darmstadt 1972, 368-
402.

Mühll, P. von der 'Isokrates und der Protreptikos des Aristoteles'. Philologus 94(1941), 259ff.

Mugnier, R. Le sens du mot THEIOS chez Platon. Paris 1930.

Newman, W.L. The Politics of Aristotle. With an introduction, two prefatory essays and notes critical and explanatory. 4 vols. Oxford 1887-1902.

Nilsson, M.P:n. Grekisk Religiositet. (2.ed.). Stockholm 1960.

Nickel, R. Das Begriffspaar Besitzen und Gebrauchen. Ein Beitrag zur Vorgeschichte der Potenz-Akt-Beziehung in der aristotelischen Ethik. Berlin 1970.

Nolte, H.J.A. Het godsbegrip bij Aristoteles. Nijmegen 1940.

Nuyens, F. L'évolution de la psychologie d'Aristote. Louvain/Paris 1948.

Oehler, K. Die Lehre vom noetischen und dianoetischen Denken bei Platon und Aristoteles. Zetemata 29. München 1962.

- 'Der Entwicklungsgedanke als heuristisches Prinzip der Philosophie-historie'. Zeitschrift für philosophische Forschung 17(1963), 604-13.

- Antike Philosophie und byzantinisches Mittelalter. Aufsätze zur Geschichte des griechischen Denkens. München 1969.

Owens, J. The Doctrine of Being in the Aristotelian Metaphysics. (2.ed.) Toronto 1963.

- 'The Grounds of Ethical Universality in Aristotle'. Man and World 2(1969), 171-93.

Patzig, G. 'Theologie und Ontologie in der "Metaphysik" des Aristoteles'. Kant-Studien 52(1960/61), 185-205.

Picht, G. Wahrheit, Vernunft, Verantwortung. Philosophische Studien. Stuttgart 1969.

Pieper, J. Musse und Kult. München 1948.

Pohlenz, M. Griechische Freiheit. Wesen und Werden eines Lebensideals. Heidelberg 1955.

Rabinowitz, W.G. Aristotle's Protrepticus and the Sources of its Reconstruction. Berkeley/Los Angeles 1957.

Ramsauer, G. Aristotelis Ethica Nicomachea (edidit et commentario continuo instruxit). Leipzig 1878.

Randall, J.H. Jr. Aristotle. New York/London 1960.

- Plato. The Dramatist of the Life of Reason. New York/London 1970.

Redlow, G. Theoria. Theoretische und praktische Lebensauffassung im philosophischen Denken der Antike. Berlin 1966.

Regenbogen, O. 'Die Geschichte von Solon und Kroisos'. Das humanistische Gymnasium 41(1930), 1-20.

Régis, L.-M. L'opinion selon Aristote. Paris/Ottawa 1935.

Reiner, H. 'Das Kantische Sittengesetz im sittlichen Bewusstsein der Antike'. Kant-Studien 39(1934), 1-26.

Ringbom, M. 'Moral Relevance in Aristotle'. Ajatus 27(1965), 83-96.

Ritter, J. Metaphysik und Politik. Studien zu Aristoteles und Hegel. Frankf. am Main 1969.

Ritter, R. Die aristotelische Freundschaftsphilosophie nach der Nikomachischen Ethik. München 1963.

Riva, G. Il concetto di Aristotele sulla felicità terrestre, secondo il libro primo e decimo dell'Etica Nicomachea. Prato 1883.

Rodier, G. Introduction et notes au livre X de l'Éthique à Nicomaque. Paris 1897.

Rolfes, E. Aristoteles. Politik. Neu übersetzt und mit einer Einleitung und erklärenden Anmerkungen versehen. Leipzig 1912.

Rose, V. Aristoteles. Fragmenta. Leipzig 1886.

Rosen, S.H. 'Thought and Touch. A note on Aristotle's De Anima'. Phronesis 6(1961), 127-37.

Ross, W.D. Select Fragments. The Works of Aristotle transl. into English. Vol.XII. Oxford 1952.

- 'The Development of Aristotle's Thought'. Aristotle and Plato in the Mid-Fourth Century (ed. by I. Düring and G.E.L. Owen). Göteborg 1960, 1-17.

- Aristotle (5.ed.). London 1966.

Routila, L. Die aristotelische Idee der Ersten Philosophie. Amsterdam 1969.

Rudberg, G. 'Hellenisches Schauen'. Classica et Mediaevalia 5(1942), 159-86.

Ryffel, H. 'Eukosmia'. Museum Helveticum 4(1947), 23-38.

Sambursky, S. The Physical World of the Greeks. London 1963.

Schadewaldt, W. 'Das Welt-Modell der Griechen'. Hellas und Hesperien
    (2.ed.). Zürich 1970, I, 601-625.

Schilling-Wollny, K. Aristoteles' Gedanke der Philosophie. München 1928.

Schmidt, L. Die Ethik der alten Griechen. 2 vols. Berlin 1882.

Schneeweiss, G. Der Protreptikos des Aristoteles. Bamberg 1966.

Schultz, W. 'Herakles am Scheidewege'. Philologus 1909, 489-99.

Seidl, H. 'Zum Verhältnis von Wissenschaft und Praxis in Aristoteles'
    Nikomachischer Ethik'. Zeitschrift für philosophische Forschung
    19(1965), 553-62.

    - Der Begriff des Intellekts (NOUS) bei Aristoteles. Meisenheim am
    Glan 1971.

Shellens, M.S. Das sittliche Verhalten zum Mitmenschen im Anschluss an
    Aristoteles. Hamburg 1958.

Siwecki, J. 'Praxis et poiesis dans l'Éthique Nicomachéenne'. Charisteria
    Przychocki. Warscau 1934, 175-89.

Snell, B. Theorie und Praxis im Denken des Abendlandes. Hamburger
    Universitätsreden 13. Hamburg 1951.

    - The Discovery of Mind. The Greek Origins of European Thought.
    Oxford 1953.

    - Leben und Meinungen der Sieben Weisen. München 1971.

Solmsen, F. Plato's Theology. New York 1942.

    - 'Leisure and Play in Aristotle's Ideal State'. Kleine Schriften. Vol.II.
    Hildesheim 1968, 1-28.

    - 'Dialectics without the Forms'. Aristotle on Dialectic (ed. by G.E.L.
    Owen). Oxford 1968, 49-68.

    - Aristotle's System of the Physical World. Ithaca 1960.

Sparshott, F.E. 'Five Virtues in Plato and Aristotle'. The Monist 54(1970),
    40-65.

Spoerri, W. Recension of R. Joly. Le thème philosophique des genres de
    vie, etc. in Gnomon 30(1958), 186-92.

Stenzel, J. Metaphysik des Altertums. Darmstadt 1971.

Stewart, J.A. Notes on the Nicomachean Ethics of Aristotle. 2 vols. Oxford
    1892.

Stigen, A. 'On the alleged primacy of sight - with some remarks on theōria and praxis - in Aristotle'. Symbolae Osloenses 37(1961), 15-44.

- The Structure of Aristotle's Thought. Oslo/New York 1966.

- Aristoteles' etikk. Oslo 1973.

- 'Aristoteles' kategorilære'. Ajatus 29(1967), 103-27.

- Aristoteliske grunnbegreper. Oslo 1974.

Stocks, J.L. 'Scholē'. Classical Quarterly 30(1936), 177-87.

Theiler, W. Zur Geschichte der teleologischen Naturbetrachtung. Berlin 1965.

Thompson, W.H. The Phaedrus of Plato. With English notes and Dissertations. London 1868.

Tomberg, F. Polis und Nationalstaat. Eine vergleichende Überbauanalyse im Anschluss an Aristoteles. Darmstadt/Neuwied 1973.

Ulmer, K. Wahrheit, Kunst und Natur bei Aristoteles. Ein Beitrag zur Aufklärung der metaphysischen Herkunft der modernen Technik. Tübingen 1953.

Vanhoutte, M. La philosophie politique de Platon dans les "Lois". Louvain 1954.

Verbeke, G. 'L'ideal de la perfection humaine chez Aristote et l'évolution de sa noetique'. Fontes Ambrosiani 25, Milan 1951, I, 79-95.

Verdenius, W.J. 'Platons Gottesbegriff'. La notion du divin depuis Homère jusqu'à Platon. Vandoeuvres/Geneve 1954, 241-93.

- 'Participation and Contemplation in Ancient Greek and in Modern Thought. Ratio 3(1960), 9-25.

- 'Traditional and Personal Elements in Aristotle's Religion'. Phronesis 5(1960), 56-70.

- 'Human Reason and God in the Eudemian Ethics'. Untersuchungen zur eudemischen Ethik (ed. by P. Moraux and D. Harlfinger). Berlin 1971, 285-97.

Walzer, R. Magna Moralia und aristotelische Ethik. Berlin 1929.

Wehrli, F. Hauptrichtungen des griechischen Denkens. Zürich/Stuttgart 1964.

– Theoria und Humanitas. Gesammelte Schriften zur antiken Gedankenwelt. Zürich/München 1972.

Welskopf, E.C. Probleme der Musse im alten Hellas. Berlin 1962.

Wheeler, M. 'Self-Sufficiency and the Greek City'. Journal of the History of Ideas 16(1955), 416-20.

Widmann, G. Autarkie und Philia in den aristotelischen Ethiken. Stuttgart 1967.

Wieland, W. Die aristotelische Physik. Göttingen 1962.

Wilpert, P. 'Aristoteles und die Dialektik'. Kant-Studien 48(1956/57), 247-57.

Wolz, H.G. 'The Protagoras Myth and the Philosophers-Kings'. Review of Metaphysics 17(1963/64), 214-34.

Wundt, M. Der Intellektualismus in der griechischen Ethik. Leipzig 1907.

– Geschichte der griechischen Ethik. 2 vols. Leipzig 1908-11.

Wyller, E.A. Der späte Platon. Hamburg 1970.

INDEX OF GREEK WORDS AND PHRASES

Kleve, K. 225

Koller, E. 228, 233, 237

Krämer, H.J. 233

Kranz, W. 216

Krohn, S. 223

Kuhn, H. 242

Kullmann, E. 242

Kullmann, W. 217

LeBlond, J.N. 165, 217ff., 230, 244

Léonard, J. 76, 79, 82, 127, 141, 148, 161, 199f., 226, 232f., 239, 242, 244, 248

Lieberg, G.

Lloyd, G.E.R. 29, 219, 220, 233

Longrigg, J. 219

McKeon, R. 217, 219

Mansion, A. 237, 239

Mansion, S. 233, 246

Margueritte, H. 166, 223, 244

Meinhardt, H. 244

Merlan, P. 225, 236

Mikkola, E. 109, 218, 237

Milobenski, E. 239

Monan, J.-D. 67, 219, 230

Morrison, J.S. 216

Mourelatos, A.P.D. 241

Müller, C.W. 135, 228, 234, 240

Müller, G. 121f., 212, 229, 239

Mugnier, R. 235

Natorp, P. 191

Newman, W.L. 80, 91, 106, 175ff., 180, 213, 218, 232, 235, 237, 240, 242, 246

Nickel, R. 223

Nilsson, M. P:n 234, 239

Nuyens, F. 186, 239, 245, 247

Oehler, K. 193f., 197, 203, 211, 218, 230, 232, 247f., 249

Owens, J. 191, 247

Parmenides 15, 100, 140, 205f.

Patzig, G. 247

Periander 133

Pericles 110f., 113, 136, 163, 165f., 229

Picht, G. 16, 214f., 220

Pindar 44, 120

Plato - passim

Pohlenz, M. 100, 225, 236

Polycrates 57

Rabinowitz, G. 212

Ramsauer, G. 13, 132, 141, 168

Randall, J.H. jr. 9, 23, 78, 125, 211f., 217, 232, 239

Redlow, G. 225, 242

Regenbogen, O. 227

Régis, L.-M. 218

Reiner, H. 223

Ritter, J. 164, 233, 244

Ritter, R. 227

Riva, G. 223

Rodier, G. 53f., 56, 68, 90, 93f., 102, 118, 125, 129, 132, 151, 163, 167f., 199f., 226f., 236, 243, 248

Rolfes, E. 177, 246

Rose, V. 232, 238

Rosen, S.H. 233

Ross, W.D. 66, 99, 166, 169, 188, 231, 233, 236, 238, 247

Routila, L. 190f., 193, 247f.

Rudberg, G. 232

Ryffel, H. 216

Sambursky, S. 235

Sardanapallus 58, 113, 151

Schmidt, L. 214, 226, 240, 242

Schneeweiss, G. 12, 212, 216, 221

Schultz, W. 227

Seidl, H. 140f., 227, 231, 238, 240f.

Shellens, M.S. 227

Simonides 76, 170

Snell, B. 15, 214, 220, 240

Socrates 17f., 19ff., 36, 50, 88, 99, 124, 157, 159, 214, 217

Solmsen, F. 88, 110ff., 156f., 216f., 234f., 237f., 243

Solon 57, 108, 113, 136, 163f., 166, 244

Sophocles 120, 220

Sparshott, F.E. 237

Speiser, A. 74

Speusippus 45, 229

Spoerri, W. 215

Stenzel, J. 83, 233

Stewart, J.A. 13, 29, 33, 40, 53f., 64, 68, 71, 80, 90, 98f., 101f., 109f., 120, 127, 137ff., 152f., 163, 166, 168, 223, 229

Stigen, A. 36, 219, 228, 230, 241, 248

Thales 15, 18, 90, 165, 205f., 240

Themistius 115, 180

Theophrastus 82, 173

Tomberg, F. 225, 236, 242

Thompson, W.H. 240

Theiler, W. 42, 223, 235

Ulmer, K. 230

Verbeke, G. 72, 221, 232

Verdenius, W.J. 164f., 168, 172, 195f., 198, 216, 234, 243ff., 248

Walzer, R. 213

Wehrli, F. 16, 203f., 211, 215, 219, 221, 227, 239, 249

Welskopf, E.C. 242

Widmann, G. 213, 225, 237, 245

Wieland, W. 67, 211, 219, 230

Wilpert, P. 217

Wolz, H.G. 216

Wundt, M. 199, 246

Wyller, E.A. 232

Xenocrates 45, 223

Xenophanes 15f., 100, 157f.

Zeller, E. 10, 147, 198, 200, 205, 212, 238

DATE DUE

SEP. 2 3 1980			
APR 1 7 1991			